MYTHS, LEGENDS, AND
FOLKTALES OF
AMERICA

MYTHS, LEGENDS, AND FOLKTALES OF AMERICA

An Anthology

David Leeming and Jake Page

New York   Oxford

OXFORD UNIVERSITY PRESS INC.

1999

Oxford University Press

Oxford   New York
Athens   Auckland   Bangkok   Bogotá   Buenos Aires   Calcutta
Cape Town   Chennai   Dar es Salaam   Delhi   Florence   Hong Kong   Istanbul
Karachi   Kuala Lumpur   Madrid   Melbourne   Mexico City   Mumbai
Nairobi   Paris   São Paulo   Singapore   Taipei   Tokyo   Toronto   Warsaw

and associated companies in
Berlin   Ibadan

Published by Oxford University Press, Inc.
198 Madison Avenue, New York, New York 10016

Oxford is a registered trademark of Oxford University Press

Library of Congress Cataloging-in-Publication Data

Leeming, David Adams, 1937–
    Myths, legends, and folktales of America: an anthology / by David Leeming and
    Jake Page.
        p. cm.
    Includes bibliographical references and index.
    ISBN 0-19-511783-2
        1. Folklore—United States.   2. Tales—United States.   3. Legends—
    United States.   4. Indians of North America—Folklore.   5. Afro-
    Americans—Folklore.   6. Ethnic folklore—United States.   7. United
    States—History.   8. United States—Social life and customs.
    I. Page, Jake.   II. Title.
    GR105.L43   1998   97-48607
    398'.0973—dc21

1 3 5 7 9 8 6 4 2

Printed in the United States of America
on acid-free paper

For
our
grandchildren

CONTENTS

MYTHS, LEGENDS, AND FOLKTALES OF AMERICA

Introduction

This is a book of peculiarly American stories. Here, as everywhere from time immemorial, stories have served to entertain and to explain. They serve as mirrors in which a group of people can see themselves. More specifically and more often, they are like those mirrors in which we apply makeup or even disguises, designing images of who we think we are, how we believe we should appear to the world, and how we think we should perform in it.

Some stories reflect the cosmos and our particular way of seeing it and understanding its mysteries. These can be classified as mythology. Mythology deals with such persistently compelling matters as origins— the beginnings of the world or of a particular people—and they are populated with deities and heroes who more often than not have supernatural powers. Myths, in this sense, are religious stories, and they are at the very least metaphorically and psychically true.

Those numerous peoples or tribes whom we call, collectively, Indians or Native Americans, the original immigrants to this continent, each had their own mythologies. The American landscape, its mountains, valleys, plains, and waters, and the sky overhead were already filled with deities and heroes when the first Europeans arrived with *their* mythologies. The Europeans brought Africans with them, usually as slaves, and the tales of Africa joined the mix. Asians, brought over as cheap labor, had their own mythologies as well. All of these stories are what might be thought of as local variations on universal religious themes.

In common parlance, another meaning has come to adhere to the word *myth:* a form of self-delusion, or more precisely a group delusion— a widely held belief that is simply not true. This usage of the word arose from the field of anthropology but can nowhere be better perceived than

3

in the myth, so eagerly and widely believed in the decade after World War II, that electricity produced in nuclear power plants would be "too cheap to meter."

In the real world, of course, these two forms of myth intercalate. But experience tends to show up the delusory stories for what they are, and they are eventually, if sometimes reluctantly, discarded as useless or even harmful. Mythology in the religious or cosmological sense generally has a longer lifetime, being a true, if poetic, reflection of the human spirit.

In this volume we have attempted to introduce, by selective example, the astonishing breadth of mythology that has guided the successive waves of inhabitants of what has become the United States. As noted, all these peoples brought their own mythologies with them, and all of them, confronting so new and astounding a place, began to adapt their mythologies to new conditions and new needs. The American Indians did not bring the animal called Coyote with them across the Bering Strait, but they did bring trickster tales.

As another example, with the arrival of the Spanish and the Roman Catholic Church in Mexico, a new ethnic group came about—the Hispano-Indian—and before long an Aztec goddess had metamorphosed into the Virgin Mary with a brown skin, Our Lady of Guadalupe.

To the many different groups of people arriving on these shores, eventually to create a new nation, it was almost all alien—enormous, wild, lush, harsh, promising, varied to the extreme, terrifying. No one dwelling in Europe, for example, had seen such unbroken expanses of forest since the time of Christ. For many of these newcomers, new gods and new heroes were called for—new explanations and meanings. New religions would spring up, and Americans would deify or try to deify people, nature, and even machines in an attempt to create a psychically true secular mythology to go along with, or supplant, the ones they brought with them. The wilderness of nature needed to be tamed, its monsters exiled, before it could be worshiped.

At the same time, to knit a nation from such various materials, Americans produced what might be thought of as sociological myths to explain and enforce the sense of "a new people." The self-made man (a phrase invented by Henry Clay to describe frontier Kentucky entrepreneurs but apotheosized in the works of Horatio Alger) is such a myth, as is the melting pot. Manifest destiny—the idea that the United States should stretch across the continent from sea to shining sea—may be thought of as another, but of course it has been fulfilled . . . and then some. The frontier may or may not have shaped our national character, if there is one, but the same is true of the myth of the city.

Certainly, the sheer scale of things that greeted Europeans and other newcomers called for new eyes, new ways of seeing the world. The first Spaniards to peer over the edge of the Grand Canyon perceived the Colorado River (a mile down) as a nearby creek and descended to replenish their water supply. They returned exhausted only after a day or two.

Or at least there is a legend to that effect—another kind of story. Somewhere along the continuum between mythology and such stories as fairy tales and jokes lie what are called legends. These tend to be based on actual events and persons and, over time, are carefully tailored, often exaggerated, and serve to express some group aspiration.

Legends find their way into the collective "folk mind" in various ways. Journalists in the American West, responding to a hunger in the East for juicily terrifying tales, turned Billy the Kid from a colorful but small-time sociopath into a mass killer, and later (reversing ground) into a modern Robin Hood. On the other hand, Davy Crockett created the Davy Crockett legend largely by himself, prodigiously exaggerating his exploits on the frontier into his own tall tales, many of which he delivered in no less a forum than the floor of the United States House of Representatives. Buffalo Bill Cody was another real-life figure who capitalized on his heroism with his Wild West show. The systematic inventions of public relations firms on behalf of corporations and celebrities have a long and time-honored history on this continent.

The tall tale is, again, something beyond a legend on the continuum of story types, and very American: a harmless exaggeration of self—or of group—to match, perhaps, the exaggerated scale of the continent and its features. Paul Bunyan may be the quintessential tall-tale hero. These are what can be called folk tales, which also include fables, fairy tales, animal tales, and the elaborate jokes called shaggy-dog stories.

American folklore, then—its continuum of mythologies, legends, and folktales—is a reflection of the reality of American experience. As rich as any in the world, and perhaps richer thanks to our polyglot existence, it is characterized by a lack of homogeneity, and also by a tendency to escape from the bounds of glib definitions. In putting together this volume from so vast and multifarious a universe of stories, we have sought to use, as an ordering principle, certain basic motifs common to all peoples of the world. These are deities and demideities, tricksters, mythical monsters, and heroes.

We are well aware that the categorization of our highly selective examples is, in some instances, arguable. It is as if the stories themselves are laughing at such an attempt to pin them down. And in putting together this volume, we have been constantly reminded that humor of all kinds, from the subtle to the slapstick, from the self-deprecating to the joke at another group's expense, is very much a part of the American experience and the American attempt to understand ourselves. We Americans—Native, European, Asian, and African—all seem to have that in common at least. If the distinct ingredients of the American experience have yet to blend in the real world pot (and would any of us enjoy a featureless gruel?), we can hope that in these pages the reader will find a nutritious and satisfying stew, all the tastier because it simmers in a savory, spicy sauce of humor.

I

DEITIES, DEMIDEITIES, DOGMAS, AND ICONS FOR A NEW LAND

Since very ancient times the human species has created images of and stories about beings who represent ultimate reality. In the myths and dogmas and images we attach to the immortals we establish a sense of our own significance in the universe. We consider the gods to be personally concerned with us; they are the creators of our tribes and our world. The gods and goddesses are projections of ourselves in that we often give them human form—male and female. Some religions tell us we are made "in the image of God." Some say God is within us, some say God is "above," others believe in a God who is in both places. There are those who have believed that the gods merely play with our lives and those who have argued that they are our protectors and saviors. Nearly all societies have assumed the existence of deities.

The stories, dogmas, and icons of the gods and/or goddesses of a given society tell us a great deal about the values and priorities of that group. They also provide insight into the group's sense of place and its role in that place. This is certainly true of the peoples who have migrated to and inhabited the area we now call the United States of America and who have brought their own understandings of deity with them—whether from Asia, Africa, Europe, or Central and South America. Naturally, these views have been colored and altered by contact with each other and by the circumstances in which the migrant peoples have found themselves.

Peaceable Kingdom, by Edward Hicks, c. 1848, oil on canvas, 23⅞ by 31⅞ inches. Courtesy Albright-Knox Art Gallery, Buffalo, NY, James G. Forsyth Fund, 1940.

Native American

When Hispanics from the south and Europeans from the east arrived in the what is now the United States, they found a large number of peoples who, for the most part, had discovered America several millennia earlier. It seems likely that most of these first Americans had come from Central Asia over the Bering Strait and that they had brought their traditions with them—complex creation myths, related shamanistic rituals, and an animistic sense of a living nature suffused with spiritual power. Gradually the old traditions were given new form based on the natural surroundings, the climate, the animals, and the long migration itself. Earth-diver creations, common in Central Asia, in which a being, directed by a creator or creatrix, dives to the depths of the primal waters to find the first materials for earth, are common in North America as well. But the settings of the American myths reflect the American landscape, and the animal characters are North American animals. As in Central Asia, creators are often assisted (or hindered) by tricksters. The creation myths most common to the Southwest, the Emergence myths, probably developed in part from the migrations themselves. In these myths, helped by deities, the people emerge from one early world into another, until they arrive in our world. Central Asian animism was translated by many American Indians into myths of a land inhabited by powerful spirits or, in many cases, made up of the bodies of deities themselves.

So it was that the gods of Central Asia became those of North America. The old creators became the Sioux Great Mystery or Great Spirit, the Athabascan Changing Woman, and the ubiquitous tricksters, Coyote, Raven, the Great Hare, and so many others. And the earth-diver creation stories became the shamanistic Cherokee Sun tale, the Iroquoian and Cherokee myths of the woman falling from the sky to assist in the animals in their search for earth, and countless other earth-diver myths adapted to the conditions of the tribes in question. And the animism of Asia was transformed into myths such as those of the Zuni Earth Mother and Sky Father, the Inuit Sedna, and the Cherokee Star Woman, whose bodies became earth's bounties.

Creation Myths

Creation myths are the most important myths for Native Americans, as they are for most peoples. A culture's creation myth is a statement of its relation to the greater powers of the cosmos. The Sky Father, the Earth Mother, and the trickster-helper of any given creation are concerned with the creation, preservation, and destiny of a particular culture. We are the Hebrews or the Egyptians or the Dineh or the Sioux because Yahweh or the Great Mystery made us so. The creation myth gives a culture significance in a universe that must otherwise be considered random and meaningless.

Zuni: The Separation of the First Parents

As in the case of so many creation myths involving a Sky Father and Earth Mother—the Egyptian and the Greek myths, for example—the world parents must be separated, or differentiated, in order that there might be room for creation to take place between earth and sky. In this story told by the Zuni Indians of the American Southwest is a classic example of this separation.

The Zuni creation culminates in a story of emergence and migration. It begins, however as an animistic tale in which the originators of life— Earth Mother and Sky Father—are themselves the elements of creation, separated from each other like the Egyptian Earth and Sky (Geb and Nut) so as to provide room for the creation between them. The Mother actually is the earth and the Father is the sky. In addition, the Mother's breath is the warm wind, the Father's the cold; the Mother's breasts are the fields that give crops, and the Father's breath brings the rain that causes the germination of the seeds in the Mother. The universe, in short, is suffused by the power of the deities.

In the fourfold womb of the world, all terrestrial life was conceived from the lying-together of Earth Mother and Sky Father upon the world waters. Soon Earth Mother grew large with progeny, pushed Sky Father away from her, and began to sink into the waters. She feared that evil might befall her offspring, just as mothers always fear for their firstborn before they emerge.

Unnerved by her ominous, foreboding thoughts, she kept her offspring within her and discussed her fears with Sky Father. They wondered how these offspring would know one place from another, even in the light of the sun. They wondered how their progeny would survive.

They were surpassing beings, these two, and therefore changeable as the smoke in the breeze. And so they took the form of a man and a woman.

Then a great bowl filled with water appeared nearby, and Earth Mother realized that every place in the world would be surrounded by mountains like the rim of the bowl that was near her. She spat in the water and, as foam formed on its surface, she said, "Look! It's from my bosom that they will find sustenance."

She blew her warm breath over the foam and some of it lifted upward, shattering in the air, sending mist and spray down in great, shimmering abundance.

"Just so will clouds form at the rim of the world where the great waters are," she said, "and be borne on the breath of the surpassing beings until your cold breath makes them shed, falling downward—the waters of life falling into my lap, where our children will nestle and thrive, finding warmth in spite of your coldness."

"Wait," Sky Father said, and he spread his hand over the bowl, setting in its crevices what looked like yellow corn grains gleaming in the dark of the early dawn of the world. He took seven grains between his thumb and fingers and said, "When the Sun is gone and all is dark in the world, our children will be guided by these lights, which will tell them the regions of space. And just as these grains shine up from the water to the sky, so will innumerable seedlings like them spring up from your bosom whenever my waters touch them, and our children will be fed."

In this way, and in many others, Earth Mother and Sky Father talked and provided for their offspring and their offspring's progeny, the people and the other creatures of the world.

A Cherokee Earth-diver Creation Myth

The creation myths of the Cherokee, who were forcibly moved from the Southeast to the Southwest, include a female sun as well as the earth-diver motif and the belief in animistic origins.

Everyone agrees that at one time almost beyond memory the world was covered with water. Whatever was alive lived in Galunlati, the vault of the sky beyond the rainbow, where it was so crowded the animals could barely move around. They sought a solution to this discomfort, and so they sent Water Beetle down to the watery world. He dove down into the waters and eventually returned to the surface with a gob of mud that began slowly to spread out. This became the earth-island, which the Great Spirit attached to the sky with four pieces of rawhide tied to the four sacred mountains that lie in the four sacred directions.

Still, the earth-island was muddy and too soft, so Buzzard was sent down to locate a dry spot. Finally he came to a place where the mud was drying out, and with great flappings of his wings he created mountains and valleys. When the land was ready, the other animals migrated down from beyond the rainbow and were dismayed to find that their new home was dark. So they decided to pull Sister Sun down from the vault of the sky and showed her the path she should follow each day.

They say that the Great Spirit, knowing things, sent the plants down to live among the animals and sustain them. He asked that the plants and the animals all stay awake for seven days. Most of the creatures fell asleep before the time was up, but Owl stayed awake and was given the power of night sight. Some of the plants also managed to stay awake the entire time, and these—pine, holly, laurel, and a few others—were permitted to keep their hair throughout the year. The other plants were told they would have to shed their leaves each year when the cold began and grow them again when the weather began to warm up.

The Great Spirit then thought to make a man and a woman. The man proceeded to press a fish against the woman, which made her grow large and eventually give birth to a child. Every seven days she gave birth to another child, until the Great Spirit rearranged things a little bit so that she could have a new child only once a year. That is how we Cherokee came to be.

A Tewa Emergence Creation Myth

The emergence origin motif is represented here by a version of a myth told by many of the Tewa-speaking people of the Rio Grande Valley in New Mexico.

In the beginning, the people lived underground in total darkness. Dissatisfied with this existence, they were glad to be visited one time by Mole, who came down from above. They asked Mole what it was like up there where he had come from, and he replied that he was blind and couldn't say exactly. But it felt different up there. Maybe they should come up and see for themselves.

Mole proceeded to dig his way up, and the dirt got in the people's way, so they piled it up behind them as they went along. Therefore, they never were able to find their way back into the old world. Finally, they emerged into a world of blinding light. In a panic, they covered their eyes and tried to find their way back to the old world. But a voice told them to be patient. Slowly, as instructed, they took their hands away from their eyes, and there before them was the old, stooped grandmother of everything: Spider Woman.

With Spider Woman were her grandsons, the War Twins. She said, "I don't want you to become like these two foolish boys who waste their time fighting each other. If you want to be happy, you won't use weapons."

She pointed to some green stalks of growing corn and told the people how to do the work to keep the corn growing each year. Next, she said the proper place for the people to live was within sight of the great Turtle Mountain to the south, which nowadays some people call Sandia Mountain. Go forth, she told them, and when they found her and Mole again, they would know they had come upon exactly the right place. Having said that, she faded away into the night. The people were terrified, and again they panicked; the next day they ignored her advice, going to another mountain instead of Turtle Mountain.

There they were set upon by Comanches, and many were killed. This mountain came to be known as Los Sangres, which means "blood." Soon the people were quarreling and making weapons and killing one another; high up in the sky, the War Twins watched and laughed.

Finally the people straggled back to the place where they had emerged into this Middle World, hoping to find Spider Woman again, but she wasn't there. Soon, though, they spotted her high up in the night sky in her beautiful shining web. She was shaking her head in sadness over their foolishness, and weeping little star tears. The people started, one by one, to go up into the sky to be with Spider Woman, and before long there were only two people left. They went south through the hard and hostile desert, traveling a long time, until they saw green trees growing in a long row and came to the Rio Grande. In the sand along the river they found a turtle. It was the turtle of Turtle Mountain. Looking closely, the man and woman saw that it had Spider Woman's sign on its back and that it left tracks in the sand like Mole's tracks.

They were home.

A Hawaiian Creation Myth

The creation myth of the Polynesian natives of Hawaii, contained in a sacred poem called the Kumulipo, contains animistic elements as well as aspects of the emergence motif.

First, out of the very nothing, there was born Kumulipo, who was male and the essence of darkness, and Po'ele, who was female and the darkness itself. They gave birth to the children of darkness, shellfish, and the plants that grow from the dark earth. Soon many kinds of creatures of this kind existed and a bit of light appeared in the world. The god Kane-i-ka-wai-ola watered the plants.

Then deep darkness (male) and darkness with a little light (female) came into being and bore the fish of the sea, which multiplied. Still, there was little light to be seen in the world. Then Po'el'ele (who was dark night and male) was born along with Pohahha, who was female: night becoming dawn. Together they brought the insects into being, as well as an egg, from which came the bird, followed by many others. At this time in the world, it looked they way it does today a little before dawn.

In this very dim light, Popanopano and Polalowehi came about and gave rise to the animals like turtles that come to the land from the sea. Next, another male and female pair of beings was born and they gave rise to the pig, Kamapua'a, dark and beautiful. His people, the pigs, began to root around and cultivate the islands that were now flourishing in the dim light.

Yet another pair gave rise to Pilo'i the rat, and this was a mistake. For the rat people scratched and ate and began to damage the land. Next, a male and female pair arose whose names meant "night leaving" and "night pregnant." They gave birth to dawn, as well as the wind . . . and the dog. It was Po-kini and Po'he'enalu who gave birth to the time when humans came into the world, and into this time La'ila'a, the woman, and Ki'i, the man, were born. It was daytime in our world.

Goddesses

The goddess figure is important to many Native American cosmologies. If creation long ago was instigated by a male figure or one of no particular gender, the actual working out of creation, especially in its relation to human society, is more often than not dominated by the female figure, whether Spider Woman, Thinking Woman, Changing Woman, White Buffalo Woman, or one of many other such beings.

A Navajo Myth of Changing Woman

For the Navajo and Apache Indians of the Southwest, the most important deity is Changing Woman, who affected human life at its origins at the time of the Emergence, but who continues to enter the world in the female puberty rites so central to the lives of the Athabascan-speaking Indians.

When First Man and First Woman and the other emergent people came into this, the Glittering World, they were followed by monsters that had been born of their self-abuse in the previous world. And before too long, the monsters had devoured everyone but First Man and First Woman and four others. First Man hoped that the gods would help them, but First Woman doubted it, saying that they didn't yet know what pleased or displeased the gods. One morning, First Man noticed that a dark cloud covered the crest of the mountain known today as Gobernador's Knob. He decided to investigate, saying that he would protect himself by surrounding himself with songs. Just as he got to the peak, amid lightning, thunder, and driving rain, he heard an infant cry. Finding the spot in spite of the blinding storms, he discovered a small piece of turquoise in the form of a female, which he took down the mountain to First Woman, instructing her to care for it.

In an elaborate ceremony, a female baby was created from the turquoise figure, and she would become Changing Woman. When she came of age, reaching puberty, a ceremony was held in order that she would be able to bear children. She was dressed in white beads and ran four times in the direction of the rising sun. Talking God, one of the Holy People, sang twelve songs.

Sometime after the ceremony, which is called a Kinaalda to this day, Changing Woman grew lonely and wandered off. She lay down on a flat rock near a waterfall with her feet facing east, and she felt the warmth of the sun come over her and fill her being. In time, she gave birth to twin boys, who would come to be known as Monster Slayer and Child Born of Water. As they grew up, they were challenged to ever greater feats by Talking God and the Wind, until they were fit to take on the greatest challenge facing the world: the monsters that still roamed the land.

In a series of great battles, they fought the monsters and slew them. Then they traveled to the four sacred mountains, from which they could see that there were no more monsters to be slain. There was now order and harmony in the world. With their father, the sun, they buried the corpses of the monsters under the blood of one of the monsters, Big Giant, which had spilled down the sides of Mount Taylor and can be seen today as what some people think of as lava.

Five days later, the Sun came to Changing Woman and asked her to go with him to the west. There, he said, he would establish a home for her, so that they could be together at the end of his daily labors. But Changing Woman would have nothing to do with him. She knew, for example, that he also had a home—and a wife—in the east. He tried to persuade her:

"What use is male without female? What use is female without male? What use are we two without each other?" Still Changing Woman resisted the sun's warm embrace, but she began to think that perhaps she was lonely after all.

After a long silence, she explained that she would want a beautiful house, as beautiful as the sun's eastern house, "floating on the shimmering water," away from war and disharmony, surrounded instead by gems and animals to keep her company during the long hours each day when the sun was away. Nonplussed, the sun asked her why she made such demands, and she said:

"You are of the sky, and I am of the earth. You are constant in your brightness, but I must change with the seasons." And she said: "Remember, as different as we are, you and I, we are of one spirit. As dissimilar as we are, you and I, we are of equal worth. As unlike as you and I are, there must always be solidarity between the two of us. Unlike each other as you and I are, there can be no harmony in the universe as long as there is no harmony between us. If there is to be such harmony, then my requests must matter to you."

So it was agreed in those olden times, and Changing Woman went to live in the west beyond the farthest shore, joined each evening by the sun. But Changing Woman soon found her days long and lonely, and she yearned for mortal company. Her breasts swelled, her hips, her abdomen. The Holy People came and laid her down, head pointing west, and rubbed her body into perfection. And by rubbing skin from her breast, her back, and under each arm, Changing Woman then created the clans who would become the Dineh, the people—the Navajo.

For the Dineh, Changing Woman remains the ideal for which all women strive. And it is remembered even today that if the sun and Changing Woman, the creatrix of the people and the goddess of the earth and the seasons, do not get along, then no Navajo can walk in beauty.

A Sioux Myth of White Buffalo Woman

The goddess traditionally teaches the people how to live properly. This is particularly so of White Buffalo Woman, who is sacred to the Lakota Sioux and other Plains Indians.

Long ago the people were starving.

Each day, scouts went forth but returned without having seen any game. One day, two young men went off to hunt and thought to climb a high hill so they could see far across the plain. Partway up the hill they saw a figure floating toward them from the distant horizon, and they knew at once that it was a holy person.

As it came closer, they saw that it was a most beautiful young woman, with red spots on her cheeks. She was clad in white buckskin that gleamed in the sun and was richly embroidered with rows of porcupine quills. As she approached, one of the young men reached out to grab her, but a bolt of lightning crackled in the air and burned the rash young man into a small pile of charred bones.

She explained to the other young man, who stood in awe, that she was White Buffalo Woman and would bring his people some good things and some holy things from the nation of the buffalo. She told him to go back to his people and tell them to erect a medicine lodge. She told him what prayers they had to say to make the lodge holy.

They did all this, and four days later White Buffalo Woman appeared, entered the lodge, and told the people to make an altar of red earth. They did so, and she drew a design on the altar and withdrew from her bundle a sacred red pipe, holding the stem in her right hand and the bowl in her left. She filled it with material made from red willow bark and lit it. The smoke they could see rising from the pipe, she told them, was the breath of the Great Mystery.

She taught them the proper way to pray, and how to lift the pipe to the sky, hold it to the earth, and hold it in the four directions. This way, the earth, the sky, and all living things are knit into one family, held together by the pipe. The bowl of red stone represents the buffalo, whose four legs are the four directions. The pipe's wooden stem represents all things that grow in the earth, and the twelve eagle feathers hanging from the stem are those of the messenger to the Great Spirit. The seven designs carved on the bowl are the seven ceremonies the people would practice from that time onward.

White Buffalo Woman explained to the women there that the work of their hands and the fruit of their bodies kept the people alive. They were of Mother Earth and were therefore as important as the warriors and hunters. Thus the pipe, its bowl carved by men and its stem made by women, bind the two together in love. From her bundle, White Buffalo Woman took corn and other food and gave them to the women. She taught them how to make fire and how to cook.

She told the children that they were the most precious and important of all the people. And she told the chief that the pipe was very sacred. She entrusted it to the people, saying that if they treated it with respect, it would see them through to the end of their road here on this earth.

Promising that she would return to them, she left, walking directly toward the red orb of the setting sun. Four times she rolled over, each time turning into a buffalo—first a black one, then a brown one, then a red one, and finally a white one. A white buffalo remains to this day the most sacred thing alive, and there is great rejoicing whenever one is born.

Once White Buffalo Woman disappeared beyond the horizon, great herds of buffalo appeared and roamed the plains, making themselves available to be killed to furnish people with all that they needed—food, skins, tools. And the red pipe that White Buffalo Woman gave to the people so long ago is still with them—still sacred, still the source of the Lakotas' knowledge of how to live and how to pray.

An Inuit Myth of Sedna

A goddess imported from Siberia who is central to the animistic mythologies of many of the Inuit peoples of Alaska and Canada is Sedna, out of whose bodily sacrifice arise the creatures of the world.

The world came from nothing, with the help of old Anguta. Anguta lived with his daughter Sedna, a beautiful and most desirable woman. Sedna loved the old man but she did not appreciate old Anguta's constant attention—he liked to pinch her. So one day, when a great seabird that today we call a fulmar flew over and urged her to follow him, she did so without another thought.

The fulmar led Sedna to his home, and the beautiful woman was horrified. His tent stank and there was nothing to eat. She called out for her father, but to no avail, and for a year lived in the foul home of the fulmar. At the end of the year, her father did come, bringing warm winds that broke up the ice. He killed the fulmar, put Sedna and her dogs in his boat, and headed for home.

When the other fulmars found that their chief had been killed, they mourned with the long sad cries you can hear them making even today. At the same time, they grew furious and searched the sea far and wide for Anguta's boat. Once they saw it, they blew up a huge, raging storm that began tossing the boat high and low on ferocious waves.

To save himself, Anguta threw his daughter overboard into the icy sea, and when she clutched at the side of the boat, he chopped her fingers off. Some of the fingers sank into the sea and became whales, fish, and other sea creatures. Sedna sank into the sea and the storm subsided, but she wasn't yet dead. Instead, she managed to haul herself back into the boat.

In the lull of the storm, Anguta had fallen asleep, and in vengeance Sedna ordered her dogs to bite off her father's hands and feet. Waking up, Anguta cursed everything and everyone, and the earth opened its great maw and swallowed him, the dogs, and Sedna. But just before she vanished, Sedna created the deer.

Now Anguta and Sedna both live beneath the world in a place called Adlivun. There Sedna rules and old Anguta hobbles around painfully on his stumps. When people die, they go to Sedna's house in Adlivun, but if they have been bad in their lives, they are forced to sleep with Anguta, who pinches them unmercifully.

Trickster Gods

The best-known archetypal figure in American Indian mythology is the trickster. The trickster is also a significant presence in African American and European American folklore. This mysterious and often outrageous character is promiscuous and amoral and often takes animal form— Spider in Africa, Brer Rabbit in the American South, and Raven and Coyote among Native American peoples. Yet he is also inventive and sometimes serves as the primary assistant to the supreme creator. Sometimes he is a culture hero or god, as in the case of the Indian Krishna or the Great Hare of the American Indian plains and woodlands. Carl Jung saw the trickster as "an earlier rudimentary stage of consciousness," possessing untamed appetites not yet tempered by a social conscience. Jung also saw in the creative aspect of the trickster a hint of later shamanic "medicine people" and savior culture heroes. Like the shaman, the trickster can change forms at will and transcend human limitations. Even his excessive eroticism suggests his creative power, his drive to create new things and ideas.

Newspaper Rock. From *Native America: Arts, Traditions, and Celebrations,* by Christine Mather. Photo © 1990 by Jack Parsons. Reprinted by permission of Crown Publishers, Inc.

A Karuk Myth of Coyote

The most widely known of the Native American tricksters is Coyote. Found in nearly all sections of the country, he is always creative—sometimes in the interest of the tribe but more often in pursuit of the objects of his extreme lechery and gluttony. Coyote is friendly with other amoral tricksters, such as the Plains Spider (Iktome). In this Karuk myth Coyote displays his transforming abilities and his creative lechery.

Coyote drew near the river and looked this way and that. Then he stooped to the water and drank. He drank a long time, drank a lot of water, and when he stood up, he fell over backward into the river.

He floated downriver, back to the center of the world, and looked to see where he was. There on the shore, he saw young women bleaching flour.

"Aha!" Coyote said. "I'll just turn myself into a pretty piece of driftwood and see what happens."

He floated downstream, now looking like a piece of pretty driftwood, and watched the women carefully as they worked. He licked his lips.

"I'll float to shore," he said, "and float in circles right before them at the river's edge. That's what I'll do."

One of the women looked out from the shore and saw the driftwood circling in the current.

"Oh, look at the pretty driftwood," she exclaimed.

"Where?" asked another.

"Right there, circling in the current."

"Oh, yes," said the other woman. "Let's hook it and bring it in so we can look at it."

"All right!"

So they went down to the water's edge and looked at it, floating in circles, and one of them fetched a stick and pulled it out of the water. It was so pretty! They were suddenly very fond of it, and took to throwing it back and forth, playing with the pretty piece of driftwood, and giggling.

Then one of the women stopped with a look of disgust on her face.

"Oh no," she said. "They say that Coyote drowned in the river, upstream. You don't suppose this is . . ."

They threw the driftwood back into the river, collected their flour, and left. The next morning they all felt sick to their stomachs and knew that they were pregnant. Coyote had done it, and now he was floating happily down the river.

A Tsimshian Myth of Raven

Another popular trickster, especially in the Pacific Northwest, is Raven. A series of myths that form what is, in effect, a Raven cycle or Raven epic was collected early in this century by a Tsimshian, William Tate. In the Tate version we find an emphasis on the creative aspect of the trickster. The myth included here contains several motifs common to many cultures around the world, themes such as the miraculous conception and the theft of fire.

At this time, the animal people lived in a village at the tip of the Queen Charlotte Islands, and it was always dark. The chief's beloved (and spoiled) son grew ill and died, and his parents wailed and moaned for days, demanding also that the others in the village join in the mourning. Then one day the mother went to the loft where the boy's body had been put and she saw a young man who shone with the brightness of fire.

The young man explained that Heaven was irritated by all the wailing and had sent him down to calm the peoples' minds and hush them up. Both parents were overjoyed, thinking that this was their son returned to them from the dead. But the young man refused to eat, and the mother began to worry. He might die again if he didn't eat. She tried one food after another, but nothing would awaken the young man's appetite.

But he had noticed two of his father's slaves—a male and a female, both named A Mouth at Each End. These two ate large quantities of food.

"You don't want to be like us," the female slave said. "We eat our own scabs to get hungry." At this, the male slave scraped a scab from his leg and gave it to the young man in a dish of whale meat. The young man tried it and grew hungry.

After that he did nothing but eat, growing bigger and bigger, until the town's entire store of food was gone. By now his father the chief was ashamed, and gave him the skin of a raven to wear, and called him Giant. He handed Giant a bladder full of seeds and told him to fly over to the mainland and plant berries on the hillsides and put fish eggs in the streams so there would be plenty for him to eat. He also gave him a round stone to rest on when he got tired.

On the way across the water Giant dropped the stone, and it became a large rock, which he rested on. Later he flew on, and after scattering the fish eggs and sowing the seeds, he thought it would be easier to collect food if there was light.

Now, he knew light was to be found in Heaven, so he flew up through the clouds in the form of the raven, and there he found the daughter of Heaven's chief about to drink from a pot of water. He changed himself into a cedar leaf and floated in the water, and the girl swallowed him and got pregnant.

So Giant was soon born into the sky chief's house and stole daylight, which he found hanging from the ceiling in a box. He took it back to earth, and where he landed, the frog people were fishing in the dark. He told them to throw him a candlefish. The frog people refused, so he opened up the box to spite them, and the world was filled with light.

People started calling him Chemsen, and as he wandered along on the earth, he had many adventures and accomplished many things. He met Stone and Elderberry, who were arguing about which of them would be first to give birth. If it was Stone who delivered first, all the creatures would live forever. But Chemsen reached over and touched Elderberry, and she delivered first. That's why people die and why elderberries grow on their graves.

In this way, Chemsen the Raven went about stealing fire for the people, making the tides come and go, making it so that the animals and the people had to couple to make children, teaching people how to cook fish. Oh, Chemsen did plenty of things on this earth before he turned into a stone shaped like his former self. But somewhere to the east, he still lives, and if you are wandering that way, he might help you.

The Indian and the White Man

A Brule Sioux Myth of the Coming of the White Man

In the nineteenth century most Indians were preoccupied by the invasion of their lands by the European Americans. Not surprisingly, a body of mythology emerged which reflected that concern.

While there were prophecies among some tribes that spoke of the arrival of light-skinned people in their midst, the earliest appearance of Europeans was surely a shock for the native populations of North America. In 1539, for example, Hernando de Soto began a four-year siege out of Florida and through the tribal lands of the American Southeast. In 1540, a Creek chief is reported to have addressed him as follows: "Very high, powerful, and good master. The things that seldom happen bring astonishment. Think, then, what must be the effect, on me and mine, of the sight of you and your people, whom we at no time have seen, astride the fierce brutes, your horses, entering with such speed and fury into my country, that we have no tidings of your coming—things altogether new as to strike awe and terror into our hearts."

Word of the arrival of these strange and potent people, the Europeans, would have spread with great speed among the native inhabitants, however, just as trade goods such as parrot feathers, turquoise, copper objects, and shells moved transcontinentally among the tribes. A Sioux tale explains (obviously long, long after the fact) that the arrival of the whites was announced by Iktome, the spider trickster who floated through the air, alerting the Arapaho, the Crow, the Shoshone, and others. Finally Iktome went to the Sioux, explaining that this new man, this white man, was coming by boat.

"He comes by boat and he is going to give you false names. He will tame you like taming dogs, and he will make you like himself. He will lie to you."

"When will he come?" asked the chief of the Sioux.

"When the prairie blooms with white flowers. You watch: The buffalo will go away to hide in the mountains. You must send your people to guard the buffalo, for the white man will try to take them all. He will bring gambling dice, sickness, and hate. He will insist that you forget Wakan Tanka and believe in his different Great Spirit, a strange one who was killed by his own people. If you believe in this new Great Spirit, you will lose your world."

"What hope have we?" the chief asked.

"I don't know. He will put a black hoop around you. Maybe one day you can break the hoop, maybe you can make this man better, wiser. You will know him as Steal-All or Fat-taker, because he will take all the fat of the land for himself. For a while, anyway."

Iktome left, having sounded his alert, and the Sioux and the other people slowly forgot about his warnings. After all, everything went along as it always had. Then, one morning after the white flowers had lit up the prairie, two Sioux women were out gathering berries when an enormous black cloud covered them. Out of the cloud, a strange creature emerged, wearing a black hat and heavy boots on his feet. He was pale of skin, yellow of hair, blue of eye. Hair grew from under his nose and fell over his mouth; hair grew from his chin, from his arms. He was hairy all over.

This ugly, hairy person was sitting on an animal large as a moose, and when he spoke he didn't sound like a human being. The women couldn't understand him. In one hand he carried a cross, and in the other was a firestick that spat out lightning with a clap of thunder. From his black cloak, he took a glittering thing that seemed to have water inside it. He offered it to the women, and when they drank from the glittering thing, the water burned their throats and made them dizzy.

Worse, a sickness no one could see leaped from the man onto the women's skin, making red blisters, and they began to die. They remembered Iktome's warning and realized that Steal-All was here with them and that everything would be different from now on.

European American

As the Native Americans centuries earlier had brought religious traditions from Central Asia to their new lands, the Europeans who arrived in North America in significant numbers in the sixteenth and seventeenth centuries brought their religious traditions with them. But the traditions of some groups of Native Americans had evolved from their Central Asian origins over a period of several thousand years in America, and their mythology changed, too, becoming inextricably connected to the landscapes, flora, and fauna of the Americas, whereas European mythology has changed much less because of the much shorter time period since their arrival only several hundred years ago. Furthermore, whereas Native American myths and religious ideas have until very recently been transmitted orally by widely scattered tribes, the Spanish and the English brought a Judeo-Christian tradition that was preached (albeit from several ritual and theological perspectives) from a single written source, the Bible. As a result, it is easier to trace the sources and development of European mythology in America than of Native American stories. Still, although still recognizable as a religious and mythological structure exported from Europe, Christianity in America, more so than other recent imports such as Judaism or East Asian religions, has taken on characteristics that are clearly influenced by local conditions. For example, peculiarly American offshoots of Christianity include Mormonism, African American deliverance-based worship, the Nation of Islam, and Hispanic phenomena such as the cult of the Virgin of Guadalupe and Penitentism. Each of these approaches to deity, and many others, has developed dogmas, rituals, icons, and mythologies with sources in the American experience.

The Landfall of Jean Nicolet, by E. W. Deming. Courtesy State Historical Society of Wisconsin.

Hispanic Visions

When the Spaniard Francisco Vásquez de Coronado explored the American Southwest in the early 1540s, he brought Franciscan friars with him, and by 1598, when the New Mexico province was made a colony, the friars were given free rein to convert Native Americans to Roman Catholicism. The methods of the friars were often brutal, and a concentrated effort was made to stamp out Indian myth and ritual. The Pueblo uprising of 1680 resulted in a revival of Indian religion, the destruction of the missions, and in some cases a direct confrontation between the Catholic priests and real-life versions of Indian religious power figures. It is said that warrior *kachinas* (spirits) among the Hopis killed friars during the revolt.

With the reestablishment of Spanish power in the 1690s, the missions were rebuilt as well but gradually, even among converted Indians, the old religious myths and rituals were revived, and many remain intact to this day—especially among the Hopi, the Zuni, and the Pueblos of the Rio Grande. If one goes to the Pueblo of San Felipe in February for the Feast of the Purification of the Virgin Mary—the Feast of Candlemass or Candelaria—for instance, one would discover going on in the plaza a complex mystery play and dance based on an ancient Indian myth of the Buffalo King and a maiden. The connection between Mary and this maiden is slight or nonexistent.

The Virgin of Guadalupe

Mary and the myths connected with her do, however, play an important role in the Americanization of Roman Catholicism. Among the Indians of Mexico and later those of the American Southwest, the Virgin Mary and particular cults associated with her stood as a tempering force against the harsh policies of the conquistadors. The tradition of the nurturing goddess had always been strong among the native peoples, and it was not particularly difficult to translate a figure such as the virgin mother of the Aztec god Huitzilopochtli into a new "goddess" such as the famous Virgin of Guadalupe. The Guadalupe, as she is called, became a cult figure in New Spain soon after her supposed appearance in 1531, not only among Mexican Indians but among the Spanish themselves. Her fame quickly spread northward, and today the Virgin of Guadalupe is a powerful religious presence not only in Mexico, where her banner has even led soldiers into battle, but in the American Southwest, particularly in Texas and New Mexico.

The Virgin of Guadalupe is a dark virgin; her skin is the color of earth and of her Indian connections: the moon goddess of the Chorti and Otomi, on whose crescent she is always depicted as standing, and the Nahuatl earth goddess Tonantzin ("Mother") on whose sacred hill she was said to have appeared and whose language she was said to have spoken. She has still older ancestors among the earth-oriented Black Madonnas of Europe. Many Mexican Indians still call Mary Tonantzin. But she is more gentle than the old Aztec goddess unless serious sins are committed, in which case she becomes a bringer of sickness and death, like the old Tonantzin or other archetypal dark relatives such as the Hindu goddess Kali.

Early on the day of December 9, 1531, an Indian peasant named Juan Diego of the village of Tolpetlac was on his way to the town of Tlatlolco near Mexico City. A convert to Christianity, Juan Diego intended to attend mass there.

This journey led him past a hill once considered one of the sacred hills of Tonantzin, the Aztec fertility goddess associated with the moon. It was still a place of great power even though the Lord Jesus and His Blessed Mother had replaced Tonantzin in the hearts of the people. And on this day, Juan Diego heard a beautiful voice singing quietly and looked up to see a bright golden cloud upon the hill.

The singing paused and a voice called to him from the cloud, beckoning him by his very name, Juan Diego. He made his way up the hill and saw at the top a dark-skinned woman—she had the complexion of an Indian, just like his. From all around her the golden cloud emanated so brilliantly that it lit up the rocks and the cacti like gemstones in the dim light of early morning. She spoke. She said she was the Virgin Mary and would help the Indian people if their bishop would build a shrine here on her hill.

Juan forgot all about the mass he planned to attend. Instead, he hastened to the bishop and finally gained an audience, explaining what he had seen and heard on the hill. But the cleric simply did not believe so outlandish a story. Perhaps something had made this peasant's mind feverish.

On his way back home that evening, Juan Diego climbed the hill and explained what had happened. The cloud-lit figure asked him to try again the next day, and Juan Diego suggested that perhaps she should send someone of more noble stature than he, who was a mere peasant. But she insisted urgently that it be Juan Diego who made her appeal to the bishop.

So the following day Juan Diego gained another interview with the bishop, who was still skeptical, saying he needed a more certain sign than the mere word of a peasant. And again, that evening, the lady on the hill reappeared and told Juan Diego he had to try once more.

It turned out that Juan Diego could not comply. He learned that his uncle had taken ill and spent the next day and night caring for him. When, at dawn, the old man took a turn for the worse, Juan Diego went out to find a priest to administer the last rites.

He took a path that avoided the hill, but the lady appeared to him yet again, saying that his uncle was cured and he should climb the hill and pick some roses he would find there on a miraculous bush. He did as she bade, and when he returned to her with the roses, she arranged them in his cloak, telling him to take the cloak to the bishop.

Once again, Juan Diego presented himself to the bishop. When he loosened his cloak, the roses fell out, and inside the cloak there appeared the likeness of Our Lady of Guadalupe.

Here was the sign the bishop required. He caused a shrine to be built on the hill, and today it is a basilica to which thousands of pilgrims come each year to behold the very cloak that Juan Diego took to the bishop so long ago. Nuestra Señora de Guadalupe, Our Lady of Guadalupe, is the patroness today of all Mexico, and her likeness is found in the homes of millions of Spanish-speaking people all over the United States. She is often pictured standing in a full-body aura on the horns of a black crescent moon, supported there by an angel. In the state of New Mexico alone, there are eight localities identified as Guadalupe in honor of the Dark Virgin. There, as shown on the flat, painted *retablos,* she is the most popular version of the Holy Mother except perhaps for Nuestra Señora de los Dolores, associated with the Penitentes. The Virgin of Guadalupe is known to intercede with general favors in sickness and against all evil, especially war.*

La Llorona

An example of the Kali side of the Hispanic version of the goddess figure is La Llorona—the Weeping Woman. Originating in Mexico, La Llorona is said to have murdered her own child and as penance must wander about looking for him. In some versions she is a femme fatale who lures men into dark places and murders them. Scholars have compared her to the arrogant and dangerous Lilith, said to have been the first wife of Adam. She is always shrouded and can be met anywhere. She should, of course, be avoided. In Oaxaca and other parts of Mexico, something of her power is expressed in a popular dance called Llorona, in which the woman lures the man with seductive movements as she looks back at him over her shoulder.

Me and my frenn Jesus, you know, Jesus Gutierrez? He works down at the Pep Boys. Use to, anyway. Well, listen, Jesus and me, we were down at the Yellow Rooster one night last month drinkin. Yeah, lookin for action too, you know.

But the place was dead, mon, dead, so we just drank for a while and then we left. We thought we'd go on over to Raphael's, that place on Seventh?

So we're walkin and Jesus says, "Hey, mon, look at that!"

Walkin along right in front of us is this chick, I mean a *chick!* She had it packed in this tight black dress, swayin back and forth. I mean a *chiquita.*

So me and Jesus, we follow her, see if we can catch up to her real casual, you know? Jesus, he's got his comb out and all that. We're walkin along watchin her and she turns right on Seventh—hey! like she's headed for Raphael's too.

We walk faster and begin to catch up, and Jesus puts away his comb, and we're only this far behind her—maybe ten feet—and then it's like

*Based on Steele, 98–107, 175. For full citation for this and all footnotes, see the Bibliography.

some kind of dream. Suddenly she's way far ahead, like maybe a hunnah feet. She goes right past Raphael's so we say forget it, forget it, we'll go in Raphael's without her. But Jesus calls out to her:

"Hey, baby, you don' know what you're missin."

You know, trash like that. Just then she turns around and stares back at us. She had these long fingernails—really long ones like claws— and they shined in the streetlight like they're made of tin or something, chrome. Yeah, but get this. Her face—she's lookin right at us—it's the face of a horse! She lets out this long, high-pitched wailing sound, like a shriek! Scary. I'm tellin you, like my chest felt like ice.

Yeah, that's right. It was La Llorona. The Weeping Woman. The one who killed her ninos. I was gonna run, but Jesus just fainted right there on the sidewalk. By the time I got him on his feet, she was gone.

It was her. We didn' go to Raphael's after that. No way, mon. I quit drinkin. I don' know about Jesus. Ain't seen him around since then.*

The Sacred Earth of Chimayo

Pilgrimages to sites sacred to the Virgin of Guadalupe and other Madonnas, such as La Conquistadora of Santa Fe, are commonplace in the Southwest. Other pilgimages to other types of sacred sites are also popular, and usually there is a myth attached to the traditions. Among the most popular of pilgimage sites in the Southwest is the little early-nineteenth-century church in northern New Mexico called the Santuario de Chimayo, to which pilgims regularly come to be restored and cured by the sacred earth over which it stands. The tradition of healing earth is by no means peculiar to Chimayo or to any single religion. Before the Santurio de Chimayo was built, the Tewa-speaking Indians of northern New Mexico had long taken mud from a pool in the area—some say from the very same spot over which the present church stands—and used it for curative purposes, and one Tewa myth tells of the Holy Twins' killing of the giant Tsi-mayo (Chimayo) near the site of the Santurio.

Also in the background of the Chimayo cult is the shrine of the Black Christ, Nuestro Señor de Esquipulas, in the village of Esquipulas in Guatemala. The Black Christ, like the Virgin of Guadelupe, has the dark skin of the indigenous population. But the color of his skin also reflects that of the earth in Esquipulas, and the Mayans of the area, like the Tewa of New Mexico, had long made use of the curative powers of

*Source for this rewritten version is Dorson, 436–38.

El Santuario de Chimayo. Ink wash drawing. © 1985 Elizabeth Kay. By permission.

the earth there. When the Spanish arrived in the sixteenth century they
assimilated the tradition into the cult of the Black Christ.

According to the myth told in El Potrero, or Chimayo, it was one Bernardo Abeyta (1771–1856), an important member of the Penitente Brotherhood (see below), who introduced the cult of the curing earth and the Black Christ crucifix to Chimayo and caused the building of the church, whose official name is El Santuario de Esquipulas. According to one of many popular versions of the myth, Bernardo discovered the sacred earth and the cross during Holy Week sometime early in the nineteenth century. As he was doing penitential rituals in the hills around El Potrero, the story goes, he saw a mysterious light coming from a spot on the ground. From the spot he dug out a crucifix that, like the one of Esquipulas, supported a Black Christ. The crucifix was carried several times to a nearby town's church but mysteriously found its way back to the sacred hole. Finally, accepting the miracle, the people of Chimayo recognized the curative powers of the earth and built the church to protect and venerate the cross and the hole containing the holy earth. In some versions of the story it was a shepherd who found the hole and the crucifix and a mule that brought the cross back to its rightful place.

The Penitentes—the Passion

In regions of the Southwest, especially New Mexico and southern Colorado, the rituals and stories of Christianity took on particular characteristics reminiscent of the practices of Spain. Los Hermanos Penitentes (Penitent Brothers)—sometimes simply the Cofradias (Confraternities) or Hermandades (Brotherhoods)—were and still are groups of laymen devoted to community and to the sacrament of penance, expressed to some extent in flagellation and in rites associated with the suffering and death, the Passion, of Jesus. Penitential confraternities had been a presence in Spain since the Middle Ages, and they were brought to the New World by the Spanish explorers and conquistadors.

It was not until the late eighteenth and early nineteenth centuries, however, that the Penitentes became a powerful force in New Mexico. Their importance grew as the number of Franciscan friars, who had been associated with Spanish rule, diminished with Mexico's independence from Spain. In the absence of the friars and a shortage of priests in general, the Penitente moradas (chapters; the word also refers to the church buildings or meeting places of the Penitentes), although made up of laymen, were in a position to provide pastoral care and ritual richness to a spiritually deprived people.

The story with which the Penitentes are most widely associated is that of the Passion of Christ, and most specifically the events of Good Friday or La Día de la Cruz (Day of the Cross). There is a meeting early in the day between Christ and his mother, represented typically by an image of Christ carried by Penitentes from their morada and a statue of Mary brought by villagers from their local church. Then there is the procession following the Stations of the Cross, including the flagellation of Christ (who is played by a Penitente), his several falls, and his crucifixion, sometimes realistically portrayed on a cross in front of the morada. La Día de la Cruz ends with Las Tinieblas, the earthquake ceremonies marking the cracking of the Temple walls after Christ's death. When a white candle signifying the living Christ is extinguished, the members of the congregation create the "earthquake" with the noise of drums, chains on pots, and their own stomping and shouting, and the Penitentes whip themselves.

The Penitente vision of the Christian Passion story is contained not only in the ritual but in the alabados (hymns) that accompany the events of La Día de la Cruz.

One must picture the brother enacting Christ.

Clad in a black cowl and white cotton drawers rolled up as a loincloth, his arms and wrists are tied to the main member of a cross with horsehair rope, with a band of linen around his chest as well. The cross is laid on the ground with its foot near a hole dug for the purpose, and raised, facing the *morada*. For up to twenty minutes the black-cowled figure hangs on the cross until its head falls forward and the body slumps. Then the *hermanos* lower the cross and bear it back into the *morada*, singing.

> On that dolorous way,
> With Dimas and Jestas,
> He fell three times,
> With the cross uphill.
>
> With gall and vinegar
> They strengthened Him,
> It was when on the cross
> Hanging there they saw Him.
>
> Adore the cross
> That He drags along
> Splashed with His blood
> That He goes shedding.
>
> Adore the garments
> With which He is dressed,
> With His own blood
> I saw Him dyed.
>
> O precious blood!
> Alleviate my suffering
> And let me drink
> From your precious chalice.*

"Anglo" Visions

In contrast to the Hispanic American approach to the religion of the European world stands that of the English immigrants of the East Coast. The Puritans, who arrived in New England in search of freedom to worship as they chose, were in fact governed by a theocracy that saw Native Americans as emissaries of Satan, whose religion was best stamped out, and non-Puritan Englishmen as people in dire need of conversion. Puritanism by the seventeenth century in America owed as much to Cal-

*Martinez, 29.

vinism as to the Anglican tradition it had attempted to reform in England. At its heart was a belief in a covenantal relationship with a stern God. The Puritan churches were gatherings of God's chosen people, capable of personal holiness or deep personal relationships with God, and America was a new Eden, the center of a new milleniarianism. As the Puritan poet Edward Taylor wrote in 1682 in his "The Glory of and Grace in the Church Set Out" from his collection entitled *God's Determinations Touching His Elect,*

> A Divine hand
> Does hand them up to glory's room—
> Where each in sweetening songs all praises shall
> Sing all o'er heaven for aye. And that's but all.

The belief in a religion of the elect working toward a perfect Christ-based society would have a strong influence on the way Americans would see themselves from the seventeenth century on. It would spawn sociological doctrines or "myths" such as those of the self-made man, manifest destiny, the work ethic, and the melting pot. Puritanism is also the ancestor of the Protestant fundamentalism and revivalism that has at various times flourished in the political and religious landscape of America. And when combined with social Darwinism—specifically, the idea that natural selection and the survival of the fittest operate in human society—the millennial doctrine of the elect has been a powerful justification for American economic power, consumption, and growth, even at the expense of the underprivileged at home and abroad.

The Edenic concept and the belief in a "new world" in European American myth was not confined to the Puritans, however. Edens sprang up all over the eastern settlements of seventeenth-century North American. For example, George Alsop saw in Maryland "Adam's realm." And the now legendary John Smith believed that in Pocahontas he had discovered Eve among the Powhatan and that the Powhatan homeland was an Eden chosen by God for a new world.

The Work Ethic—Cotton Mather

Like his father and fellow minister, Increase Mather (1629–1723), Cotton Mather (1663–1728) was a believer in the sacredness of New England. Both preached the "New England Way" as opposed to the European way. Cotton Mather's sermons are collected in The Biblia Americana, *and he hoped that the Second Coming of Christ would occur in New England, which would thus literally become the new Jerusalem.*

Like many Puritans, Mather preached the Protestant work ethic," as in his 1701 essay "A Christian at His Calling." Striving at work and saving were godly.

'Tis not honest nor Christian that a Christian should have no business to do. . . . A Christian should follow his occupation with industry. . . . It seems a man slothful in business is not a man serving the Lord. . . .

'Tis a sin, I say, 'tis ordinarily a sin, and at length it will be a shame, for a man to spend more than he gets, or make his layings out more than his comings in. . . .

Truly, justice, justice must be exactly followed in that calling by which we go to get our living. . . . Well, then, don't conceal from any customer that which you ought in equity or charity to acquaint him withal; and, more especially, if your customer do rely upon your sincerity. Don't exceed the truth, either in commendations or disparagements of commodities. Don't assert anything that is contrary to truth about the kind or price of them. . . .

Oh, let every Christian walk with God when he works at his calling.*

The Almighty Dollar—Benjamin Franklin

Perhaps the most famous secular exponent of the work ethic and its moral basis in what might be called natural capitalism is Benjamin Franklin. The almighty dollar and the work ethic are not narrative myths, but they are what might be called conceptual or sociological myths, containing beliefs central to the national character. In 1748 Franklin published his American edition of an English book called The Instructor; or A Young Man's Best Companion. *In his edition he added material particularly addressed to American acquaintances. His "Advice to a Young Tradesman" is an example.*

Remember that time is money. He that can earn ten shillings a day by his labor, and goes abroad, or sits idle, one-half of that day, though he spends but sixpence during his diversion or idleness, ought not to reckon *that* the only expense; he has really spent, or thrown away, five shillings besides.

Remember that credit is money. If a man lets his money lie in my hands after it is due, he gives me the interest. . . .

Remember that money is of the prolific, generating nature. Money can beget money, and its offspring can beget more, and so on. Five

*Van Doren, 32.

shillings turned is six, turned again it is seven and threepence, and so on till it becomes a hundred pounds. . . .

In short, the way to wealth, if you desire it, is as plain as the way to market. It depends chiefly on two words, "industry" and "frugality"; that is, waste neither time nor money, but make the best use of both.*

God and the Elect—Jonathan Edwards

In the mid-eighteenth century a religious revival, sometimes called the first Great Awakening, swept through America. One of its leading preachers was Jonathan Edwards (1703–1758). His famous sermon, "Sinners in the Hands of an Angry God," preached in 1741 at Enfield, Connecticut, is an example of the emotionalism of the revival combined with the old piety of Puritanism. It provides a picture of the latter-day Puritan's vision of the Calvinist sovereign God, of sinners among the elect, and of the ancient myth of Hell.

The God that holds you over the pit of hell, much as one holds a spider or some loathsome insect over the fire, abhors you, and is dreadfully provoked. His wrath toward you burns like fire; He looks upon you as worthy of nothing else but to be cast into the fire; He is of purer eyes than to bear to have you in His sight; you are ten thousand times so abominable in His eyes as the most hateful and venomous serpent is in ours. You have offended Him infinitely more than a stubborn rebel did his prince; and yet it is nothing but His hand that holds you from falling into the fire every moment. It is ascribed to nothing else that you did not go to hell the last night; that you were suffered to wake again in this world after you closed your eyes to sleep; and there is no other reason to be given why you have not dropped into hell since you arose in the morning, but that God's hand has held you up. There is no other reason to be given why you have not gone to hell, since you have sat here in the house of God, provoking His pure eyes by your sinful, wicked manner of attending His solemn worship; yea, there is nothing else that is to be given as a reason why you do not this very moment drop down into hell.†

The Melting Pot—Crèvecoeur

The work ethic, a belief in the essential morality of capitalism, the feeling of sinfulness, Puritan piety, and an Edenic vision of the New World

*Von Doren, 38.
†Van Doren, 35.

populated by a chosen people all contributed to the development of what European Americans have meant by the word American. The conceptual myth of the melting pot, in which a new race of chosen people, a new nation, would be created from various stock, has always been a European American myth, and the pot has not always welcomed indigenous spices or those that were imported from Africa, Asia, or even certain sections of Europe.

The French aristocrat Michel-Guillaume-Jean de Crèvecoeur (1735–1813) took the pseudonym J. Hector St. Jean when he became a citizen of the Colony of New York in 1765. Crèvecoeur traveled extensively in the colonies and the western wilderness before settling down for some years as a farmer. In his 1782 Letters from an American Farmer, he describes the product of the melting pot.

What then is the American, this new man? He is either a European or the descendant of a European; hence that strange mixture of blood which you will find in no other country. . . . He is an American who, leaving behind him all his ancient prejudices and manners, receives new ones from the new mode of life he has embraced, the new government he obeys, and the new rank he holds. He becomes an American by being received in the broad lap of our great alma mater.

Here individuals of all nations are melted into a new race of men whose labors and posterity will one day cause great change in the world. . . .

The American is a new man, who acts upon new principles; he must, therefore, entertain new ideas and form new opinions. From involuntary idleness, servile dependence, penury, and useless labor he has passed to toils of a very different nature, rewarded by ample substance. This is an American.*

Manifest Destiny—Richard Yates and William Gilpin

By the mid-nineteenth century America had come into its own as an economic and military power. Many in the new nation carried the old idea of God's elect into the realm of international politics and land policy. The age of a new conceptual myth, that of American manifest destiny, had begun.

On April 23, 1852, Illinois congressman Richard Yates used the term "manifest destiny" in connection with United States land policy.

*Von Doren, 69.

Mr. Chairman, the population of the the Valley of the Mississippi already constitutes more than one-third of the entire population of the Union. And, sir, the time is not distant when the seat of empire, the stronghold of numerical power, will be west of the Alleghenies. The handwriting is on the wall. It is *manifest destiny,* sir. It is written on the signs of the times in clear, fresh and unmistakable lines. . . .

Within the last five years three new States have been added to the Union, and there is the territory at the head of the Missouri and the Arkansas, the Territory of Nebraska, New Mexico, Utah, and Oregon—and the vision of an ocean-bound Republic is now a reality. Sir, what a mighty theater for American enterprise! What a mighty course for the race of democratic liberty!*

As Wallace Stegner would write in Beyond the Hundredth Meridian, *Governor William Gilpin of the Colorado Territory, a great booster of western settlement and expansion, could quote everything from frontier folklore to government geologists in support of the theory that was essential to persuade people to try to populate the arid lands of the west, what Zebulon Pike had earlier called the Great American Desert. This central "scientific" myth was that settlement and agriculture improves the climate:* Rain follows the plow.†

What an immense geography has been revealed! What infinite hives of population and laboratories of industry have been electrified and set in motion! The great sea has rolled away its somber veil. Asia is found and has become our neighbor. . . . North America is known to our people. Its concave form and homogenous structure are revealed. Our continental mission is set to its perennial frame. . . .

In other speeches, Gilpin discerned "this much of eternal truth":

The democratic republican empire of North America is then predestined to expand and fit itself into the continent; to control the oceans on either hand, and eventually the continents beyond them. . . . Behold, then, rising now, as in the future, the empire which industry and self-government create. The growth of half a century, hewed out of the wilderness—its weapons, the axe and plough; the tactics, labor and energy; its soldiers,

---

*Botkin, 284–85.
†Stegner, 2.

free and equal citizens. Behold the oracular goal to which our eagles march and whither the phalanx of States and people moves harmoniously on to plant a hundred States and consummate their civic greatness.*

Religions and mythologies tend to have icons peculiar to themselves. Statues of the Virgin of Guadalupe are ubiquitous in Mexico and the American Southwest, and Native Americans make various uses of animal icons. In the Puritan tradition, icons were generally eschewed, but as the new United States developed in the eastern part of the North American continent, the folk of the nation created several genuinely American icons that, while not specifically religious, reflected the mythology and the values of the "chosen people" of the New World.

Miss Liberty

To commemorate the centennial of American independence, the French people gave the American people a gigantic statue, which the American people and immigrants to America quickly endowed with the emotional and psychological power of an icon. The Statue of Liberty, or "Liberty Enlightening the World," as it was originally called, is an allegorical expression of the centerpiece of American mythology, the idea of liberty. Standing as she does in New York Harbor, Miss Liberty also stands for the ideals of the melting pot and the promised land of the new "chosen people."

Liberty is represented in the statue as a woman dressed in classical clothes, reminding us both of Greco-Roman ideals of democracy and of the classically draped female figure so often used by French artists to represent the ideals of the revolution and the republic, primarily the ideals of liberté, egalité, and fraternité (liberty, equality, and fraternity). La Belle France is the ancestor of the crowned Miss Liberty, who stands over the broken shackles of slavery, who holds a law book in her left hand, and whose raised torch signifies the enlightenment that the new nation proposes to bring to the world. In the mythology of America Miss Liberty is the new Eve in a new Eden dedicated to the possibility of a fresh start without Old World encumbrances.

In 1903 Emma Lazarus's 1883 sonnet to Miss Liberty was inscribed on a plaque on the statue's pedestal.

*Still, 182–183.

Here at our sea-washed sunset gates shall stand
A mighty woman with a torch, whose flame
Is the imprisoned lightning, and her name
Mother of Exiles. From her beacon-hand
Glows world-wide welcome; her mild eyes command
The air-bridged harbor that twin cities frame.
"Keep, ancient lands, your storied pomp!" cries she
With silent lips. "Give me your tired, your poor,
Your huddled masses yearning to be free,
The wretched refuse of your teeming shore.
Send these, the homeless, tempest-tost to me,
I lift my lamp beside the golden door."

Uncle Sam

The icon—a semicomic one—most commonly associated with the United States is a caricature we call Uncle Sam.

It is generally thought that Uncle Sam came into actual being in 1813 (during the War of 1812) as a counterpart to England's John Bull. The name seems to come from an anonymous interpretation of the letters US on barrels of beef supplied to the army by a Troy, New York, meatpacker named "Uncle Sam" Wilson. (The US actually meant "property of the United States.") Congress recognized this origin in 1961.

Uncle Sam is, as a symbolic personage, also said to have derived from the Yankee tradition of Brother (or Cousin) Jonathan and Yankee Doodle.

U.S. cartoonists started using Uncle Sam in 1830, and he was taken up by the British in Punch. *But it was Thomas Nast who in the 1870s first drew the familiar image of Uncle Sam. James Montgomery Flagg's "I Want You" recruitment poster for (World War I and used in World War II as well) is the most famous representation of Uncle Sam.*

Uncle Sam's meaning has probably never been more grandiosely drawn than by Governor Robert L. Taylor of Tennessee in a speech to the Fourth Tennessee Volunteeers in 1897.

The most striking and picturesque in all history is the picture of a lean and sinewy old man, with long hair and chin whiskers, and wearing an old-fashioned plug hat. His pantaloons are in stripes of red and white, and his blue swallow-tail coat is bespangled with stars. He is the personification of the United States and we call him Uncle Sam.

He is the composite of the wild-cat and the cooing dove, the lion and the lamb, and "summer evening's latest sigh that shuts the rose."

❧ *Uncle Sam at 100* ❧

Uncle Sam. From *Leslie's Illustrated,* January 8, 1876, p. 276.

He is the embodiment of all that is most terrible. The world stands appalled at his wonderful power, and bows in admiration to his matchless magnanimity.

He is the tallest figure on this mundane sphere, and when he steps across the continent and sits down on Pike's Peak, and snorts in his handkerchief of red, white, and blue, the earth quakes and monarchs tremble on their thrones. . . . He is boss of the Western Hemisphere, Sheriff of Cuba, Justice of the Peace of Porto Rico, and guardian *ad litem* of the Philippine Islands. He is as brave as Caesar and as meek as Moses.

He is fierce as a tiger, and cool as a cucumber. He wears the tail feathers of the eagle of France in his hat, the scalp of Mexico in his belt. He laughs at the roar of the Russian bear, and is always ready for a schooner of German beer.

Yankee Doodle

Still another comic patriotic icon—this one primarily musical—is "Yankee Doodle." According to one legend, the words were composed by a Revolutionary War–era English army doctor to make fun of the ragged Continental army. Ironically, the well-known tune to which the words were set, a tune that was earlier associated with an English folk dance, was taken over by the Americans as a signature tune and was even played when General Cornwallis surrendered at Yorktown in 1781. Yankee Doodle, then, is a kind of allegory for the badly dressed, unprofessional, but brave and successful American soldier. It was common in the early days of the nation to make up new stanzas, so the song grew by word of mouth. This is one version of the extended song, containing several familiar verses and some not so familiar.

Father and I went down to camp
Along with Captain Goodwin,
And there we saw the men and boys
As thick as hasty pudding.

Yankee Doodle, keep it up,
Yankee Doodle dandy!
Mind the music and the steps,
And with the girls be handy!

There was Captain Washington
Upon a slapping stallion,
Giving orders to his men,
I guess there was a million.

And there they had a swamping gun
As big as a log of maple,
On a deuced little cart,
A load for father's cattle.

And every time they fired it off,
It took a horn of powder;
It made a noise like father's gun,
Only a nation louder.

And there I saw a little keg,
Its heads were made of leather—
They knocked upon it with little sticks
To call the folks together.

The troopers, too, would gallop up
And fire right in our faces,
It scared me almost half to death
To see them run such races.

But I can't tell you half I saw,
They kept up such a smother,

So I took off my hat, made a bow,
And scampered home to mother.

Yankee Doodle, keep it up,
Yankee Doodle dandy!
Mind the music and the steps,
And with the girls be handy!

VARIATIONS

Yankee Doodle went to town
A-riding on a pony,
He stuck a feather in his hat
And called it macaroni!

Yankee Doodle went to town,
He bought a bag of peaches,
He rode so fast a-coming back,
He smashed them all to pieces!

Yankee Doodle, find a girl,
Yankee Doodle dandy,
Take her to the fair today
And buy a box of candy!*

The Transcendental Deity—Ralph Waldo Emerson

In contrast to the Calvinist God and the materialist and patriotic myths and icons that emerged from Puritanism, the works of Ralph Waldo Emerson (1803–1882) expressed a belief system that was born of a combination of European romanticism and Asian religion and mysticism, a blend that was most fully articulated in America. Emerson's brand of transcendentalism, emerging from a Unitarianism that stressed the educability of man to a Christ-like state, involved the natural ability of the individual to transcend religious orthodoxy by discovering behind the beautiful veil of nature something he called the Oversoul, with which the individual could merge. The result would be an inner freedom, which would create a new type of human being. In his essay "Self-Reliance" he writes, "A nation of men will for the first time exist, because each believes himself inspired by the Divine Soul which also inspires all men." In the sense that he saw in America the potential for a new Eden and a new humanity, then, Emerson resembled his Puritan ancestors. But

*Battle, p. 98–99

Emerson's Oversoul was nothing like the Puritan God. It was a version of the mystical Hindu concept of the nonpersonal Brahman Emerson had read about in the Upanishads and the Bhagavad Gita, the all and nothing, that which is everywhere and nowhere, the very basis of existence.

One mode of the divine teaching is the incarnation of the spirit in a form,—in forms, like my own. I live in society; with persons who answer to thoughts in my own mind, or express a certain obedience to the great instincts to which I live. I see its presence to them. I am certified of a common nature; and these other souls, these separated selves, draw me as nothing else can. They stir in me the new emotions we call passion; of love, hatred, fear, admiration, pity; thence comes conversation, competition, persuasion, cities, and war. Persons are supplementary to the primary teaching of the soul. In youth we are mad for persons. Childhood and youth see all the world in them. But the larger experience of man discovers the identical nature appearing through them all. Persons themselves acquaint us with the impersonal. In all conversation between two persons, tacit reference is made as to a third party, to a common nature. That third party or common nature is not social; it is impersonal; is God. And so in groups where debate is earnest, and especially on high questions, the company become aware that the thought rises to an equal level in all bosoms, that all have a spiritual property in what was said, as well as the sayer. They all become wiser than they were. It arches over them like a temple, this unity of thought, in which every heart beats with nobler sense of power and duty, and thinks and acts with unusual solemnity. All are conscious of attaining to a higher self-possession. It shines for all. There is a certain wisdom of humanity which is common to the greatest men with the lowest, and which our ordinary education often labors to silence and obstruct. The mind is one, and the best minds who love truth for its own sake, think much less of property in truth. They accept it thankfully everywhere, and do not label or stamp it with any man's name, for it is theirs long beforehand, and from eternity. The learned and the studious of thought have no monopoly of wisdom. Their violence of direction in some degree disqualifies them to think truly. We owe many valuable observations to people who are not very acute or profound, and who say the thing without effort, which we want and have long been hunting in vain. The action of the soul is oftener in that which is felt and left unsaid, than in that which is said in any conversation. It broods over every society, and they unconsciously seek for it in each other. We know better than we do. We do not yet possess ourselves, and we know at the same time that we are much more. I feel the same truth how often in my trivial conversation with my neighbors, that somewhat higher in each of us overlooks this by-play, and Jove nods to Jove from behind each of us. . . .

Ineffable is the union of man and God in every act of the soul. The simplest person, who in his integrity worships God, becomes God; yet forever and ever the influx of this better and universal self is new and unsearchable. It inspires awe and astonishment. How dear, how soothing to man, arises the idea of God, peopling the lonely place, effacing the scars of our mistakes and disappointments! When we have broken our god of tradition, and ceased from our god of rhetoric, then may God fire the heart with his presence. It is the doubling of the heart itself, nay, the infinite enlargement of the heart with a power of growth to a new infinity on every side. It inspires in man an infallible trust. He has not the conviction, but the sight that the best is the true, and may in that thought easily dismiss all particular uncertainties and fears, and adjourn to the sure revelation of time, the solution of his private riddles. He is sure that his welfare is dear to the heart of being. In the presence of law to his mind, he is overflowed with a reliance so universal, that it sweeps away all cherished hopes and the most stable projects of mortal condition in its flood. He believes that he cannot escape from his good. The things that are really for thee, gravitate to thee. You are running to seek your friend. Let your feet run, but your mind need not. If you do not find him, will you not acquiesce that it is best you should not find him? for there is a power, which, as it is in you, is in him also, and could therefore very well bring you together, if it were for the best. You are preparing with eagerness to go and render a service to which your talent and your taste invite you, the love of men, and the hope of fame. Has it not occurred to you, that you have no right to go, unless you are equally willing to be prevented from going? O believe, as thou livest, that every sound that is spoken over the round world, which thou oughtest to hear, will vibrate on thine ear. Every proverb, every book, every by-word that belongs to thee for aid or comfort, shall surely come home through open or winding passages. Every friend whom not thy fantastic will, but the great and tender heart in thee craveth, shall lock thee in his embrace. And this, because the heart in thee is the heart of all; not a valve, not a wall, not an intersection is there anywhere in nature, but one blood rolls uninterruptedly, an endless circulation through all men, as the water of the globe is all one sea, and, truly seen, its tide is one.

Let man then learn the revelation of all nature, and all thought to his heart; this, namely; that the Highest dwells with him; that the sources of nature are in his own mind, if the sentiment of duty is there. But if he would know what the great God speaketh, he must 'go into his closet and shut the door,' as Jesus said. God will not make himself manifest to cowards. He must greatly listen to himself, withdrawing himself from all the accents of other men's devotion. Even their prayers are hurtful to him, until he have made his own. Our religion vulgarly stands on numbers of believers. Whenever the appeal is made,—no matter how indirectly,—to numbers, proclamation is then and there made, that religion is not. He that finds God a sweet, enveloping thought to him, never counts his company. When I sit in that presence, who shall dare to come in? When I rest in perfect humility, when I burn with pure love,—what can Calvin or Swedenborg say?

It makes no difference whether the appeal is to numbers or to one. The faith that stands on authority is not faith. The reliance on authority, measures the decline of religion, the withdrawal of the soul. The position men have given to Jesus, now for many centuries of history, is a position of authority. It characterizes themselves. It cannot alter the eternal facts. Great is the soul, and plain. It is no flatterer, it is no follower; it never appeals from itself. It believes in itself. Before the immense possibilities of man, all mere experience, all past biography, however spotless and sainted, shrinks away. Before that heaven which our presentiments foreshow us, we cannot easily praise any form of life we have seen or read of. We not only affirm that we have few great men, but absolutely speaking, that we have none; that we have no history, no record of any character or mode of living, that entirely contents us. The saints and demigods whom history worships, we are constrained to accept with a grain of allowance. Though in our lonely hours, we draw a new strength out of their memory, yet pressed on our attention, as they are by the thoughtless and customary, they fatigue and invade. The soul gives itself alone, original, and pure, to the Lonely, Original and Pure, who, on that condition, gladly inhabits, leads, and speaks through it. Then is it glad, young, and nimble. It is not wise, but it sees through all things. It is not called religious, but it is innocent. It calls the light its own, and feels that the grass grows, and the stone falls by a law inferior to, and dependent on its nature. Behold, it saith, I am born into the great, the universal mind. I the imperfect, adore my own Perfect. I am somehow receptive of the great soul, and thereby I do overlook the sun and the stars, and feel them to be the fair accidents and effects which change and pass. More and more the surges of everlasting nature enter into me, and I become public and human in my regards and actions. So come I to live in thoughts, and act with energies which are immortal. Thus revering the soul, and learning, as the ancient said, that "its beauty is immense," man will come to see that the world is the perennial miracle which the soul worketh, and be less astonished at particular wonders; he will learn that there is no profane history; that all history is sacred; that the universe is represented in an atom, in a moment of time. He will weave no longer a spotted life of shreds and patches, but he will live with a divine unity. He will cease from what is base and frivolous in his life, and be content with all places and with any service he can render. He will calmly front the morrow in the negligency of that trust which carries God with it, and so hath already the whole future in the bottom of the heart.

Technology Apotheosized—Henry David Thoreau

A man who attempted in his much-celebrated stay at Walden Pond (described in his classic work Walden, or Life in the Woods) *to experience and express transcendentalism through practical experience, Henry David Thoreau (1817–1862) was always an exponent of the values to be found in nature as opposed to those represented by the economic and technological growth that marked early-nineteenth-century America. Yet although he stood against the inevitable future, he could not help but recognize the new deity in the very technology he feared.*

Walden is generally taken as the work of an inspired loner seeking truth from isolation in pure nature, and Walden Pond and its woody surround have come to represent the very soul of the universe. But as Thoreau pointed out, "The Fitchburg Railroad touches the pond about a hundred yards south of where I dwell. I usually go to the village along its causeway, and am, as it were, related to society by this link."

When I meet the engine with its train of cars moving off with planetary motion,—or, rather, like a comet, for the beholder knows not if with that velocity and with that direction it will ever revisit this system, since its orbit does not look like a returning curve,—with its steam cloud like a banner streaming behind in golden and silver wreathes, like many a downy cloud which I have seen, high in the heavens, unfolding its masses to the light,—as if this traveling demigod, this cloud-compellor, would ere long take the sunset sky for the livery of his train; when I hear the iron horse make the hills echo with his snort like thunder, shaking the earth with his feet, and breathing fire and smoke from his nostrils (what kind of winged horse or fiery dragon they will put into the new Mythology I don't know), it seems as if the earth had got a race now worthy to inhabit it. . . .

The stabler of the iron horse was up early this winter morning by the light of the stars amid the mountains, to fodder and harness his steed. Fire, too, was awakened thus early to put the vital heat in him and get him off. . . . All day the fire-steed flies over the country, stopping only that his master may rest, and I am awakened by his tramp and defiant snort at midnight, when in some remote glen in the woods he fronts the elements incased in ice and snow; and he will reach his stall only with the morning star. . . .

We have constructed a fate, an *Atropos,* that never turns aside. (Let that be the name of your engine.)*

The Dynamo—Henry Adams

Another American who saw in the emergence of technology a replacement of old deities was Henry Adams (1838–1918), the grandson and great-grandson of American presidents, whose autobiography, The Education of Henry Adams, *is, in a sense, an attempt to understand his role and America's role in a new world dominated by technology.*

Adams frequented the great expositions of 1893 and 1900 seeking answers to explain whatever was the force driving American society— as the Virgin had driven medieval European society, focusing the energies of virtually everyone in both common daily endeavors as well as the building of grand cathedrals. By Adams's time, invisible forces had been uncovered—X rays, radium's emissions, and the like. Even Adams's physicist friends could not really explain the nature of electricity, though it had long been successfully harnessed in such devices as the electric tram. Nowhere did these forces strike Adams more deeply as mysterious than when he stood before the exhibitions in the hall of dynamos.

To Adams the dynamo became a symbol of infinity. As he grew accustomed to the great gallery of machines, he began to feel the forty-foot dynamos as a moral force, much as the early Christians felt the Cross. The planet itself seemed less impressive, in its old-fashioned, deliberate, annual or daily revolution, than this huge wheel, revolving within arm's length at some vertigious speed, and barely murmuring—scarcely humming an audible warning to stand a hair's breadth further for respect of power—while it would not wake the baby lying close against its frame. Before the end, one began to pray to it; inherited instinct taught the natural expression of man before silent and infinite force. Among the thousands of symbols of ultimate energy, the dynamo was not so human as some, but it was the most expressive. . . .

In these seven years [from 1893 to 1900] man had translated himself into a new universe which had no common scale of measurement with

*Thoreau, 91ff.

the old. He had entered a supersensual world, in which he could measure nothing except by chance collisions of movements imperceptible to his senses, perhaps even imperceptible to his instruments, but perceptible to each other, and so to some known ray at the end of the scale. . . .

[These rays] were occult, supersensual, irrational; they were a revelation of mysterious energy like that of the Cross; they were what, in terms of medieval science, were called immediate modes of the divine substance. . . .

The force of the Virgin was still felt at Lourdes, and seemed to be as potent as X rays; but in America neither Venus nor Virgin ever had value as force—at most as sentiment. No American had ever been truly afraid of either.*

The Book of Mormon

The clash between American liberal ideals of equality and inner freedom and those of the sometimes ruthless growth and development of the new technological society gave rise to a religious revival early in the nineteenth century. The so-called second Great Awakening reached out especially to those families unable to keep up with or capitalize on the boom that was sweeping the country. The Joseph Smith family of Palmyra, New York, was one such family, and we are told that when young Joseph junior prayed in a grove of trees for divine guidance, God and Jesus Christ appeared to him warning him away from existing orthodoxies; in later visions they directed him to form what he saw as the true church of Christ.

Of the cults that emerged in the United States in its first century the most successful has been Mormonism, the Church of Jesus Christ of Latter-day Saints. The Mormons possess a rich and complex mythology in addition to the stories and traditions contained in the Old and New Testaments. That mythology, developed primarily by way of visions that came to Smith, is contained in the Book of Mormon, first published in 1830, and in various apocryphal narrative traditions.

According to Mormon mythology, Christ came to America after his crucifixion and preached a church dedicated to Jesus, "the Christ, the Eternal God, manifesting himself to all nations."

Mormonism, like the Puritanism that preceded it, saw in the New World a new Eden, a new beginning. America was the center of the universe. It was here that Jesus had quite naturally come after his crucifixion. And it was he, through John the Baptist and the apostles Peter,

*Adams, 380–83.

James, and John, who authorized Joseph Smith and Oliver Cowdrey as priests of the new faith in 1829. For many who have been moved by the Edenic vision and the millenarianism inherent in the American worldview, Mormonism represented the Second Coming of Christ. Communities of "saints" were founded—a new elect, the chosen people of God, like the Puritans before them. In the Mormon temple in Kirkland, Ohio, Jesus himself, accompanied by Moses, Elias, and Elijah, is said to have come to Smith and Cowdrey in 1836 and to have ordered them to establish a society based on Old Testament patriarchal values. Missionaries were sent out into the world, as they have continued to be sent, to bring nonbelievers into the true Kingdom of the Latter-day Saints.

It was in the Mormon settlement of Nauvoo, Illinois, that Smith's new mythology came into conflict with more traditional beliefs. Smith had begun to preach the possibilty of achieving divinity through Mormonism, among other radical ideas, and in 1844 he was murdered by an angry mob. At this point a split developed, with Smith's son Joseph junior establishing the more liberal Reorganized Church of Jesus Christ of Latter-day Saints in Independence, Missouri. Brigham Young, a follower of the murdered Smith's beliefs, including polygamy, led the Mormons to Salt Lake City, where to this day their temple stands as the central monument of Mormonism.

Jesus Christ did show himself unto the people of Nephi, as the multitude were gathered together in the land Bountiful, and did minister unto them; and in this wise did he show himself unto them.

CHAPTER 11.

The Eternal Father proclaims the Christ—The Resurrected Christ appears—The multitude permitted to feel his wounds—Mode of baptism prescribed—Contention and disputation forbidden—Christ the rock.

1. And now it came to pass that there were a great multitude gathered together, of the people of Nephi, round about the temple which was in the land Bountiful; and they were marveling and wondering one with another, and were showing one to another the great and marvelous change which had taken place.

2. And they were also conversing about this Jesus Christ, of whom the sign had been given concerning his death.

3. And it came to pass that while they were thus conversing one with another, they heard a voice as if it came out of heaven; and they

cast their eyes round about, for they understood not the voice which they heard; and it was not a harsh voice, neither was it a loud voice; nevertheless, and notwithstanding it being a small voice it did pierce them that did hear to the center, insomuch that there was no part of their frame that it did not cause to quake; yea, it did pierce them to the very soul, and did cause their hearts to burn.

4. And it came to pass that again they heard the voice, and they understood it not.

5. And again the third time they did hear the voice, and did open their ears to hear it; and their eyes were towards the sound thereof; and they did look steadfastly towards heaven, from whence the sound came.

6. And behold, the third time they did understand the voice which they heard; and it said unto them:

7. Behold my Beloved Son, in whom I am well pleased, in whom I have glorified my name—hear ye him.

8. And it came to pass, as they understood they cast their eyes up again towards heaven; and behold, they saw a Man descending out of heaven; and he was clothed in a white robe; and he came down and stood in the midst of them; and the eyes of the whole multitude were turned upon him, and they durst not open their mouths, even one to another, and wist not what it meant, for they thought it was an angel that had appeared unto them.

9. And it came to pass that he stretched forth his hand and spake unto the people, saying:

10. Behold, I am Jesus Christ, whom the prophets testified shall come into the world.

11. And behold, I am the light and the life of the world; and I have drunk out of that bitter cup which the Father hath given me, and have glorified the Father in taking upon me the sins of the world, in which I have suffered the will of the Father in all things from the beginning.

12. And it came to pass that when Jesus had spoken these words the whole multitude fell to the earth; for they remembered that it had been prophesied among them that Christ should show himself unto them after his ascension into heaven.

13. And it came to pass that the Lord spake unto them saying:

14. Arise and come forth unto me, that ye may thrust your hands into my side, and also that ye may feel the prints of the nails in my hands and in my feet, that ye may know that I am the God of Israel, and the God of the whole earth, and have been slain for the sins of the world.

15. And it came to pass that the multitude went forth, and thrust their hands into his side, and did feel the prints of the nails in his hands and in his feet; and this they did do, going forth one by one until they had all gone forth, and did see with their eyes and did feel with their hands, and did know of a surety and did bear record, that it was he, of whom it was written by the prophets, that should come.

16. And when they had all gone forth and had witnessed for themselves, they did cry out with one accord, saying:

17. Hosanna! Blessed be the name of the Most High God! And they did fall down at the feet of Jesus, and did worship him.

18. And it came to pass that he spake unto Nephi (for Nephi was among the multitude) and he commanded him that he should come forth.

19. And Nephi arose and went forth, and bowed himself before the Lord and did kiss his feet.

20. And the Lord commanded him that he should arise. And he arose and stood before him.

21. And the Lord said unto him: I give unto you power that ye shall baptize this people when I am again ascended into heaven.

22. And again the Lord called others, and said unto them likewise; and he gave unto them power to baptize. And he said unto them: On this wise shall ye baptize; and there shall be no disputations among you.

23. Verily I say unto you, that whoso repenteth of his sins through your words and desireth to be baptized in my name, on this wise shall ye baptize them—Behold, ye shall go down and stand in the water, and in my name shall ye baptize them.

24. And now behold, these are the words which ye shall say, calling them by name, saying:

25. Having authority given me of Jesus Christ, I baptize you in the name of the Father, and of the Son, and of the Holy Ghost. Amen.

26. And then shall ye immerse them in the water, and come forth again out of the water.

27. And after this manner shall ye baptize in my name; for behold, verily I say unto you, that the Father, and the Son, and the Holy Ghost are one; and I am in the Father, and the Father in me, and the Father and I are one.

28. And according as I have commanded you thus shall ye baptize. And there shall be no disputations among you, as there have hitherto been; neither shall there be disputations among you concerning the points of my doctrine, as there have hitherto been.

29. For verily, verily I say unto you, he that hath the spirit of contention is not of me, but is of the devil, who is the father of contention,

and he stirreth up the hearts of men to contend with anger, one with another.

30. Behold, this is not my doctrine, to stir up the hearts of men with anger, one against another; but this is my doctrine, that such things should be done away.

31. Behold, verily, verily, I say unto you, I will declare unto you my doctrine.

32. And this is my doctrine, and it is the doctrine which the Father hath given unto me; and I bear record of the Father, and the Father beareth record of me, and the Holy Ghost beareth record of the Father and me; and I bear record that the Father commandeth all men, everywhere, to repent and believe in me.

33. And whoso believeth in me, and is baptized, the same shall be saved; and they are they who shall inherit the kingdom of God.

34. And whoso believeth not in me, and is not baptized, shall be damned.

35. Verily, verily, I say unto you, that this is my doctrine, and I bear record of it from the Father; and whoso believeth in me believeth in the Father also; and unto him will the Father bear record of me, for he will visit him with fire and with the Holy Ghost.

36. And thus will the Father bear record of me, and the Holy Ghost will bear record unto him of the Father and me; for the Father, and I, and the Holy Ghost are one.

37. And again I say unto you, ye must repent, and become as a little child, and be baptized in my name, or ye can in nowise receive these things.

38. And again I say unto you, ye must repent, and be baptized in my name, and become as a little child, or ye can in nowise inherit the kingdom of God.

39. Verily, verily, I say unto you, that this is my doctrine, and whoso buildeth upon this buildeth upon my rock, and the gates of hell shall not prevail against them.

40. And whoso shall declare more or less than this, and establish it for my doctrine, the same cometh of evil, and is not built upon my rock; but he buildeth upon a sandy foundation, and the gates of hell stand open to receive such when the floods come and the winds beat upon them.

41. Therefore, go forth unto this people, and declare the words which I have spoken, unto the ends of the earth.*

*Book of Mormon, 3 Nephi, ch. 11.

The Devil in the West—Charles O. Brown

*Supernatural beings could sometimes be treated humorously by Euro-
pean Americans, as in the poem "Arizona: How It Was Made and Who
Made It; or the Land that God Forgot."*

*Charles Brown, a Tucson bartender, wrote this paean to the Arizona
territory in 1879. Like other poems comparing tracts of western land to
Hell, it suggests that one must be a tough hombre indeed to put up with
such a place—a kind of reverse bragging in which the Devil himself is
the subject of a tall tale of sorts.*

The Devil was given permission one day
To select him a land for his own special way;
So he hunted around for a month of more
And fussed and fumed and terribly swore,
But at last was delighted a country to view
Where the prickly pear and the mesquite grew.
With a survey brief, without further excuse,
He took his stand on the Santa Cruz.
He saw there were some improvements to make,
For he felt his own reputation at stake;
And an idea struck him—he swore by his horns,
To make a complete vegetation of thorns.
He studded the land with the prickly pears
And scattered the cactus everwhere,
The Spanish dagger, sharp-pointed and tall,
And at last—the cholla—the worst of all.
He imported the Apaches direct from Hell,
And the ranks of his sweet-scented train to swell,
A legion of skunks, whose loud, loud smell
Perfumed the country he loved so well.
And then for his life he could not see why
The rivers should carry even water supply,
And he swore if he gave it another drop
You might take his head and his horns for a mop.
He filled the river with sand till it was almost dry,
And poisoned the land with alkali
And promised himself on its slimy brink
The control of all who from it should drink.
He saw there was one more improvement to make,
He imported the scorpion, tarantula and rattlesnake,
That all who might come to his country to dwell

Would be sure to think it was almost hell.
He fixed the heat at one hundred and seven,
And banished forever the moisture from heaven
But remembered as he heard his furnace roar,
That the heat might reach five hundred or more.
And after he fixed things so thorny and well,
He said, "I'll be damned if that don't beat hell."
Then he flapped his wings and away he flew
And vanished from earth in a blaze of blue.
And now, no doubt, in some corner of hell
He gloats over the the work he has done so well,
And vows that Arizona cannot be beat
For scorpions, tarantulas, snakes and heat.
For his own realm compares so well
He feels assured it surpasses hell.*

*Griffith, 113–14.

African American

The myths of African Americans have generally reflected the condition of blacks in America, first as slaves and then as people rejected by the melting pot. The Africans brought to America as slaves naturally brought religious traditions with them, and they also tended to reinterpret the rituals, myths, and other religious traditions of their owners to fit their own needs and their own heritage. So, for instance, Christian baptism could be related easily to African initiation rites, and the new Christian God, like the old African ones, could be a god who "possessed" the worshiper. Furthermore, southern Protestant revivalism appealed to a people longing for a better life and provided a religious tradition centered in ecstatic practices. This ecstaticism took root in the mainline Protestant black churches of later years and especially in the Holiness-Pentecostal movement, characterized by extreme emotionalism in worship.

It was also natural that the slaves and the early black religious movements in America would have taken the condition of the Jews in the Old Testament as the source of their own mythology. It was logical to associate themselves with the Jews as a chosen people and their white oppressors with the Egyptians, the Babylonians, or the Philistines. African American religion quickly became a deliverance religion based on the myth of a promised land for people freed from bondage by a strong Father God aided by Moses-like heroes.

The Spiritual—"Go Down, Moses"

The mythology of the early black churches was not spelled out in written documents so much as in ecstatic sermons and in the musical form we know as the Negro spiritual. These were songs such as "Didn't My Lord Deliver Daniel," "Walk Around Zion, I Believe," and "In that Great Getting-Up Morning." Spirituals became a part of general American folklore when Slave Songs of the United States *appeared in 1867 and when the Jubilee Singers from Fisk University in Tennessee took the songs on tour in 1871. Spirituals were religious; that is, they were concerned with spiritual salvation. But they also clearly expressed a dream of freedom in this world. One of the most popular of the spirituals, "Go Down, Moses," implicitly associates the Hebrews and Moses with the condition of the slaves.*

> Go down, Moses,
> Way down in Egyptland
> Tell old Pharaoh
> To let my people go.
>
> When Israel was in Egyptland
> Let my people go
> Oppressed so hard they could not stand
> Let my people go.
>
> Go down, Moses,
> Way down in Egyptland
> Tell old Pharaoh
> "Let my people go."
>
> "Thus saith the Lord," bold Moses said,
> "Let my people go;
> If not I'll smite your first-born dead
> Let my people go."
>
> Go down, Moses,
> Way down in Egyptland,
> Tell old Pharaoh,
> "Let my people go!"

God and the Devil—"The Devil's Doing"

The African American concept of deity was also expressed in fablelike origin myths that are generally comic in tone. As is the case with many Central Asian and Native American myths also, this origin myth from the American South involves a conflict between God and a trickster Devil.

When the Devil gets a good hold of you he's bound to leave his mark on you; and what's more, he'll leave that mark on your children and your grandchildren.

And that's the way it was with the catfish. If he'd kept out of the Devil's hands, he'd been a whole lot better-looking than what he is, and so would his children. You've noticed that the catfish doesn't have any scales like the other fish, but he wasn't always that way. It happened more or less like this.

It was a Friday morning that the Good Lord created the fish, and when he turned them all loose in the river it was a mighty fine sight, I'll tell you. And there wasn't any more handsome fish in the crowd than the catfish. He was all covered with red and yellow and blue scales according to the kind of catfish he was, and he was one of the finest fishes in the river.

Well, the Good Lord created all the different kinds of fish in the forenoon, and he set out to make all the chickens and the turkeys and the geese in the afternoon. When it come dinner time, he put away the tools and locked the door and put the key in his pocket and went along up to the Big House to get something to eat.

After dinner, the Good Lord and the Angel Gabriel were walking along back down the Big Road, picking their teeth, and talking about whether they ought to make the birds with scales, like the fish, or with feathers, when who did they bump into by the side of the road but Old Nick, and he was scraping the scales off some catfish he had just caught. And the Good Lord said: "Look here, Nick, what in the name of common sense are you doing with those fish?"

Old Nick said, "Well, I noticed it was Friday, and I thought I'd just have a fine fish dinner, and so when I saw how crowded the fish were in the river, I thought it would sort of help matters if I'd just thin them out a bit. So I reached down and grabbed a few of the catfish that were handiest, and I was just getting them ready to fry when you came along."

And the Good Lord came right back: "Well, you look here; you just put those fish back in the water and go on about your business, you trifling good-for-nothing black rascal!"

He made Old Nick put all the fish back in the water. Now, where the scales had been scraped off it hurt so that the catfish went down to the bottom and rolled over in the mud to try and do something about the pain. Bye and bye, the pain went away, but the scales never grew back, and from that time on the catfish haven't had scales.

And that's what makes me tell you that you better always keep out of reach of the Devil, because if you don't, he'll make trouble for you and all your kinfolks.*

"The Creation"—James Weldon Johnson

The creation story of Genesis has always been a popular subject for African American sermons. James Weldon Johnson, the great African American statesman, poet, novelist, and composer (with his brother John Rosamond Johnson he composed "Lift Every Voice and Sing," often called the national anthem of African Americans), wrote this version of the creation, making use of black language patterns, particularly those that had evolved in the context of the inspired improvisational sermon. In fact, the book from which it is taken is entitled God's Trombones: Seven Negro Sermons in Verse.

And God stepped out on space,
And he looked around and said:
I'm lonely—
I'll make me a world.

And far as the eye of God could see
Darkness covered everything,
Blacker than a hundred midnights
Down in a cypress swamp.

Then God smiled,
And the light broke,
And the darkness rolled up on one side,
And the light stood shining on the other,
And God said: That's good!

Then God reached out and took the light in His hands,
And God rolled the light around in His hands
Until He made the sun;
And He set that sun a-blazing in the heavens.
And the light that was left from making the sun
God gathered it up in a shining ball
And flung it against the darkness,
Spangling the night with the moon and stars.
Then down between
The darkness and the light

*Abrahams, 62–63.

He hurled the world;
And God said: That's good!

Then God himself stepped down—
And the sun was on His right hand,
And the moon was on His left;
The stars were clustered about His head,
And the earth was under His feet.
And God walked, and where He trod
His footsteps hollowed the valleys out
And bulged the mountains up.

Then He stopped and looked and saw
That the earth was hot and barren.
So God stepped over to the edge of the world
And He spat out the seven seas—
He batted His eyes, and the lightnings flashed—
He clapped His hands, and the thunders rolled—
And the waters above the earth came down,
The cooling waters came down.

Then the green grass sprouted,
And the little red flowers blossomed,
The pine tree pointed his finger to the sky,
And the oak spread out his arms,
The lakes cuddled down in the hollows of the ground,
And the rivers ran down to the sea;
And God smiled again,
And the rainbow appeared,
And curled itself around His shoulder.

Then God raised His arm and He waved His hand
Over the sea and over the land,
And He said: Bring forth! Bring forth!
And quicker than God could drop His hand,
Fishes and fowls
And beasts and birds
Swam the rivers and the seas,
Roamed the forests and the woods,
And split the air with their wings.
And God said: That's good!

Then God walked around,
And God looked around
On all that He had made.
He looked at His sun,
And He looked at His moon,
And He looked at His little stars;
He looked on His world
With all its living things,
And God said: I'm lonely still.

Then God sat down—
On the side of a hill where He could think;
By a deep, wide river He sat down;
With His head in His hands,
God thought and thought,
Till He thought: I'll make me a man!

Up from the bed of the river
God scooped the clay;
And by the bank of the river
He kneeled Him down;
And there the great God Almighty
Who lit the sun and fixed it in the sky,
Who flung the stars to the most far corner of the night,
Who rounded the earth in the middle of His hand;
This Great God,
Like a mammy bending over her baby,
Kneeled down in the dust
Toiling over a lump of clay
Till He shaped it in His own image;

Then into it He blew the breath of life,
And man became a living soul.
Amen. Amen.*

The Nation of Islam

The need for delivering heroes—a Moses to lead the people out of Egypt to the promised land—has been expressed in various ways. Figures such as Father Divine (George Baker, 1877–1965) and Bishop Emmanuel "Daddy" Grace were spiritual leaders to whom were attributed godlike

*African American Literature, 119ff.

powers of healing and prophecy. They advocated the right to a better life in this world rather than the next. And not surprisingly, there were those who looked for a more appropriate mythology to replace what was seen as the white Christian religion. Noble Drew Ali (Timothy Drew, 1886–1929) founded the Moorish Science Temple in Newark, New Jersey, claiming that American blacks were not "Negroes" but "Moors." Their natural religion was Islam, and according to Moorish Science mythology, Ali had been sent directly by Allah himself to bring true religion to African Americans, whose identity had been stolen by Europeans. Ali and his followers even wrote their own version of the Koran.

But it is the Nation of Islam, begun under Elijah Muhammad (Elijah Poole, 1897–1975), that has been most successful in establishing Allah as an African American deity. The Black Muslims, as they are often called, have attempted to create a "nation" within the United States, one committed to the psychological, spiritual, and economic welfare of African Americans. The theological justification for the movement is contained in a complex mythology that begins with the appearance in Detroit in 1930 of Wallace D. Fard (Walli Farrad or Farrad Mohammed). As Joseph Smith said he was instructed by Jesus, Fard claimed to have been sent by Allah himself from Mecca to bring Islam back to the "lost-found tribe of Shabbazz." When Fard disappeared mysteriously in 1934, his position as leader of the Nation was taken over by Elijah Muhammad. It was Elijah Muhammad who provided the details of Black Muslim mythology. Fard, he announced, had been an incarnation of Allah and he, Elijah Muhammad, was his prophet or messenger. Muhammad informed his followers that humankind had originally been black until an evil scientist called Yakub created a race of white devils whose religion was Christianity and who would rule the world for six thousand years. Once again, as in much of American mythology, millenarianism is an important aspect of Muslim lore. Muhammad predicted that after the six-thousand-year period the rule of the true believers, the Black Muslims, would be achieved.

These are Elijah Muhammad's own words on the subject as contained in his The Supreme Wisdom, *a bible of sorts for the Nation of Islam, and in his newspaper,* Mr. Muhammad Speaks.

Who is better knowing of whom we are than God himself? He has declared that we are descendants of the Asian Black Nation and of the tribe of Shabazz [which] came with the earth . . . sixty-six trillion years ago. . . .

The original man, Allah has declared, is none other than the Black

Man. He is the first and the last, and maker and owner of the universe; from him come all—brown, yellow, red, and white. . . . The true knowledge of black and white should be enough to awaken the so-called Negroes.*

Who are the white race? "Why are they white-skinned?" Answer: Allah (God) said this is due to being grafted from the Original Black Nation, as the Black Man has two germs (two people) in him. One is black and the other brown. The brown germ is weaker than the black germ. The brown germ can be grafted into its last stage, and the last stage is white. A scientist by the name of Yakub discovered this knowledge . . . 6,645 years ago, and was successful in doing this job of grafting after 600 years of following a strict and rigid birth control law. . . .

The human beast—the serpent, the dragon, the devil, and Satan—all mean one and the same; the people or race known as the white or Caucasian race.†

A leader who was at first seen as Elijah Muhammad's logical successor and as a Moses to lead African Americans out of political, economic, and social bondage was Malcolm X (Malcolm Little, 1925–1965), who was brutally murdered after a break with Messenger Muhammad and a denial of much of the Nation's mythology.

Voodoo

A mythic tradition that comes to America from Africa, primarily by way of the West Indies and Haiti, is Voodoo. Voodoo is a religion of spirits, or groups of spirits called nanchon *(nations), for whom elaborate ceremonies are held. Two of the most important* nanchon *are the* rada *and the* petro, *the first sweet and the second hot.*

Death is made much of in Voodoo. In Haiti the gede *are spirits of death and of sex, suggesting a connection with the West Indian trickster god Gede, who is the god of death and sexuality. The connection between death and sexuality suggests a crossing over or passing through, and tricksters always penetrate to the unknown realm. They are above all messengers, connectors between the other world and this one, the sacred and the profane. Perhaps not surprisingly, then, there is a trickster*

---

*Elijah Muhammad, *Wisdom*, 38.
†Elijah Muhammad, *Mr. Muhammad Speaks*, December 13, 1958, and July 4, 1959.

aspect to Jesus as a messenger or to figures such as Father Divine, Daddy Grace, Wallace Fard, and even Elijah Muhammad.

The primary effect of Voodoo (sometimes called "hoodoo") in the American South is a large number of conjuring tales and traditions, such as these ones collected by Newbell Puckett in the 1920s.

Conjure material is sometimes put into a person's shoes. "One instance is of a girl who detects her father-in-law putting something into her shoes after she is supposed to have gone to sleep. She burns the shoes and so avoids the trick; the shoes in burning make a noise like a bunch of fireworks." Conjures may be set in sweet potatoes in the field, among chips in the woodshed, in perfume (a bottle of cologne presented to a girl by her unsuccessful rival puts her eyes out when she smells of it), or even on a carving knife, the first one to use it being the one to receive the harm. A girl was given a bunch of roses on her wedding day and her attention was called to their sweet fragrance. That girl fell dead when going into the church. A common method of conjure is by means of things put in a person's hat. "To conjure by means of a hat, take a toad, dry and powder, and put the powder in the hat, or the dried toad may be put up all over the door or under the steps. Toads, frogs, lizards, etc., must be all procured at night on the waste of the moon, as that will insure a wasting away of the body." Even the wind may be the innocent bearer of "devilment." Find out the direction of the wind and stand so that it will blow from you towards your enemy. Having dusted your hands with powdered devil's shoe string and devil's snuff, hold them up so that the wind will blow from them towards the man coming towards you. The dust will be carried into his eyes and your opponent will be at least temporarily blinded. . . . A way of locating a thief is to put a rooster under a pot and let all suspects touch the pot. When the thief touches it the rooster will crow. There is a Negro story of a clever slaveowner who tried this out on his slaves, after some chickens had been stolen, telling them in advance that the rooster would crow when the thief touched the upturned pot. He ordered them all to touch the pot, but the rooster did not crow. Then he made them all show their hands—all had their fingers blackened with soot, with the exception of one man. That one was the thief who was afraid to touch the pot. In another case two chairs are placed back to back in such wise that a sifter resting between them, edge on edge, is balanced so lightly that a breath will serve to disturb its equilibrium. The diviner (not necessarily a hoodoo) stands some distance away from the chair and sifter and with lifted hands chants slowly:

By Saint Peter, by Saint Paul,
By the Lord who made us all,
If John Doe did thus and so,
Turn, sifter, turn and fall.

If the person is innocent the sifter remains motionless; if an accomplice, it merely trembles; if guilty it turns and drops.*

*Puckett, 223–24, 281–82.

Asian American

American conditions appear to have had little effect on the concept of deity or the mythologies brought to America by Asian immigrants. As in the case of American Jews, Asian Americans have tended to attach themselves to traditional religious structures, perhaps both because of the occasional reluctance of the melting pot to assimilate them or because of a desire to preserve old ways and ethnic integrity. Buddhists, Taoists, Confucianists, or Christians from China, Buddhists and Shintoists from Japan, or Hindus and Muslims from India and Pakistan, for instance, have for the most part not allowed their experience in America to alter the rituals and myths of their forebears. There is, therefore, a shortage of what can genuinely be called Asian American mythology. The myths and legends of Asian Americans are, rather, the myths and legends of Asia.

An interesting development, however, has been the effect of Asian religions and mythologies on Americans in general. Few Americans are unfamiliar with the ancient Chinese yin-yang symbol of harmony between opposites or with the saffron-clad Hare Krishna chanters. The Beats of the 1950s, the hippies and flower people of the 1960s and 1970s, and New Age people of the 1980s and 1990s have all been attracted to Asian religious and mythological concepts, and America has long been fertile ground for the work and cults of Asian gurus and mystics, whether Brahmanists, Sufis, Zen masters, or traditional Buddhist monks. Often the interest in Asian myth and religion has been the result of a dissatisfaction of the young, in particular, with what is seen as the conservatism, materialism, and excessive worldliness of mainline Christianity and Judaism.

Hare Krishna and Other Movements

An example of the importation of Asian mythology to America is the International Society for Krishna Consciousness, a form of Hinduism brought to New York City by guru A. C. Bhaktivedanta in 1965. The guru's taken name itself has mythoreligious implications. *Bhakti* is Sanskrit for "devotion," which leads to *moksa*, "liberation" or "enlightenment." *Vedanta* refers to the teachings of the Hindu holy scripture called the Upanishads, the culmination of the earlier Vedas. Bhaktivedanta's goal was to convert Americans to the "God-consciousness" of the Upanishads and Vedas. He gradually attracted a following of sixties youth who became a common sight on the streets of New York, Los Angeles, and other cities. Dressed in saffron robes, their heads shaved, the Hare Krishnas joyfully chant *mantras* (hymns) in honor of the Lord Krsna (Krishna), avatar of the god Visnu. Krsna, who represents divine love, also has a playful trickster side and is sometimes a lover in the non-Platonic sense. The myth of his life reveals the Hindu belief in life as *lila,* or divine play—thus the joyfulness of the Hare Krishnas.

Another importer of Asian concepts of ultimate reality to America was D. T. Suzuki (Suzuki Daisetsu Teitaro, 1870–1966), a Japanese student of Zen Buddhism who translated and analyzed Zen texts for his American audience and who, with the help of Alan Watts, an Anglo-American guru of the 1960s and 1970s, popularized the Zen movement, especially within the counterculture movement of the time. More traditional Buddhism had long been important to American mystics. H. P. Blavatsky and H. S. Olcott founded the Buddhist-inspired Theosophical Society in New York in 1875. And, as we have seen, Brahmanism through the Upanishads greatly influenced the thinking of the American transcendentalists of the nineteenth century.

Perhaps the most articulate of contemporary Americans influenced by Asian myth and religion were poets Allen Ginsberg (1929–1997) and Gary Snyder (b. 1930). Ginsberg turned the harsh and seemingly bland reality of his America into ironical *sutras,* or Buddhist scriptures, as in his famous "Sunflower Sutra."

"Amitabha's Song"—Gary Snyder

Gary Snyder, in his series of poems called Myths and Texts, *implicitly identifies himself with Amitabha, a Buddha figure of the Mahayana tradition. Like Ginsberg, he turns the conditions of life of the Beat gener-*

ation in America into the subject matter for ironic and somewhat comic Buddhist preaching.

Amitabha's Vow

"If, after obtaining Buddhahood, anyone in my land
 gets tossed in jail on a vagrancy rap, may I
 not attain highest perfect enlightenment.

 wild geese in the orchard
 frost on the new grass

"If, after obtaining Buddhahood, anyone in my land
 loses a finger coupling boxcars, may I
 not attain highest perfect enlightenment.

 mare's eye flutters
jerked by the lead-rope
 stone-bright shoes flick back
 ankles trembling: down steep rock

"If, after obtaining Buddhahood, anyone in my land
 can't get a ride hitch-hiking all directions, may I
 not attain highest perfect enlightenment.

 wet rocks buzzing
 rain and thunder southwest
 hair, beard, tingle
 wind whips bare legs
 we should go back
 we don't

II

NEW WORLD
MYTHICAL MONSTERS AND
FABULOUS CREATURES

Monsters and various forms of fabulous creatures are probably as old as human dreams. It is logical to assume that early humans expressed their fear of wild animals by exaggerating their size and malevolence in their dreams and that eventually they clothed other, more complex fears in the characteristics both of real wild beings and of even more terrifying composite ones. As early as circa 3000 B.C.E. we find Egyptian gods depicted with animal heads and Mesopotamian beings we recognize as the centaur, the sphinx, the dragon, and others. The ancient Greeks would conceive of Sirens, Cyclopes, and the Harpies. And Christians of the Middle Ages developed monsterlike gargoyles, fabulous unicorns, and complex bestiaries with allegorical significance. Later fantasy artists from Hieronymus Bosch to Marc Chagall and beyond have made rich use of strange creatures that are part human and part animal. Science fiction, too, has been a breeding ground for mythical monsters and fabulous creatures.

The fascination with such creatures is expressed in American myth and folklore as well. Native Americans have their ogres and man-eating monsters. Asian Americans brought their good dragons, their evil demons, and their shape-shifting mythical animals with them. European Americans and African Americans have created some particularly odd beings that in various ways reflect life in the New World.

Native American

Monsters—nearly always large and vicious, often composite in nature—play a role in many Native American mythologies. Burr Woman lodges herself in the backs of heroes and refuses to let go. Cliff Ogre kicks people off cliffs. The Winter Dances of several Northwest Coast tribes are based on myths of cannibal monsters. The Iroquois have several monsters, including ogres and man-eating females. The Algonkian of the Northeast make much of the *windigo* syndrome. A *windigo* is a type of monster with characteristics of witches and ghosts. It is said that when individuals become crazed, especially when lost and hungry in the woods, they sometimes turn into *windigos*—cannibalistic ice-hearted giants who haunt and threaten and sometimes eat their former fellow tribe members, especially, according to some Ojibwa, children who have been naughty. A *windigo* can sometimes be "cured" by being made to swallow hot tallow.

Monsters can be positive as well. Indians of northern California told of the Earth Dragon, which had great horns and whose body was used animistically as the basis for the creation.

Almost always, however, monsters represent the frightening nightmare side of reality, and there are several examples of heroes who, like Herakles and other heroes around the world, prove themselves by destroying such beings. The Athabascan Apache and other tribes tell of the Vagina Girls, monster vaginas that chew up their male victims. The Vagina Girls are conquered and detoothed by Monster-slayer or Killer-of-enemies, important deities among Navajos and Apaches. The Plains Indians have a myth of the dragon husband of Old Woman (the Moon), who is slain by the son of the Sun god. The Blackfoot tell of the hero Kutoyis, who traveled the world slaying monsters of many kinds, in-

cluding a cannibalistic one and a terrifying Wind Sucker whose heart
Kutoyis stabbed after being swallowed by the monster. In this last act
Kutoyis is one of many heroes from Africa, Siberia, Europe, and other
parts of North America who kill monsters from within.

Hopi Ogres

*Ogres have always been popular mythological figures. They are some-
times animal in form, sometimes humanlike females. Often they eat living people, sometimes corpses. They are always frightening even when,
as in the case of the Hopi Indians of Arizona, they are assimilated into
tribal ritual.*

*For half of the year—from winter solstice till late July—nature spir-
its callled* katsinas *visit Hopi villages in northeastern Arizona. The katsinas are multifarious in form, and their dances in the Hopi plazas in
the summer months are widely known. They appear at other times as
well during the Hopi ceremonial cycle, always blessed arrivals, benign
celebrations of the gift of life in all its forms and messengers that are
asked to bring rain to the dry lands in which the Hopi must grow their
corn and other crops.*

*But one group of katsinas are not so benign: the mean ogre spirits,
or* soo'so'yoktu, *who make their appearance in the icy chill of February
during the ceremonies of purification. On a gloomy night, So'yokwuuti,
the sister of the ogres, suddenly appears in the village, demanding that
young girls prepare certain sacred foods and that young males hunt large
game animals, all in great quantities, to feed the ogres. Here, in the
words of Alph Secakuku, a Hopi snake priest, is a description of these
events.*

Only if [these sacred foods] are provided will individual life be spared
to enjoy the blessings manifested by the completed ceremonies. Within
about a week, the *soo'so'yoktu* appear from the So'yok'ki [spiritual
home of the Ogres] and proceed to each house, insisting on the food.
The *Soo'so'yoktu* fill the villages with eerie and terrifying hoots and
snarls. The peacefulness of the village is shattered. The Ogres say that
if the food demanded is not forthcoming, they will take the children and
eat them instead. The children wail and cry in terror. Everybody looks
into themselves to see what they may have done wrong during the year
to deserve this terrifying disruption.

At each house and *kiva*, [underground social and religions space for
clans] everyone (including *kiva* members) is loudly and publicly ridi-

Hopi Ogre. © Susanne Page. By permission.

culed, harshly disciplined for not living up to the high standards of life. Especially important is the maintenance of the spiritual life crucial for one's "Hopiness." Once the ridicules and punishments are over, everyone is given a special blessing: a social dance is held as a healing process. The Ogre family is forcibly removed from the village as an antidote for their ridicule and punishments.*

The Iroquois Flying Head

A particularly terrifying myth is this popular Iroquois tale of the Flying Head.

Of all the monsters who lurked in the forest, of all the spirits who slipped silently through the dark to menace the people, the most fearsome was

*Secakuku, 30.

the Flying Head. Along with the others, it would emerge from its den on stormy nights and go on the hunt.

The Flying Head was a grimacing, snarling head that had no body— only great wings protruding from its cheeks. Even though it was only a winged head, it was four times as tall as a man, and its mouth was filled with fangs with which it seized, tore into shreds, and ate anything alive, including human beings, which it evidently preferred above all other meat.

One such night when the wind blew foul, thunder rumbled, and lightning struck, a man spotted the Flying Head soaring through the treetops, merely a shadow against the dark sky, but lit for an instant by a bolt of distant lightning. In fear, the man told the people in his longhouse to flee, and they all did—except for one young woman who sat alone with her baby, thinking that someone had to make a stand against this awful scourge of the night.

The woman sat beside the hearth and built the fire up into a great blaze, then heated some stones to a red-hot glow. Suddenly the Flying Head appeared, its horrible mouth slavering as it looked into the longhouse from the far end.

Not giving any sign that she noticed it, the young woman began to pretend she was eating a meal. She picked up the red-hot rocks with a forked stick and pretended to put them in her mouth. With each "bite," she said how good it tasted, what wonderful meat this was.

The monster watched, growing hungrier and hungrier, his horrid mouth drooling until he could wait no longer. He stuck his head far into the longhouse and swallowed the entire heap of burning rocks.

A horrible scream pierced the night, and another, and the monster frantically beat its wings and flew off into the dark, screaming in agony and rage. He screamed so loud that the trees he flew past all trembled. People scattered here and there in the forest fell to the ground, covering their ears. The monster kept screaming as he flew farther and farther away from the longhouse, until his screams could be heard no longer, and the people rose up from the ground and went home, finally safe.

No one ever saw the Flying Head again, and nobody knows whatever happened to it. Maybe it died. Maybe it went to the sea and cooled its mouth down and is bothering those people there now.

The Chinook Ship Monster

When the Chinook of the Washington state coast first saw Europeans— white men, or wasichu—*they mistook the ship in which they came for a monster. Given the effect of the diseases and the materialism of the white "civilization" of which this ship was the first experience, the monster interpretation was not far wrong. This is a tale based on the ship's arrival.*

In a village near the mouth of Big River, an old woman grieved for her son who had died. For a whole year she wept. One day, trying to think of happier days when her son was alive, she took a walk along the beach. She walked a long way south along the strand of the ocean, making her way among the great rocks and the driftwood on the shore. Finally, feeling better, turned around and headed for home. It was then that she saw something strange out in the water—maybe a whale.

But as she drew closer, she saw it had two spruce trees standing erect on its back.

It must be a monster, she thought.

Coming even closer, she saw this strange creature had copper on its sides and ropes strung up to the spruce trees. She saw a bear appear from inside it—a bear with a human face. The people told stories of monsters from the sea, and she wailed now: "Oh, my son is dead and here is the thing, the monster, they tell about."

She ran back to her village, crying, and her people came out, thinking she had been hurt or attacked. But she explained that there was a monster just offshore to the south, so everyone ran down there with their bows and arrows. When they got there, they saw two bearlike creatures standing on the monster. The creatures seemed to be asking for water to drink.

One of the people climbed up on the monster and looked inside, seeing boxes and other things. He also saw that the monster had caught on fire, so he leaped off, and the two bearlike creatures followed him. They took the two creatures to their village, and soon people from all around heard about them and came to see them. The people of the village had noticed that everything on the monster burned up except the copper and other metal, so they traded the metal for deerskins and necklaces, slaves, and other useful things. The people of the village grew rich, trading and selling the metals that no one else had ever seen before, and the two bearlike creatures were kept in separate villages.

European American

European Americans brought European tales of monsters with them to the New World. But the very mystery of this largely uncharted world, with its endless forests, towering mountains, killing deserts, and unfamiliar animals and plants, encouraged the production of new monsters. These monsters and fabulous beings became characters in a favorite European American art form, the tall tale.

A time-honored part of tall-tale telling has been what might be called *un*natural history, the creation of an improbable bestiary inhabiting the wilderness. The amusement of these tales also often arose from the gullibility of the visiting greenhorn, who would spend anxiety-filled and wakeful nights near the campfire, fearing the arrival not just of such real animals as bears but of even more ferocious creatures.

(Greenhorns to this day are invited on snipe hunts. The snipe is variously described, most often vaguely but more or less like a highly tasty woodchuck. The locals provide the greenhorn with a sack, perhaps a burlap bag, and tell him to wait in a particular place in the dark while they go forth to locate a snipe and drive it, by beating the brush, to the place where the greenhorn can catch it in the bag.)

The forests where Paul Bunyan worked and played (see page 135) were filled with otherwise little-known animals like the harmless stone-eating gyascutus, a sordid beast with ears like a rabbit and the teeth of a lion. Its telescopic legs permit it to graze on hillsides, where it feeds on rocks and lichens. Like many other woodland beasts of this kind, it is rarely seen except after a case of snakebite or a jug of whiskey. Among birds are the gillygaloo, which lays square eggs so they won't roll down the steep inclines where it nests (boiled, the eggs made dice for the lumberjacks), and the goofus bird, which always flies backward, needing to know only where it has been and not where it is going. The venomous hoop snake puts its tail in its mouth and rolls after its prey with lightning speed; escape is achieved only by leaping through its hoop.

The black hodag *(Bovinus spiritualis)* is a rare creature found only in the swamps of Wisconsin. Its primary food is mud turtles, water snakes, and muskrats, but it also eats human flesh. A ferocious animal, it has horns on its head, huge bulging eyes, and sharp claws, along with a line of sharp spines that runs along its back and long tail. It is not known ever to lie down; instead, it sleeps leaning against the trunk of a tree.

Bigfoot

Throughout the world, people dwelling in or near forests have spoken of windigo-like forest monsters and also more humanlike creatures with hairy pelts, walking upright on two legs, usually gigantic in size. In the Mongolian steppes, the creature is called the almas; *in China it is known as the Wildman; and European forests were believed to harbor wild men—hairy, nocturnal, and dangerous. In the upper (and unforested) reaches of the Himalayas, it is known as Yeti, or the legendary Abominable Snowman, and in North America it is called Sasquatch (a name derived from the Indians of the Northwest) or—because of the giant tracks it seems to leave behind—Bigfoot.*

One can speculate that these wild giants of the wilderness are some form of archetypal dream or nightmare, or a nearly species-wide recollection from the time protohumans left the forests of Africa and the resident apes behind and went timidly off to make a living in the nearby savanna. But with Bigfoot and its other cousins around the world, we enter a realm that may be considered legend but is also called cryptozoology.

Here the bogeyman, designed perhaps to scare children into good behavior, becomes instead a distinct possibility. As in the case of the Loch Ness monster, or "Nessie," there are earnestly reported sightings, even putative photographs, the sort of "evidence" that no one expects in discussing such folkloric beasts as Paul Bunyan's giant blue ox or the hodag. In 1887, for example, a Russian explorer named Nicolai Przewalski collected reports of "wild men" (almas) on an expedition to Mongolia and also, pursuing other local legends about small untamed horses, discovered what we now know as Przewalski's horse. Several large animals, including a relative of the giraffe called the okapi, have come to light only in the twentieth century. That some secretive, perhaps mostly nocturnal, humanlike relative might still wander mostly unseen in the few yet-to-be-overrun wildernesses of the planet remains a scientific pos-sibility, though less likely with every passing year as forests are detim-bered and satellites look with increasingly fine resolution down on the earth's most intimate affairs.

In the United States (and Canada), reports of a giant, humanlike creature are rife, from the early nineteenth century till today, and from as far east as Pennsylvania to the main Bigfoot region, the Pacific North-west, where vast tracts of relatively untrammeled forest still exist. Some-times a sighting may consist only of the perception of an unpleasant odor and a shadowy movement in the dark; others report seeing the creature briefly before it disappears into the trees.

The Mount Vernon monster, which for a few years in the late 1970s, inhabited the area near George Washington's home in Virginia, was known only by its nocturnal roar, a very low rumbling sound that terrified local inhabitants and brought to mind the notion of a Bigfoot-type monster roaming this exurban neighborhood. It was widely re-ported in local papers and on television. Assiduous investigators taped the roars and brought the tape to Eugene Morton, an ornithologist at the National Zoo in Washington, D.C., and an expert at interpreting sonograms (voice prints) of animal sounds. It turned out to be the chirp of a baby robin played at one-eighth normal speed, turning it into a low rumble, and once this finding was announced it was never heard again in the Mount Vernon area.*

In the Pacific Northwest, however, Bigfoot is not so easily disposed of. There are hundreds of reports (and castings) of tracks—prints left in mud or snow of feet more than sixteen inches long. Some of these tracks may well have been elaborately faked, occurring (as do some of the sightings) not far from human activity. But other prints have been found in wilderness areas where no hoaxer would expect his work to be dis-covered. And some of the tracks seem to exhibit whorls of fingerprintlike markings, which would be nearly impossible for a hoaxer to produce. So overwhelming are the number of prints found in the northwestern forests that Sir John Napier, a primatologist who was employed by the Smithsonian during the 1960s, said flatly that "Sasquatch exists."†

Only a handful of other scientists agree, and few will even discuss the matter seriously, finding the existence of a gigantic hominid remain-ing in our midst so long after humans evolved as at best implausible. Why, after all these years during which several adventurers have dili-

---

*Personal communication from Eugene Morton to Jake Page, February 24, 1997.
†This quote is from Napier. The rest of this account derives from *Mysterious Creatures.* The chapter on Bigfoot in that book was written by Jake Page.

gently sought out Bigfoot, is there no direct and incontrovertible physical evidence—bones, for example? But to others who prefer to think that the planet may still harbor surprises, that there is room not only for monsters of the imagination but real giants in the thickets that range from Oregon north into British Columbia, twenty-four feet of motion picture film taken in October 1967 still give heart.

Roger Patterson was a onetime rodeo rider, a part-time inventor, and a firm believer in the existence of Bigfoot. Short and sinewy, he had been looking for the giant for years, and this October he was at it again with a friend named Bob Gimlin, a construction worker and a good horseman.

They had been out in the highland forests of northern California, near the Oregon border, for more than a week, looking for tracks. A bulldozer operator named Jerry Crew had reported tracks near there only a few months earlier; others in the area—road builders—had made casts of tracks with humanlike sixteen-inch-long feet, and the Eureka newspaper had published the finds as a front-page story.

It was Friday, October 21, in the early afternoon, and Patterson and Gimlin were making their way on horseback along the hundred-foot-wide, shallow bed of Bluff Creek, which flows eventually into the Klamath River. The waters of springs past had kicked up a fifteen-foot-high tangle of logs and trees ahead of them, which obscured their view, so the two horsemen made their way toward the tangle, and then came abreast of it.

And then they saw her.

She was crouched over a fallen tree. At the snort of one of the horses, she stood erect and stared across the water at the two men. Maybe it was her smell or just her looming presence, but the horses screamed and backed away, one of them rearing so high it threw its rider, the seasoned horseman Patterson, onto the ground.

Immediately he grabbed from his horse's saddlebag the 16-millimeter camera he had been using to photograph the scenery as part of a documentary he aspired to produce of a Bigfoot sighting. He started the camera and ran through the wet sand toward the creature, which moved off behind some low piles of logs.

"Cover me!" Patterson shouted to his companion, who readied his rifle as a precaution. Patterson crouched and kept the camera runnning, pointed at the creature. At one point she swiveled her torso and head around and looked back at her pursuer while still striding away.

"Oh, my God," Patterson now shouted. "I'm out of film!"

By now the horses had bolted, and the two men decided it was wiser to catch them than to pursue the Bigfoot. Once they collected them and returned to the site, the creature was long gone, but they made plaster casts of the inch-deep footprints it left in the ground as it disappeared. They were fourteen inches long each and showed a stride of forty-two inches.

The unprecedented find, of course, was the film. About a minute of film showed a broad-shouldered creature with pendulous breasts. She was covered with dark reddish hair, except for her face, nipples, palms and soles, and she appeared neckless, with a forehead that sloped back to a point on her head, not unlike the crested skull of a gorilla. As she loped off, the camera showed long thick arms and strong legs moving in a strikingly smooth gait, each knee bending like that of a cross-country skier as it received her weight.

Millions saw this brief moment of cryptozoological history on their televisions, and most scientists assumed the film was an elaborate hoax. A British expert in biomechanics named Donald Grieve said that if the film had been shot at the standard speed of 24 frames per second (fps), the creature could have been—and probably was—a human in disguise. But, he added, "the possibility of fakery is ruled out if the speed of the film was 16 or 18 fps. In these conditions a normal human being could not duplicate the observed pattern."

Patterson could not remember the setting. He knew that 24 fps was more acceptable for television use, but thought it might have been changed when his horse spooked. There was no way of telling.

But there was a way of telling. Russian analysts noted that the film also recorded the manner in which Patterson ran toward the creature, bobbing up and down with each step. If the film had been shot at the standard 24 fps, Patterson would have to have been taking six steps per second, faster than an Olympic sprinter. So, according to the Russians, the film had to have been shot at 16 fps; therefore it was not a hoax.

Subsequently, upon analyzing the film, technicians at the Walt Disney studios said that if Patterson's film was a hoax, it was a better hoax than they could have perpetrated themselves. They could not find "the zipper in the suit." And later an anthropologist at Washington State University named Grover Krantz pointed out a detail that no rodeo rider would probably have known enough about to include in a hoax: Given the creature's apparent size and weight, it would require a foot formed differently than a human's—notably a heel that extended farther back from the ankle. And this is just what the creature on the film possessed.

There the matter rests. Legend or evolutionary relic? A recurrent dream or a hoax—or a real offshoot from the human family tree? People still seek it out, whatever it is, and in several local jurisdictions in the Pacific Northwest, Sasquatch is listed as a legally protected species.

The Jersey Devil

The Jersey Devil, or Leed's Devil (it is said to have been born at Leed's Point), is a fabulous being of the South Jersey shore. He or she (no one knows its gender) has long haunted people along the shore. Its footprints are often found on the beaches and its screams are heard at night.

There once was an old woman, so the story goes, who had ten or twelve children and dreaded having any more. In a rash moment she said she hoped that if she had another child it would be a devil. When a monster was, in fact, born to her she kept it hidden in an old house until it grew large and escaped. Now it peers into the windows of innocent shore inhabitants and does other sorts of mischief.

Moby Dick

Americans found adventure and riches in their exploration of their new land. They also found both as they sailed the seas in search of fish and other sea animals, especially the whale. Stories of gigantic whales and the perils of hunting them were common in nineteenth-century America. Author Herman Melville made good use of these stories in his creation in the novel Moby Dick *of the sometimes diabolical Captain Ahab and his obsessive quest for dominance over a white whale. The whale's attitude to Ahab cannot, of course, be known, but its character is ambiguous—is it merely whalelike in its self-defense, or does it act in a consciously malevolent manner as the representative of some dark force or of a Calvinist God bent on breaking the obstinate Ahab and perhaps humanity itself? Whatever the meaning of the whale and its whiteness (and Melville and his charcters speculate a great deal on this question), it appears to us and to the common sailors on Ahab's ship as a monster from the deep with all the supernatural qualities of such beings.*

And as for those who, previously hearing of the White Whale, by chance caught sight of him; in the beginning of the thing they had every one of them, almost, as boldly and fearlessly lowered for him, as for any other whale of that species. But at length, such calamities did ensue in these assaults—not restricted to sprained wrists and ankles, broken limbs, or devouring amputations—but fatal to the last degree of fatality; those repeated disastrous repulses, all accumulating and piling their terrors

All in a Day's Work, by C. A. Raleigh. Courtesy of the Kendall Whaling Museum.

upon Moby Dick; those things had gone far to shake the fortitude of many brave hunters, to whom the story of the White Whale had eventually come.

Nor did wild rumors of all sorts fail to exaggerate, and still the more horrify the true histories of these deadly encounters. For not only do fabulous rumors naturally grow out of the very body of all surprising terrible events,—as the smitten tree gives birth to its fungi; but, in maritime life, far more than in that of terra firma, wild rumors abound, wherever there is any adequate reality for them to cling to. And as the sea surpasses the land in this matter, so the whale fishery surpasses every other sort of maritime life, in the wonderfulness and fearfulness of the rumors which sometimes circulate there. For not only are whalemen as a body unexempt from that ignorance and superstitiousness hereditary to all sailors; but of all sailors, they are by all odds the most directly brought into contact with whatever is appallingly astonishing in the sea; face to face they not only eye its greatest marvels, but, hand to jaw, give battle to them. Alone, in such remotest waters, that though you sailed a thousand miles, and passed a thousand shores, you would not come to any chiselled hearthstone, or aught hospitable beneath that part of the sun; in such latitudes and longitudes, pursuing too such a calling as he does, the whaleman is wrapped by influences all tending to make his fancy pregnant with many a mighty birth.

No wonder, then, that ever gathering volume from the mere transit over the widest watery spaces, the outblown rumors of the White Whale did in the end incorporate with themselves all manner of morbid hints, and half-formed fœtal suggestions of supernatural agencies, which eventually invested Moby Dick with new terrors unborrowed from anything that visibly appears. So that in many cases such a panic did he finally strike, that few who by those rumors, at least, had heard of the White Whale, few of those hunters were willing to encounter the perils of his jaw.

But there were still other and more vital practical influences at work. Not even at the present day has the original prestige of the Sperm Whale, as fearfully distinguished from all other species of the leviathan, died out of the minds of the whalemen as a body. There are those this day among them, who, though intelligent and courageous enough in offering battle to the Greenland or Right whale, would perhaps—either from professional inexperience, or incompetency, or timidity, decline a contest with the Sperm Whale; at any rate, there are plenty of whalemen, especially among those whaling nations not sailing under the American flag, who have never hostilely encountered the Sperm Whale, but whose sole knowledge of the leviathan is restricted to the ignoble monster primitively pursued in the North; seated on their hatches, these men will hearken with a childish fireside interest and awe, to the wild, strange tales of Southern whaling. Nor is the pre-eminent tremendousness of the great Sperm Whale anywhere more feelingly comprehended, than on board of those prows which stem him . . .

One of the wild suggestings referred to, as at last coming to be linked with the White Whale in the minds of the superstitiously inclined, was the unearthly conceit that Moby Dick was ubiquitous; that he had actually been encountered in opposite latitudes at one and the same instant of time.

Nor, credulous as such minds must have been, was this conceit altogether without some faint show of superstitious probability. For as the secrets of the currents in the seas have never yet been divulged, even to the most erudite research; so the hidden ways of the Sperm Whale when beneath the surface remain, in great part, unaccountable to his pursuers; and from time to time have originated the most curious and contradictory speculations regarding them, especially concerning the mystic modes whereby, after sounding to a great depth, he transports himself with such vast swiftness to the most widely distant points. . . .

But even stripped of these supernatural surmisings, there was enough in the earthly make and incontestable character of the monster to strike the imagination with unwonted power. For, it was not so much his uncommon bulk that so much distinguished him from other sperm whales, but, as was elsewhere thrown out—a peculiar snow-white wrinkled forehead, and a high, pyramidical white hump. These were his prominent features; the tokens whereby, even in the limitless, uncharted seas, he revealed his identity, at a long distance, to those who knew him.

The rest of his body was so streaked, and spotted, and marbled with the same shrouded hue, that, in the end, he had gained his distinctive appellation of the White Whale; a name, indeed, literally justified by his vivid aspect, when seen gliding at high noon through a dark blue sea, leaving a milky-way wake of creamy foam, all spangled with golden gleamings.

Nor was it unwonted magnitude, nor his remarkable hue, nor yet his deformed lower jaw, that so much invested the whale with natural terror, as that unexampled, intelligent malignity which, according to specific accounts, he had over and over again evinced in his assaults. More than all, his treacherous retreats struck more of dismay than perhaps aught else. For, when swimming before his exulting pursuers, with every apparent symptom of alarm, he had several times been known to turn round suddenly, and, bearing down upon them, either stave their boats to splinters, or drive them back in consternation to their ship. . . .

Is it that by its indefiniteness it shadows forth the heartless voids and immensities of the universe, and thus stabs us from behind with the thought of annihilation, when beholding the white depths of the milky way? Or is it, that as in essence whiteness is not so much a color as the visible absence of color, and at the same time the concrete of all colors; is it for these reasons that there is such a dumb blankness, full of meaning, in a wide landscape of snows—a colorless, all-color of atheism from which we shrink? And when we consider that other theory of the natural philosophers, that all other earthly hues—every stately or lovely emblazoning—the sweet tinges of sunset skies and woods; yea, and the gilded velvets of butterflies, and the butterfly cheeks of young girls; all these are but subtile deceits, not actually inherent in substances, but only laid on from without; so that all deified Nature absolutely paints like the harlot, whose allurements cover nothing but the charnel-house within; and when we proceed further, and consider that the mystical cosmetic which produces every one of her hues, the great principle of light, for ever remains white or colorless in itself, and if operating without medium upon matter, would touch all objects, even tulips and roses, with its own blank tinge—pondering all this, the palsied universe lies before us a leper; and like wilful travellers in Lapland, who refuse to wear colored and coloring glasses upon their eyes, so the wretched infidel gazes himself blind at the monumental white shroud that wraps all the prospect around him. And of all these things the Albino whale was the symbol. Wonder ye then at the fiery hunt?

African American

African folklore and mythology, like that of Native Americans, is
heavily populated by animal figures who are fabulous and sometimes monsterlike in that they combine animal agility and power with
human wile and trickery. The slaves who were brought to America from
Africa naturally carried these animal tales in their memories. Tales of
the African spider-trickster Anansi continued to be told in the American
South, as were tales of the rabbit trickster who, also influenced by American Indian tales, emerged as the ubiquitous Brer Rabbit, perhaps the
prime African American trickster (see the Brer Rabbit story in Part 3).
Still another fabulous beast with trickster characteristics is the monkey,
or *jigue,* who has pointed teeth, long hair, and dark skin, and who
terrifies those he watches with his "eyes of live coals." Many of these
animal trickster figures have in common the fact that, though small and
seemingly powerless, they manage to outwit the powerful. As in many
other cultures, such stories mirror the secret wishes of an oppressed
people.

"A Boarhog for a Husband"

*While monster stories per se are rare in African American mythology,
there are fairytalelike legends of beasts disguised as humans. A well-
known tale of the sort is this "Beauty and the Beast"–style tale told in
the Bahamas and also in the American South.*

> Scalambay, scalambay
> Scoops, scops, scalambay

> See my lover coming there
> Scoops, scops, scalambay.

Once upon a time—it was a very good time—Massa King had an
only daughter. And all the young fellows were constantly talking with
each other about who was going to be able to marry her. They all came
by to call on her, but none of them suited her. Each time one would
come, her father would say "Now this is the one!" But she kept saying,
"No, Daddy, this fellow here, I just don't like him," or "No, Mommy,
this one really doesn't please me." But the last one to come along was
a handsome young fellow, and she fell in love with him right away. And
of course, when she fell in love, it was deep and wide—she just lost her
head altogether. What she didn't know was that she'd actually chosen
a boarhog who had changed himself into a human to go courting.

Now the Massa King had another child, a little Old Witch Boy who
lived there and did all the nasty stuff around the palace. He was always
dirty and smelly, you know, and no one liked to be around him, especially the King's beautiful daughter. One day after work the young
fellow came in to visit his bride, and the Old Witch Boy whispered,
"Daddy, Daddy, did you know that the fellow my sister is going to
marry is a boarhog?" "What? You better shut your mouth and get back
under the bed where you belong." (That's where they made the Old
Witch Boy stay, you see, because he was so dirty.)

Now when they got married, they moved way up on the mountain
up where they plant all those good things to put in the pot, roots like
dasheen, tania, and all those provisions that hogs like to eat, too. One
day, Massa King came up there and showed him a big piece of land he
wanted his daughter and her husband to have for farming. The husband
really liked that because he could raise lots of tanias—which is what
boarhogs like to eat most.

So one day he went up to work, early early in the morning. Now
there was this little house up by the land where he could go and change
his clothes before he went to work. He went into one side of the little
house, and he started singing:

> Scalambay, scalambay
> Scoops, scops, scalambay
> See my lover coming there
> Scoops, scops, scalambay.

And with each refrain he would take off one piece of clothing. And with
every piece he took off he became more of a boarhog—first the head,
then the feet, then the rest of the body.

> Scalambay, scalambay
> Scoops, scops, scalambay
> See my lover coming there
> Scoops, scops, scalambay.

Well, about noon, when he thought the time was coming for lunch to arrive in the field, he went back into the house and put back on his clothes, took off the boarhog suit and put back on the ordinary suit he came in. And as he got dressed he sang the same little song to change himself back into a handsome man.

> Scalambay, scalambay
> Scoops, scops, scalambay
> See my lover coming there
> Scoops, scops, scalambay.

After a while, the Old Witch Boy as usual came with the food, but this day he came early and saw what was going on, heard the singing, and saw the man changing. So he rushed home and told his father again, "Daddy, this fellow who married my sister up there really is a boarhog. It's true!" Massa King said "Boy, shut your mouth," and his sister said, "Get back underneath the bed, you scamp you."

The next day, the Old Witch Boy got up very early and went up the mountain and heard the song again:

> Scalambay, scalambay
> Scoops, scops, scalambay
> See my lover coming there
> Scoops, scops, scalambay.

All right, he thought, and he went down again and he told his father what he had seen and heard. He even sang the song. Now Massa King didn't know what to think. But he knew he was missing a lot of tanias from his other fields, so he loaded up his gun and went to see what was going on up there in his fields. Mr. Boarhog was up there changing and didn't know he was being watched, but he thought he heard something so he kind of stopped. The Old Witch Boy started to sing, and Mr. Boarhog couldn't do anything but join in with him. And so there they both were, singing:

> Scalambay, scalambay
> Scoops, scops, scalambay
> See my lover coming there
> Scoops, scops, scalambay.

And the man slowly changed into a boarhog. When the King saw this he couldn't believe his eyes. He took his gun and he let go, *pow!* And he killed Mr. Boarhog, and carried him down the mountain. The King's beautiful daughter couldn't believe what she saw and began to scream and cry, but Massa King told her what he had seen and what he had done, and then she had to believe it.

They cleaned Mr. Boarhog's body and had him quartered. And I was right there on the spot, and took one of the testicles and it gave me food for nearly a week!*

"The Poor Man and the Snake"

Readers of the fables of Aesop or the Reynard the Fox tales of medieval Europe will not be surprised by the prevalence of animal tales with a moral among African Americans. The main beast character in this tale from the American South is Brer Snake.

One poor man was making a living by splitting long shingles and cutting timber in the swamp. He had a wife but no children. Every day, from sunrise till sundown, he went to the swamp to cut. Though he tried his best, he scarcely could make enough for his everyday bread to eat.

Once, a very big snake—the father of all those other snakes that lived in the swamp—noticed the man. He saw how hard he worked and how little he made and he took pity on him. One evening, just before the poor man left working, this snake crawled up to the log where the man had been chopping and said, "Brother, how you making out?" The man answered, "I don't make out. I work in this swamp from day till dark, day in and day out, and I try my best, but I can scarcely make vittles enough for me and my wife to eat." Then the snake said, "I am sorry for you and willing to help." The man thanked him and asked him how, and the snake said, "Do you have any children?" The man said, "No!" The snake asked "Do you have a wife?" The man said, "Yes." The snake said, "Can you keep a secret from your wife?" The man answered that he could. Brer Snake told him he was afraid to trust him; but when the man begged the snake very hard to try him, the snake agreed to do so. The snake told him he was going to give him some money the next day, but he mustn't tell his wife where he got the money. The man made a strong promise, and they parted.

The next day, just before the poor man finished working, the snake crawled up to him. His belly and his mouth were puffed out. He spit out two quarts of silver money on the ground right there in front of the poor man, and he said, "Do you remember what I told you last night? Well, sir, here is some money I brought to help you. Take it. But remember, if you tell your wife where you got it, or who gave it to you, it won't do you any good, and you will die a poor man." The man was so glad to get the money, he kept saying, "Thank you, thank you, thank you, my brother; I won't ever tell anyone where I got this money." After he left the swamp to go home, the snake suspected that he was going to go back on his promise and tell his wife, so he made up his mind to follow him and see what happened.

It was dark when he reached the man's house. He crawled up and lay down under the window where he could hear everything that was said inside the house. The wife was turned around and cooking supper. After she and her husband ate, her husband said, "I had a lot of work today, look at this money." Then he pulled out the silver and spread it on the table. Well now, his wife was amazed. She jumped with happiness and said, "Tell me where you got this money." The man said, "A friend gave it to me." His wife said, "what friend?" The man said he had promised not to tell. The wife begged so hard that the man forgot his promise and went and told everything that had happened. Then the wife said, "That snake must have a belly full of silver money, and I will tell you what to do tomorrow. When the snake comes to talk to you, you pick a moment and chop off his head with your ax, and take all the money out of him." And the husband agreed!

Brer Snake heard every word they spoke, and he went to his house in the swamp very vexed because the man that he had befriended had gone back on his promise and made an evil plan to kill him.

The next day, the man watched for the snake. When the sun lay far down, and the man was very tired from splitting one big log, Brer Snake crawled up alongside of the log and showed himself to the man. They talked together, and the snake asked the man, "Have you shown your wife the money I gave you?" The man answered, "Yes, I did." And then he asked him, "Did you tell your wife where you got it?" The man said, "No." The snake asked him again, "Are you sure you didn't tell her you got it from me?" The man said, "I told you once already. What makes you ask again? You think I am lying to you?" With that, he tried to chop off the snake's head. But the snake had had his eyes on him and he drew back against the log. The ax missed the snake and glanced back off the log and cut the man's own leg off. The poor man hollered for someone to come help him. But he was way in the middle of the swamp and out of everybody's hearing. Well, he was bleeding to death, and just before he died, Brer Snake said to him, "Didn't I tell you when you got that silver from me, that if you told your wife you would die a poor man? You promised me you would keep the secret. You went home to your wife and you showed her the money and you told her where you got it. More than that: you and she fixed a plan to kill me, me who had been your friend, and to rob me of the money I had left. Now you see the judgment that comes to you. When you tried to chop off my head, you cut your own foot off. You are going to die in these here woods. No man nor woman is ever going to find you. The buzzards are going to eat you."

And it happened just as the snake said. The man broke his word, and he died a poor man.

Anybody who goes back on his promise and tries to harm the person who has done him a favor is sure to meet up with big trouble.*

*Abrahams, 130–32.

Asian American

Monsterlike beings of various kinds are common in Asian folklore. A red candle keeps ghosts from entering the body of a newborn Chinese child. A small knife worn around the neck will prevent demons from threatening the child within a pregnant Chinese woman. In both Chinese and Japanese mythology foxes are dangerous shape-shifters who can become bewitching women. But of all the monsters or fabulous beasts of Asia that have become a part of the American or Asian American landscape, none can compare with the dragon.

The Dragon

Dragons are common to many cultures. In ancient Mesopotamia the dragon was a female primeval essence destroyed by the god Marduk. In Europe the dragon protected treasure and was an evil, fire-breathing, scaly monster who was slain by the likes of Saint George and King Arthur. Virgins must sometimes be sacrificed to dragons. Dragons are often associated with the Devil himself. But in China the dragon is for the most part a helpful beast associated with the Chinese New Year celebrations that continue to take place not only in China but in Chinatowns all over the world, including America. At such celebrations the benevolent dragon is paraded through the streets, and dragon kites are flown. Different-colored dragons traditionally represent different values of leadership—white for purity, blue for compassion, and so forth.

III

NEW WORLD
HEROES AND HEROINES

Heroes are common to all cultures. Some are essentially adventurers out to prove themselves or to avenge crimes in war or individual confrontation. The great figures of Homer's epics are such heroes, for the most part. Other, more altruistic heroes lead their people unselfishly. Religious heroes such as Moses, Jesus, Buddha, and Mohammed fall under this category, as do secular nationalistic heroes such as Joan of Arc or Simón Bolívar. There are also culture heroes, who often take animal form and are usually trickster-transformers living in the ancient mythic age who aid in or direct the creation. Typically, they teach the people how to procreate, how to use language, and how to obtain food, shelter, and medicine. They kill the monsters that threaten the tribe, and they sometimes steal light and/or fire for their followers. Prometheus is a culture hero of sorts among the Greeks.

Heroes are always in one way or another a reflection of their people. The brave but arrogant and prideful Achilles expresses the value system of a male-dominated pirate culture. So does the famous Herakles (Hercules). The heroes of the epics of India reflect a strict caste and ritual system and a particular sense of ultimate reality. The Buddha and other religious heroes speak to the inner needs of human culture in general, but each begins from within the traditions of a particular people. Heroes are external expressions of aspects of a culture's collective psyche. And, as Joseph Campbell and others have pointed out, heroes tend to follow a path of archetypal or universal events—the miraculous birth, the search (for the father, for example, or for some boon for the tribe), the descent to the underworld—that allow heroes of particular cultures to become meaningful to all people. At the universal level the hero is each of us on his or her journey toward some sort of wholeness or meaningfulness.

American heroes run the gamut of heroes from trickster-creator to arrogant adventurer, from selfless giver to proud leader. They represent the multifarious reality that is the American character.

Native American

Heroes abound in Native American myth and legend, but the majority of these fall into the culture hero category and must therefore also be considered gods in some sense. Figures such as Raven and Coyote, stories about whom we treated earlier, are tricksters known not only for their humorous and amoral escapades but for their role in creation and in bringing knowledge to their people. Other Indian culture heroes include Mink and Bluejay on the Pacific, Rabbit in the Southeast, and more humanlike figures such as Glooskap in the Northeast and Killer-of-enemies or Monster-slayer in the Southwest. These mythic heroes, whose function is in a sense religious, should be differentiated from the purely human heroes who also exist among the Native Americans—heroes such as Hiawatha or Geronimo—and also from fictional heroes such as Water Jar Boy and Kutoyis, who are essentially human but possess certain mythic characteristics of the culture hero.

The Wabanaki Glooskap—The Fight with the Water Monster

Glooskap (Glooscap, Gluskap), the popular mythic hero of many tribes of the Northeast, including the Wabanaki-speaking Indians, is an example of the culture hero who is both man and god, who was there at the creation, who ordered the lives of his people, and who lives forever. In this story we find Glooskap behaving like many heroes from different parts of the world. When his people are confronted by a monster he, like Saint George with the dragon or Oedipus with the Sphinx, comes to their rescue. The story is also an origin story, telling how bullfrogs came to be.

He was known as Glooskap and he was a spirit, a shaman, a clown, and a warrior. He created his village and the animals around it. The village had a spring that ran clear and cold year in and year out. But one day it began to dry up and only a slimy muck oozed from it. The people of the village thought hard about this and decided to send a man to the north to find the source of the spring and maybe discover why it had dried up.

The man went a long way north and came upon a village where the people had webbed hands and feet. They had a little brook in their village that ran with yellow water that smelled bad. But it was water.

The man asked the webbed people for some of their water and they said no, they couldn't give him any. Their chief wanted it all. The man asked to see the chief, and the people said he lived far upstream. Again, the man headed north.

Finally he saw the chief and began to shake with terror. The chief was so huge a monster you couldn't see his head if you stood at his feet. He had dammed up the valley that he lived in and nearly filled with his own vast body, and he had made the water smelly and yellow. He had enormous warts and yellow eyes.

"What do you want, little man?" he croaked.

The man explained that his village needed water but their spring had dried up because of the monster's dam. The monster roared that he didn't care about that. "Don't bother me," he croaked in a huge and horrid voice. "Go away!"

He opened his mouth, and the man could see all the things the monster had already eaten. The monster smacked his lips, and the man ran off as fast as he could go. He told the people of his village about the monster and his dam, and they all lamented that there was nothing more they could do.

But Glooskap heard all this lamentation and girded himself for war, painting his body red, with yellow rings around his eyes, and adorning himself with eagle feathers. From a mountain he made himself a flint knife, and while thunder and lightning crashed around him he made his way north.

Finally reaching the valley of the monster, he demanded water, and the monster roared at him to go away or die. Glooscap called the monster a slimy lump of mud and other things, and they fought. The monster's great mouth flew open—a mile wide—but Glooskap made himself even larger and slit the monster's belly with his mountainous flint knife. From the gaping wound, a vast river gushed and flowed south, right past the village with the people with webbed feet, and down through Glooskap's village to the sea.

Not finished, Glooskap seized the monster in his hand and squeezed him into a lump and threw him into a swamp. He had squeezed the monster into a bullfrog, and ever since the bullfrog's skin has been wrinkled.

The Tewa Water Jar Boy

Water Jar Boy is a Tewa hero whose miraculous conception and childhood and eventual search for his father reveal him as a relative of Quetzalcoatl, Jesus, King Arthur, and many other versions of the "hero with a thousand faces."

A woman at Sikyatki had a beautiful daughter who refused to get married. The mother spent her days making water jars, and one day she asked the daughter to help mix some clay while she went for water. The girl put some clay on a flat stone and stepped on it and somehow some of the clay entered her, making her pregnant.

He mother was angry to hear about this, and when she looked again she saw that her daugher had given birth not to a regular child but to a water jar. Her father came in and said he was glad, especially when he found out the baby was a water jar. He liked the water jar and watched it grow.

In twenty days, the child was big enough to run around with the other children, and they came to like the creature, finding out that he was called Water Jar Boy. His mother cried all the time because Water Jar Boy had no arms or legs, just a mouth they could feed him by.

Later, Water Jar Boy begged to go rabbit hunting, but his grandfather said he couldn't, not without any arms or legs. But the boy pleaded and his grandfather took him. He was rolling along under the mesa when he saw a rabbit and rolled after it, fetching up against a rock, where he broke. Up jumped a boy, glad his old skin was broken. He was a fine-looking boy, handsomely dressed, with a lot of turquoise beads around his neck. He was fleet of foot and that day killed four rabbits before he went to the foot of the mesa to meet his grandfather.

"Who are you?" the old man asked, and didn't believe it when the handsome boy said he was his grandson. But when he explained what had happened, the old man accepted the boy and they went home. When they got there, his mother thought her father had come back with a handsome suitor for her, but they explained that it was her son, Water Jar Boy.

Her son went off with the other boys, but one day he came and asked who his father was.

"I don't know," his mother said.

"Well, I'm going to go find him."

"You can't," his mother said. "I've never been with a man, so there isn't anywhere you can look."

"I know where he lives," Water Jar Boy said, and he left, walking southwest toward Horse Mesa Point, where he came to a spring. An old man was walking near the spring and asked the boy where he was going.

"To the spring, to see my father."

"You'll never find your father," the old man said, but the boy insisted he would find him.

"Who is your father?" the man asked, and the boy said, "I think you are."

The man glared at the boy, trying to scare him, but the boy kept on saying, "You are my father." Finally the man put his arms around the boy and said he was glad, and took him down into the spring. There he saw all his father's relatives, and they all ran up and put their arms around him. He stayed with them one night, and then went home the next day and told his mother what had happened.

Soon his mother got sick and died, and the boy thought there was no reason for him to stay, so he went back to the spring. There he found his mother with all the other women. His father told him he didn't want the boy living over at Sikyatki, so he had made his mother die and come over to the spring to live. So they all lived together there.

The Iroquois Hiawatha

The real Hiawatha, as opposed to the one used by Longfellow in his famous poem of that name, was a sixteenth-century follower of Dekanawida, founder of the Iroquois League. Longfellow's Hiawatha is based on the mistaken research of Henry Rowe Schoolcraft, who confused Hiawatha with the Ojibwa culture hero.

It was Ta-ren-ya-wa-gon, the Upholder of the Heavens, who came down to save the people from the monsters and man-eating giants, and led them toward the rising sun. Along the way, he made some of his band Mohawks and gave them corn, beans, squash, and dogs to help them hunt game. He taught them all the ways they needed to know to live.

Continuing east, he created the Oneida, then the Onondaga, the Cayuga, and the Seneca. To each of these nations he gave special gifts— swiftness, the canoe, the knowledge of eternal laws, the making of bows and arrows.

Then Ta-ren-ya-wa-gon decided to become a human himself and live among the Onondaga, taking the name Hiawatha. He married an Onondaga woman and they soon had a daughter, Mnihaha. The Onondaga and all the other tribes grew, prospered, and were happy.

But after happiness comes sorrow. Wild tribes appeared from the north, people with no skills or knowledge of laws, but only the desire to prey on the five nations that had been founded by Ta-ren-ya-wa-gon long before. The marauders wreaked devastation through the land, and the people turned to Hiawatha, asking for help.

Hiawatha told them to assemble beside a lake, build a great council fire, and wait for him. On the fourth day, Hiawatha appeared in his gleaming white canoe, floating above the mists that rose in the lake. With him was his daughter.

As Hiawatha and his daughter disembarked, a tremendous roar was heard and a huge bird descended, bigger than a hundred eagles, his wings flapping louder than the loudest thunder. The people cowered, but Hiawatha stood calmly, his hands on his daughter's head in blessing. She then bade him farewell and seated herself on the bird. They spiraled up into the clouds and disappeared.

After four days of mourning, Hiawatha announced to the people that his time among them was now limited, that it was the future that was important—not the past. He noted that the five tribes he had founded from a single band had drifted apart, each acting in its own particular interests.

"Now," he said, "you must reunite. You must act as one people. Our enemies are too great, too powerful to be held off by only one tribe at a time. You are brothers—with one fire, one pipe. You should be as one hand with five fingers."

The wise men of the tribes met and agreed. Hiawatha gathered up some white feathers the great bird had left behind and distributed them among the leaders. "By these feathers, you will be known from now on," he said. "You will be called the Iroquois."

Thus was born the mighty League of Five Nations that held sway between the sea to the east and the great river to the west. The leaders all called for Hiawatha to stay among them, but he protested that he had to leave them. If they followed his teachings, he said, they would survive.

With that, he stepped into his white canoe and, amid a rush of beautiful sounds, rose slowly into the sky and disappeared.

The Ojibwa Corn Hero

Schoolcraft's work on "Hiawatha" includes this Ojibwa hero myth of the boy Wunzh, who wrestles with a corn spirit, Mondawmin, much as Jacob wrestles with the angel in the biblical tale. The result of Wunzh's test is the gift of corn for his people.

When the youth Wunzh reached the proper age, his father built him a lodge in a remote place where he could fast undisturbed and find his guardian in life. It was spring of the year and, in the first days of his fast, Wunzh walked the woods each morning, musing on the first shoots of plants and flowers, coming alive in the warming earth.

He hoped this would store his mind with pleasant thoughts for his dreams each night. Often, on these strolls, he found himself wondering how these plants grew, some of them sweet like berries, others poisonous, yet others full of medicine. Perhaps, if he knew more about such things, he could help his people. Perhaps they might not have to rely on the luck of the hunt or the occasional fish caught from opaque waters.

As the days went by, Wunzh grew too weak for such wanderings and instead lay in his lodge, praying that he would dream of something that would help his people. In his increasing dizziness, he permitted himself the thought that while the Great Spirit had made all things, including the people, he could have made things a bit easier for them.

On the third day of his fast, as he lay in his lodge, he saw a figure descend from the sky—a figure richly dressed in yellow and green garments of many shades, with a great plume of golden feathers waving on its head. With dreamlike grace, it arrived in Wunzh's lodge.

"The Great Spirit sent me to you, my friend," said the figure. "He takes note that your prayers are unusual. You don't seem to want the glory of the warrior, but instead merely something for the good of your people." The visitor went on to explain that this was possible. The condition was that Wunzh wrestle with his visitor.

At first, Wunzh's heart sank. He was already weak from fasting.

What hope did he have . . . ? But gathering his courage, he engaged the figure, and they wrestled until Wunzh felt utterly exhausted. Abruptly, the figure stopped, smiled, and said, "That's enough for now. You did well, I will come again to try you." He disappeared, ascending into the light of the sun.

The following day he came again, and once again challenged Wunzh who by now was even weaker. But it seemed that the weaker his body was, the greater his courage and determination. Again they wrestled, long and hard, and again the visitor broke it off, promising to come again for the final trial. Wunzh collapsed in an exhaustion near death.

The next day, after the third and final trial had begun, the heavenly visitor stopped and declared himself beaten. He sat down next to the youth and told him the Great Spirit was pleased with his courage. Now he would receive the instructions he had prayed for.

"Tomorrow," the visitor said, "is your seventh day of fasting. Your father will come with some food for strength and I will come again and you will win. Afterward, you must strip my clothes from me, put me on the ground, and take away all the weeds. Then you must bury me there. Do not let weeds grow there, but come from time to time and see if I have returned. And then you will have your wish and be able to teach your people what you want them to know."

In the morning, Wunzh's father came with food, and the youth said he would wait until sundown to eat it. And when the visitor came again, Wunzh seized him with strength that amazed the youth, threw him down on the ground and stripped away his rich yellow and green clothes. Seeing that the figure was dead, he buried him as he had been told to, and returned to his father's lodge to eat.

In the days that followed, Wunzh would go off unannounced to the spot where he had buried his friend and kept the weeds away. Toward the end of summer, he came to the spot and found that his old lodge had disappeared. In its stead was a tall, graceful plant, with clusters of yellow on its side, long green leaves, and a graceful plume of gold nodding from the top.

"It is my friend," Wunzh said to himself, and suddenly knew his friend's name: Mondawmin. He ran to fetch his father and told him that this was what he had dreamed for in his fast. If the people cared for his friend the way Wunzh had been instructed, they would no longer have to rely only on the hunt or the waters. With that, he showed his father how to tear off the yellow clusters, as he had torn off the garments before, and he showed how to hold the ears to the fire to turn them brown. The whole family then gathered for a feast upon this newly grown presence in their lives, and expressed their lasting thanks to the spirit, the beautiful visitor, who had given it to them.

And so corn came into this world.

An Oneida Maiden Hero

In spite of the fact that males are traditionally the warriors and adventurers in Native American societies heroines do exist in the lore of American Indians. This Oneida story is the legend of a maiden whose willingness to sacrifice herself saved the tribe.

In the old days before the white man came, the Oneida people had their traditional enemies, the Mingoes, who invaded their villages, burned their houses and fields, killed the men and boys, and took away the women and girls. In one such raid, the Oneida who managed to escape hid in a high cave in the forest, protected there by the Great Spirit. But the people began to starve; they either had to die in their hiding place or search for food, thus attracting the attention of their enemies.

During the great council that was held to decide what to do, a young woman called Aliquispo came forward, saying that the spirits had come to her in a vision and told her that her destiny was to save the people. "Stay here in the cliff cave," she told the Oneida, "while I lead the Mingoes to the space below. Then you will be able to crush them." The elders all praised Aliquispo for her bravery and for understanding the role given to her by the Great Spirit.

The girl made her way to the old Oneida village, where the Mingoes now lived. The Mingoes threatened to burn her alive if she did not lead them to her people. To allay their suspicions, Aliquispo refused and was immediately tied to a stake. After enduring the torture of the hot flames for an amazingly long time, she pretended to give in and with her hands tied behind her back she led the Mingoes to the space below the cliff hiding place. She whispered to the Mingoes that they should gather close to her so that she could show them the secret path that would lead to her sleeping friends and relatives. As soon as the enemies were massed around her she cried out in a loud voice, "My people, your enemies are here; destroy them." The Mingoes struck her down but were themselves struck down by a huge rain of boulders and rocks thrown from the hiding place above.

So Aliquispo died to save her people from the Mingoes. The Great Spirit turned her hair into woodbine and made honeysuckle grow from her body. Woodbine is fine medicine, and the Oneida still call honeysuckle "brave women's blood."

Geronimo—Apache Hero

Geronimo (c. 1829–1906), whose true Chiricahua Apache name was Goyathlay or Goyakla ("he who yawns"), was perhaps the most famous—and legendary—of all Indian "outlaw" warriors. When he was a young man, his entire family was wiped out during a surprise raid by Mexican troops, and Geronimo swore vengeance, which he continued to fulfill for most of his life. Something of a maverick, he became known as one who had spiritual power and could tell where the enemy was well before they came into view. While he never was the actual leader of a band in the political sense, he became a fierce leader of raids upon the Mexicans and later the Americans who began to filter into Chiricahua territory. He was no more (or less) fierce than many other Apache war leaders, but his exploits came to be better known and more exagerrated than others'.

Several times he and the people he was with were caught, arrested, and placed on reservations, and each time he broke out and went on the warpath again. Finally, leading a group of some fifty Apaches (mostly women and children), he eluded five thousand U.S. troops for about a year and then, in September 1886, was persuaded to surrender. The U.S. army then rounded up all the remaining Chiricahuas—not just renegades, but those who had been living peacefully on the reservation, and even those who had served the army as scouts—and sent them all as prisoners of war to Florida, then Alabama, and finally Fort Sill, Oklahoma.

At the time, Geronimo was the very emblem of the hated Apaches in the minds of the Anglos and Mexicans in southern Arizona, and his exploits were the topic of perfervid tales in the penny press. In captivity, Geronimo came to be lionized in non-Arizonan circles and enjoyed his fame, visiting the St. Louis World's Fair and riding in the front of Teddy Roosevelt's inaugural parade in 1905. Americans have always had a peculiar admiration for outlaws, especially those who are old, tame, or dead.

Thus did the man who was perceived for a time internationally as the worst of the "bad Indians" become something of a hero to the people who had pillaged his land and been pillaged in return.

Custer's Last Stand—Two Versions

Many stories have been told—in writing and in film—about the death of George Armstrong Custer at the hands of Native Americans. "Cus-

Big Wolf, by Howling Wolf, Southern Cheyenne, 1849–1927. From *Oberlin Ledger,* p. 64. Gift of Mrs. Jacob D. Cox, 04.1180. Courtesy of The Allen Memorial Art Museum, Oberlin College.

ter's last stand" *has become a part of American legend—mostly European American legend—as in this song of the 1930s:*

Across the Big Horn's crystal tide, against the savage Sioux;
A little band of soldiers charged, three hundred boys in blue;
In front rode blond-haired Custer bold, pet of the wild frontier,
A hero of a hundred fights, his deeds known far and near.
. . .
The night came on with sable veil and hid those sights from view,
The Big Horn's crystal tide was red as she wound her valleys through;
And quickly from the fields of slain those gloating redskins fled—
But blond-haired Custer held the field, a hero with his dead.

Another version is told from the point of view of the Cheyenne and Arapaho, who, with all Indian resisters of American oppression, are the collective heroes here. This story was told to Indian researchers Alice Marriott and Carol K. Rachlin by Mary Little Bear Inkanish, John Stands-in-the-Timber, and John Fletcher, members of the Cheyenne tribe, and Richard Pratt, an Arapaho.

After the treaty of Medicine Lodge Creek, in 1871, the Cheyennes and the Arapahos, who were old allies, sat in the council tipi together. All the leading chiefs were unhappy and disturbed, for among the white men present at the signing of the treaty had been Yellow Hair—George Armstrong Custer.

Custer was known to have a Cheyenne wife and a half-Cheyenne son. The same man who disobeyed his commanding officer's orders so that he might make a dash to Fort Riley, Kansas, to see his white wife, also spent many nights in a Cheyenne tipi. How could the chiefs trust him? He would trick women, disavow his son's parentage, and lie to his friends. He could not be trusted.

They sent a young man, as messenger, with a word that Custer should come to Black Kettle's camp and smoke with him. Black Kettle was a peace chief of the Cheyennes—an old man, loved and respected by everybody. His wife prepared a feast for the visitors and they all sat down and ate together.

After the feast, the young messenger brought Black Kettle a pipe bag. It was of the finest fawn skin, and was beaded in horizontal red, yellow, black, and white bands. Black Kettle's wife belonged to the women's secret society, and she had the right to make that kind of beadwork.

From the bag, Black Kettle drew out a T-shaped pipe of red pipestone, with a straight white dogwood stem. He fitted the stem to the pipe bowl, and filled the pipe with native tobacco mixed with shredded sumac bark. Very carefully Black Kettle lifted a coal from the tipi fire, using a pair of sticks for tongs, and lighted the pipe. When he had blown smoke to Maheo above, to mother the Earth, and to the four corners of the world, Black Kettle spoke.

"Yellow Hair," he said, "we have called you to our council because we all wish to make a peace and keep the peace. We have set our marks on paper, but that is the white man's way. Now we ask you to swear the peace in the Indian way, too. Smoke with us, Yellow Hair."

Custer tossed back the long yellow locks that lay on the shoulders of his fringed and beaded buckskin shirt. He never wore a uniform if he could help it and that was another thing the Indians didn't like. If he joined the soldiers, if he gave orders to the soldiers, then he should dress like them. The yellow locks might be thinning on top, but they still hung thick from the sides and back, and fell across his shoulders.

One thing every Indian knew about Custer, he never smoked. Even smelling tobacco smoke, he said, made him feel sick. But success and advancement depended on his control of these Indians, so Yellow Hair put out his hand for the pipe.

Yellow Hair followed Black Kettle's motions, and let a little smoke trickle from his mouth to each of the six directions. He didn't swallow any smoke, but he put the pipe to his mouth six times, and blew out six puffs of tobacco smoke. Now Custer was joined to the Cheyennes and the Arapahos in what the Indians hoped would be a lasting and safe peace. The other chiefs smoked in their turns.

"Now, Yellow Hair," Black Kettle said, "you have smoked with us, and promised us peace. You may go."

Custer left the tipi, denting the ground with the heels of his boots. Black Kettle shook the dottle from the pipe into the palm of his hand, and sprinkled a pinch of it in every heel print.

"Yellow Hair has gone," he said. "Hear me, my chiefs. If he breaks the promise he has made us today, he will die, and he will die a coward's death. No Indian will soil his hands with Yellow Hair's scalp."

"Hah-ho," said all the other chiefs. "So be it. If Yellow Hair breaks the promise he has sworn in the peace treaty, then let him die a woman's death."

Two years later Black Kettle and his band made their winter camp on the banks of the Washita River. It was a peace camp, a settled camp. There were brush windbreaks around many of the tipis, and the children played in safety. In the center of the camp stood the beautifully beaded tipi where Black Kettle and his wife lived, and to one side of them and to the other were the keepers of the Cheyenne sacred medicines.

The weather was bitterly cold, for a blue norther had swept across the plains that afternoon, and everyone shivered under its weight of hail and sleet. People huddled inside their tipis, away from the force of the wind; sat close to their fires, and, after they had eaten dinner, told stories of the old days and the old ways. It was a rich camp. The women of Black Kettle's band worked hard, and they were well supplied with dried meat, fine clothes, and painted, beaded, and quill-embroidered robes.

By midnight the camp was silent, and then Yellow Hair struck. He and his troopers, with the storm at their backs, had ridden the seventy miles from Camp Supply in two days, and now, in the darkness, they attacked the peace camp.

Custer had divided his forces, sending a small detachment of troopers downstream to attack a camp of visiting Arapahos. He, with the main body of troops, struck at Black Kettle's camp. The old man died in the ruins of his flaming tipi and fell with the United States flag—given him at Medicine Lodge as a token of the peace he was to keep—still clutched in his hand. Black Kettle's wife stabbed herself and fell dead across her husband's body.

Downstream there was shooting at the Arapaho camp, and then there was no more shooting.

The troops of the Seventh Cavalry gathered together all the wealth of Black Kettle's camp and set fire to every beautiful thing those Cheyennes possessed. Even some of the soldiers cried when they saw the destruction of robes and food belonging to women and children.

By daylight, with Sharp's carbines, the troopers shot all the horses in the great herds pastured across the river.

And still there was no more shooting from downstream. Yellow Hair sent a detachment to see if the Arapahos had been wiped out like the Cheyennes. The troops found that the Arapahos and their camp were gone. On the ground were the bodies of Major Joel Eliot and his men—all scalped.

Yellow Hair had broken the peace, but his men had died like men.

Now the proud Cheyennes became for a time a broken people. They suffered imprisonment, and death from disease and starvation. Yellow Hair reported his great victory over Black Kettle, but he also had to report that he had let men be killed without sending them support. Even "Woosinton" could not let that go by. They sent for Yellow Hair to go east, and they punished him by making him stay there for one whole year.

Then Yellow Hair and his white wife came back to Fort Abraham Lincoln. His Cheyenne wife had died of grief, and her sisters had taken her son and hidden him, so he could be raised as an Indian. Fort Abraham Lincoln was far away, north on the Yellowstone, so the southern Cheyennes sat and waited and worked out a plan.

Quietly, messengers moved from tribe to tribe, up and down the plains. They went to the Arapahos, of course, and to the many different bands of Sioux. The Crows and the Pawnees, who had taken the white man's uniforms, and served the Army as scouts, the messengers avoided.

In time, just as quietly, the villages moved. A few camps at a time drifted into the territory of Sitting Bull, the Hunkpapa Sioux chief. Here the groups spread out, along the Little Big Horn and Tongue Rivers, and waited until all the men were armed and ready.

The Crows and Pawnees came into Fort Abraham Lincoln with word that the tribes were gathering. They might attack the white settlements or the fort. Trouble was on its way.

There was a council of the white soldiers, and General Terry, the commanding officer at the post, gave his orders. Yellow Hair would go one way, he himself would go another, and Major Marcus Reno would go the third. They would all come together to surround the great camp on the Little Big Horn.

With Custer would ride his brother, Lieutenant Tom Custer, and Captain Myles W. Keogh. Captain Keogh was famous everywhere for his devotion to his big bay gelding, Comanche. The two talked to each other like brothers, and Comanche seemed to know what the Captain thought before the words had formed in the man's mind.

The night before they set out, these three men, with some other officers, gathered in Custer's quarters for a farewell dinner. Elizabeth Custer and her Negro cook, Eliza, provided a good one, of venison, and roast sage hens, and any other game the men had brought in. Late in the evening, Tom Custer, Yellow Hair, and Keogh shaved their heads with horse clippers. Elizabeth wept when she saw the fading golden locks fall to the floor; then she comforted herself with the thought that perhaps the Indians would be less likely to recognize and attack her husband if they did not see his long hair.

Early in the morning, the troops rode out of the fort, and the women watched them go. Some women wept, and others held back their tears and bravely waved their handkerchiefs in good-by. As the women and the post guard watched and the band played "The Girl I Left Behind Me" and the regimental marching song, "Garry Owen," one of those miracles of plains light appeared. Riding above the troopers were their images, mirrored against the sky by a mirage. Someone cried, "They are riding to their death!" but the shout was quickly stilled.

If the Pawnees and the Crows knew what was happening in the Indian camps, the Sioux, the Cheyenne, and the Arapaho knew what was happening at Fort Abraham Lincoln. They were prepared, and when the charge came the Indians met it like rocks.

Custer and his troops were driven back, and took refuge on top of a steep hill, almost a bluff, north of the Little Big Horn. There the Indians could surround them, and slowly, methodically, tear them to pieces. Major Reno was pinned downstream by the Arapahos. General Terry had not yet come up in support. Yellow Hair died as Major Eliot had died, in the center of a ring of soldiers, killed by "the finest light cavalry in the world."

The Indian women struck camp and loaded their horses while the battle still went on. When victory came, the Indians melted away into the Black Hills. By the time General Terry relieved Major Reno, and rescued his detachment, the only being left alive on the hilltop was Captain Keogh's great horse, Comanche. The dead man's hand still clutched the reins. Those two were like brothers and no Indian would separate them. Later, General Terry took Comanche to Fort Riley, Kansas, and there he lived until he died of old age—no rider ever mounted him again, but he was led in every review on the post. Comanche's body is still preserved in the Kansas State Historical Museum.

Whether, as the Cheyennes say, no one recognized Yellow Hair with

his head shaved; whether, as the Arapahos say, he was a coward and
not worth scalping, we do not know. We do know that his body, unlike
others on that battlefield, was not mutilated. Yellow Hair lay on his
back, with a woman's knife thrust through his chest, but he was dead
before that Cheyenne woman struck him, so they say.*

*Marriott, 187–93.

European American

The European American hero is a product of the experience of the European adventurers, explorers, pilgrims, frontiersmen, and settlers in the New World. There are patriotic heroes who emerged from the Revolution and other major events in American history; worker heroes who grew out of the building of the new nation's infrastructure; lone heroes who in legend and fiction represent American ideals such as rugged individualism and "freedom and justice for all"; outlaw and gangster heroes who represent the American fascination with lawlessness and with what can be called the rags-to-riches or self-made man myth, which is the essence of the so-called American dream. There are poor-boy-become-rich heroes who represent that myth also. In the American dream a poor boy can either "make good" or "make bad." And there are trickster heroes and bigger-than-life heroes, some with historical foundation, some purely fictional, who reflect the very vastness of the American landscape, the myth of manifest destiny, and the immense variety of American experience. These bigger-than-life heroes form the basis of a particular aspect of American folklore that is essentially comic and primarily based on exaggeration by way of a fictional form called the tall tale.

Patriotic Heroes

Patriotic heroes have always been important to Americans. These are actual political figures whose lives have been endowed with legendary dimensions that express what are popularly seen as American values. In several cases the people have immortalized them in the kinds of monuments associated in ancient times with hero-kings and gods. Statues of Lincoln and Jefferson are housed in classical temples; Washington is represented by a gigantic obelisk reminiscent of the gods and heroes of ancient Egypt and Rome; huge heads of Washington, Jefferson, Lincoln, and Theodore Roosevelt are carved into the side of Mount Rushmore in South Dakota, dominating a landscape that has always been sacred to the Sioux (a rival statue of Chief Crazy Horse is in process nearby).

The list of patriotic heroes is long. Betsy Ross (1752–1836) is said to have been commissioned by George Washington to sew the first American flag. John Hancock, because of his signature on the Declaration of Independence, is remembered still when we say "put your John Hancock on the dotted line." Many legends are told about Ben Franklin and about Patrick Henry, who proclaimed the famous words "Give me liberty or give me death." We have our modern patriotic heroes as well. John Kennedy's presidency was compared to King Arthur's Camelot, and his assassination and funeral were nothing if not mythic in tone.

George Washington—"I Cannot Tell a Lie"

Many legends grew up around the imposing figure of George Washington. Most of these stories can be attributed to the imagination or the folkloric interests of Mason Locke Weems (1759–1825), better known as "Parson" Weems. Weems was an Anglican priest turned bookseller and writer of biographies. His subjects, in addition to Washington, included Ben Franklin and William Penn. Parson Weems's biographies have been termed "hero worship." His purpose was clearly to instill patriotic fervor in the American young.

This is the famous story of the cherry tree, meant to celebrate the honesty of "the Father of our Country" and, by extension, of our country itself.

Never did the wise Ulysses take more pains with his beloved Telemachus, than did Mr. Washington with George, to inspire him with an *early love of truth.* "Truth George," said he, "is the loveliest quality of youth. I would ride fifty miles, my son, to see the little boy whose heart is so *honest,* and his lips so *pure,* that we may depend on every word he says. O how lovely does such a child appear in the eyes of everybody! his parents doat on him. His relations glory in him. They are constantly praising him to their children, whom they beg to imitate him. They are often sending for him to visit them; and receive him, when he comes,

Parson Weems's Fable by Grant Wood. Oil on Canvas, 1939. © Amon Carter Museum, Fort Worth, TX, 1970.43.

with as much joy as if he were a little angel, come to set pretty examples to their children.

"But, Oh! how different, George, is the case with the boy who is given to lying, that nobody can believe a word he says! He is looked at with aversion wherever he goes, and parents dread to see him come among their children. Oh, George! my son! rather than see you come to this pass, dear as you are to my heart, gladly would I assist to nail you up in your little coffin, and follow you to your grave. Hard, indeed, would it be to me to give up my son, whose little feet are always so ready to run about with me, and whose fondly looking eyes, and sweet prattle make so large a part of my happiness. But still I would give him up, rather than see him a common liar."

"Pa," said George very seriously, "do I ever tell lies?"

"No, George, I *thank* God you do not, my son; and I rejoice in the hope you never will. At least, you shall never, from me, have cause to be guilty of so shameful a thing. Many parents, indeed, even compel their children to this vile practice, by barbarously beating them for every little fault: hence, on the next offence, the little terrified creature slips out a *lie!* just to escape the rod. But as to yourself George, you know I have *always* told you, and now tell you again, that, whenever by accident, you do anything wrong, which must often be the case, as you are but a poor little boy yet, without *experience* or *knowledge*, you must never tell a falsehood to conceal it; but come *bravely* up, my son, like a *little* man, and tell me of it: and, instead of beating you, George, I will but the more honour and love you for it, my dear."

This, you'll say, was sowing good seed!—Yes, it was: and the crop, thank God, was, as I believe it ever will be, where a man acts the true parent, that is, the *Guardian Angel*, by his child.

The following anecdote is a *case in point*. It is too valuable to be lost, and too true to be doubted; for it was communicated to me by the same excellent lady to whom I am indebted for the last.

"When George," said she, "was about six years old, he was made the wealthy master of a *hatchet!* of which, like most little boys, he was immoderately fond, and was constantly going about chopping every thing that came in his way. One day, in the garden, where he often amused himself hacking his mother's pea-sticks, he unluckily tried the edge of his hatchet on the body of a beautiful young English cherry-tree, which he barked so terribly, that I don't believe the tree ever got the better of it. The next morning the old gentleman, finding out what had befallen his tree, which, by the by, was a great favourite, came into the house; and with much warmth asked for the mischievous author, declaring at the same time, that he would not have taken five guineas for his tree. Nobody could tell him anything about it. Presently George and his hatchet made their appearance. 'George,' said his father, 'do you know who killed that beautiful little cherry tree yonder in the garden?' This was a *tough question*; and George staggered under it for a moment; but quickly recovered himself: and looking at his father, with the sweet face of youth brightened with the inexpressible charm of all-conquering truth, he bravely cried out, 'I can't tell a lie, Pa; you know I can't tell a lie. I did cut it with my hatchet.'—'Run to my arms, you dearest boy,' cried his father in transports, 'run to my arms; glad am I, George, that you killed my tree; for you have paid me for it a thousand fold. Such an act of heroism in my son is more worth than a thousand trees, though blossomed with silver, and their fruits of purest gold.' "

It was in this way by interesting at once both his *heart* and *head*, that Mr. Washington conducted George with great ease and pleasure along the happy paths of virtue.*

*Weems, 256–58.

Abraham Lincoln—"Honest Abe"

The theme of honesty among American leaders is perpetuated in stories about probably the most admired American president, Abraham Lincoln. The story of young Abe as a shopkeeper is at once a morality tale and a part of a larger rags-to-riches saga. It is told by Horatio Alger (1832–1899), himself a legend of the American dream. Alger worked in New York at the Newsboy's Lodging House, whose homeless inhabitants became the inspiration for his many novels about boys—Ragged Dick, Tattered Tom, and others—who managed to rise out of poverty to financial success.

As a clerk [Abraham Lincoln] proved honest and efficient, and my readers will be interested in some illustrations of the former trait which I find in Dr. Holland's interesting volume.

One day a woman came into the store and purchased sundry articles. They footed up two dollars and six and a quarter cents, or the young clerk thought they did. We do not hear nowadays of six and a quarter cents, but this was a coin borrowed from the Spanish currency, and was well known in my own boyhood.

The bill was paid, and the woman was entirely satisfied. But the young store-keeper, not feeling quite sure as to the accuracy of his calculation, added up the items once more. To his dismay he found that the sum total should have been but two dollars.

"I've made her pay six and a quarter cents too much," said Abe, disturbed.

It was a trifle, and many clerks would have dismissed it as such. But Abe was too conscientious for that.

"The money must be paid back," he decided.

This would have been easy enough had the woman lived "just round the corner," but, as the young man knew, she lived between two and three miles away. This, however, did not alter the matter. It was night, but he closed and locked the store, and walked to the residence of his customer. Arrived there, he explained the matter, paid over the six and a quarter cents, and returned satisfied. If I were a capitalist, I would be willing to lend money to such a young man without security.

Here is another illustration of young Lincoln's strict honesty:

A woman entered the store and asked for half a pound of tea.

The young clerk weighed it out, and handed it to her in a parcel. This was the last sale of the day.

The next morning, when commencing his duties, Abe discovered a four-ounce weight on the scales. It flashed upon him at once that he had used this in the sale of the night previous, and so, of course, given his customer short weight. I am afraid that there are many country merchants who would not have been much worried by this discovery. Not so the young clerk in whom we are interested. He weighed out the balance of the half pound, shut up store, and carried it to the defrauded customer. I think my young readers will begin to see that the name so often given, in later times, to President Lincoln, of "Honest Old Abe," was well deserved. A man who begins by strict honesty in his youth is not likely to change as he grows older, and mercantile honesty is some guarantee of political honesty.*

Paul Revere—The Midnight Ride

Paul Revere (1735–1818) was a great silversmith who practiced his art in Boston. He is much better known, however, for the famous ride he took with William Dawes on April 18, 1775. The ride, made legendary by Henry Wadsworth Longfellow, was one of several made by Revere as an express messenger. On April 16 he rode to Lexington to warn Samuel Adams and John Hancock that they were about to be arrested and to Concord to warn patriots there to hide their weapons stores. Two days later Revere alerted the countryside towns of the arrival of the British. During the first years of the war he continued to ride as a messenger. This is his tale as made famous by Longfellow.

> Listen, my children, and you shall hear
> Of the midnight ride of Paul Revere,
> On the eighteenth of April, in Seventy-five;
> Hardly a man is now alive
> Who remembers that famous day and year.
>
> He said to his friend, "If the British march
> By land or sea from the town to-night,
> Hang a lantern aloft in the belfry arch
> Of the North Church tower as a signal light,—
> One, if by land, and two, if by sea;
> And I on the opposite shore will be,
> Ready to ride and spread the alarm
> Through every Middlesex village and farm,
> For the country folk to be up and to arm."

*Alger, 256–59.

Then he said, "Good night!" and with muffled oar
Silently rowed to the Charlestown shore,
Just as the moon rose over the bay,
Where swinging wide at her moorings lay
The Somerset, British man-of-war;
A phantom ship, with each mast and spar
Across the moon like a prison bar,
And a huge black hulk, that was magnified
By its own reflection in the tide.

Meanwhile, his friend, through alley and street,
Wanders and watches with eager ears,
Till in the silence around him he hears
The muster of men at the barrack door,
The sound of arms, and the tramp of feet,
And the measured tread of the grenadiers,
Marching down to their boats on the shore.

Then he climbed the tower of the Old North Church,
By the wooden stairs, with stealthy tread,
To the belfry-chamber overhead,
And startled the pigeons from their perch
On the sombre rafters, that round him made
Masses and moving shapes of shade,—
By the trembling ladder, steep and tall,
To the highest window in the wall,
Where he paused to listen and look down
A moment on the roofs of the town,
And the moonlight flowing over all.

Beneath, in the churchyard, lay the dead,
In their night-encampment on the hill,
Wrapped in silence so deep and still
That he could hear, like a sentinel's tread,
The watchful night-wind, as it went
Creeping along from tent to tent,
And seeming to whisper, "All is well!"
A moment only he feels the spell
Of the place and the hour, and the secret dread
Of the lonely belfry and the dead;
For suddenly all his thoughts are bent
On a shadowy something far away,
Where the river widens to meet the bay,—

A line of black that bends and floats
On the rising tide, like a bridge of boats.

Meanwhile, impatient to mount and ride,
Booted and spurred, with a heavy stride
On the opposite shore walked Paul Revere.
Now he patted his horse's side,
Now gazed at the landscape far and near,
Then, impetuous, stamped the earth,
And turned and tightened his saddle-girth;
But mostly he watched with eager search
The belfry-tower of the Old North Church,
As it rose above the graves on the hill,
Lonely and spectral and sombre and still.
And lo! as he looks, on the belfry's height
A glimmer, and then a gleam of light!
He springs to the saddle, the bridle he turns,
But lingers and gazes, till full on his sight
A second lamp in the belfry burns!

A hurry of hoofs in a village street,
A shape in the moonlight, a bulk in the dark,
And beneath, from the pebbles, in passing, a spark
Struck out by a steed flying fearless and fleet:
That was all! And yet, through the gloom and the light,
The fate of a nation was riding that night;
And the spark struck out by that steed, in his flight,
Kindled the land into flame with its heat.

He has left the village and mounted the steep,
And beneath him, tranquil and broad and deep,
Is the Mystic, meeting the ocean tides;
And under the alders that skirt its edge,
Now soft on the sand, now loud on the ledge,
Is heard the tramp of his steed as he rides.

It was twelve by the village clock,
When he crossed the bridge into Medford town.
He heard the crowing of the cock,
And the barking of the farmer's dog,
And felt the damp of the river fog,
That rises after the sun goes down.

It was one by the village clock,
When he galloped into Lexington.
He saw the gilded weathercock
Swim in the moonlight as he passed,
And the meeting-house windows, blank and bare,
Gaze at him with a spectral glare,
As if they already stood aghast
At the bloody work they would look upon.

It was two by the village clock,
When he came to the bridge in Concord town.
He heard the bleating of the flock,
And the twitter of birds among the trees,
And felt the breath of the morning breeze
Blowing over the meadows brown.
And one was safe and asleep in his bed
Who at the bridge would be first to fall,
Who that day would be lying dead,
Pierced by a British musket-ball.

You know the rest. In the books you have read,
How the British Regulars fired and fled,—
How the farmers gave them ball for ball,
From behind each fence and farm-yard wall,
Chasing the red-coats down the lane,
Then crossing the fields to emerge again
Under the trees at the turn of the road,
And only pausing to fire and load.

So through the night rode Paul Revere;
And so through the night went his cry of alarm
To every Middlesex village and farm,—
A cry of defiance and not of fear,
A voice in the darkness, a knock at the door,
And a word that shall echo forevermore!
For, borne on the night-wind of the Past,
Through all our history, to the last,
In the hour of darkness and peril and need,
The people will waken and listen to hear
The hurrying hoof-beats of that steed,
And the midnight message of Paul Revere.

American Loners, Frontiersmen, and Tall Tales

A typical American hero-type is the lone individualist who prefers the mystery and beauty of nature, the adventure of the wilderness, or the pleasures of self-examination to a life of marriage, domesticity, and safety. Henry David Thoreau in *Walden* created an autobiographical transcendentalist version of this hero when he recorded selectively his time alone at Walden Pond, near Concord, Massachussets. For Thoreau, heroism consisted of an honest facing of life:

> I went to the woods because I wished to live deliberately, to front only the essential facts of life, and see if I could not learn what it had to teach, and not, when I came to die, discover that I had not lived. . . . I wanted to live deep and suck out all the marrow of life . . . to drive life into a corner, and reduce it to its lowest terms.

James Fenimore Cooper and many writers after him created heroes who, while not as gentle as Thoreau and more adventuresome, followed the frontier on its movement westward, sometimes helping those settlers who struggled to find the American dream, but never opting to settle with them. Often these characters have sidekicks; Native American companions were particularly useful because they were close to the land. Cooper's Natty Bumppo (or Deerslayer, Hawkeye, Leatherstocking, or Pathfinder) is one such hero who represents the rugged individualism in the American psyche. His companion is the Indian Chingachgook, whom Mark Twain wryly called "Chicago."

Another example of the celibate individualist hero is the mysteriously masked Lone Ranger, whose faithful Indian is Tonto. However close Natty or the Masked Man come to love, he always rides off into the sunset with his faithful Indian companions. For D. H. Lawrence the American loner myth, as expressed especially by Cooper, was "a wish-fulfillment, an evasion of actuality," a nostalgic return to adolescence or preadolescence rather than a facing of reality.

If the European fictional "happy ending" is the achievement of family and home, often the European American version, then, is the freedom of the road "with the boys." Modern-day examples of the tendency are to be found in the much-mythologized lives of the Beat writers of the 1950s, who took to the road looking for a new kind of frontier, one of the mind, one of the inner self, a freedom that would carry them beyond the mundane realities of life in bourgeois America. Beat novelist Jack Kerouac's (1922–1969) most famous works, *On the Road* (1957) and

The Dharma Bums (1960), suggest a somewhat ironic American quest for truth that echoes that of the Beat generation's own hero, poet Walt Whitman, the individualist par excellence, whose greatest work was "Song of Myself." The beginning of his poem is a transcendental statement of the sacredness of individual being and of the possibility of true union through that sacredness:

> I celebrate myself, and sing myself
> And what I assume you shall assume,
> For every human atom belonging to me as good belongs to you.

Johnny Appleseed

Among the most popular of the lonely heroes of the road is John Chapman (1774–1845), better known as Johnny Appleseed, a precursor of the gentle flower child or hippie hero of the 1960s and a genuine holy man of his time. His story is told here by W. D. Haley, writing in Harper's New Monthly Magazine *in 1871.*

The first reliable trace of our modest hero finds him in the Territory of Ohio, in 1801, with a horse-load of apple seeds, which he planted in various places on and about the borders of Licking Creek, the first orchard thus originated by him being on the farm of Isaac Stadden, in what is now known as Licking County, in the State of Ohio. During the five succeeding years, although he was undoubtedly following the same strange occupation, we have no authentic account of his movements until we reach a pleasant spring day in 1806, when a pioneer settler in Jefferson County, Ohio, noticed a peculiar craft, with a remarkable occupant and a curious cargo, slowly dropping down with the current of the Ohio River. It was "Johnny Appleseed," by which name Jonathan Chapman was afterward known in every log-cabin from the Ohio River to the Northern lakes, and westward to the prairies of what is now the State of Indiana. With two canoes lashed together he was transporting a load of apple seeds to the Western frontier, for the purpose of creating orchards on the farthest verge of white settlements. With his canoes he passed down the Ohio to Marietta, where he entered the Muskingum, ascending the stream of that river until he reached the mouth of the Walhonding, or White Woman Creek, and still onward, up the Mohican, into the Black Fork, to the head of navigation, in the region now known as Ashland and Richland counties, on the line of the Pittsburgh and Fort Wayne Railroad, in Ohio. A long and toilsome voyage it was, as a glance at the map will show, and must have occupied a great deal of time, as the lonely traveler stopped at every inviting spot to plant the seeds and make his infant nurseries. These are the first well-authenticated facts in the history of Jonathan Chapman, whose birth, there is good reason for believing, occurred in Boston, Massachusetts, in 1775. According to this, which was his own statement in one of his less reticent moods, he was, at the time of his appearance on Licking Creek, twenty-six years of age, and whether impelled in his eccentricities by some absolute misery of the heart which could only find relief in incessant motion, or governed by a benevolent monomania, his whole after-life was devoted to the work of planting apple seeds in remote places. The seeds he gathered from the cider-presses of Western Pennsylvania; but his canoe voyage in 1806 appears to have been the only occasion upon which he adopted that method of transporting them, as all his subsequent journeys were made on foot. . . .

Johnny would shoulder his bag of apple seeds, and with bare feet penetrate to some remote spot that combined picturesqueness and fertility of soil, and there he would plant his seeds, place a slight inclosure around the place, and leave them to grow until the trees were large enough to be transplanted by the settlers, who, in the meantime, would have made their clearings in the vicinity. The sites chosen by him are, many of them, well known, and are such as an artist or a poet would select—open places on the loamy lands that border the creeks—rich, secluded spots, hemmed in by giant trees, picturesque now, but fifty years ago, with their wild surroundings and the primal silence, they must have been tenfold more so.

In personal appearance Chapman was a small, wiry man, full of restless activity; he had long dark hair, a scanty beard that was never shaved, and keen black eyes that sparkled with a peculiar brightness. His dress was of the oddest description. Generally, even in the coldest weather, he went barefooted, but sometimes, for his long journeys, he would make himself a rude pair of sandals; at other times he would wear any cast-off foot-covering he chanced to find—a boot on one foot and an old brogan or a moccasin on the other. It appears to have been a matter of conscience with him never to purchase shoes, although he was rarely without money enough to do so. On one occasion, in an unusually cold November, while he was traveling barefooted through mud and snow, a settler who happened to possess a pair of shoes that were too small for his own use forced their acceptance upon Johnny, declaring that it was sinful for a human being to travel with naked feet in such weather. A few days afterward the donor was in the village that has since become the thriving city of Mansfield, and met his beneficiary contentedly plodding along with his feet bare and half frozen. With some degree of anger he inquired for the cause of such foolish conduct, and received for reply that Johnny had overtaken a poor, barefooted family moving Westward, and as they appeared to be in much greater need of clothing than he was, he had given them the shoes. His dress was generally composed of cast-off clothing, that he had taken in payment for apple-trees; and as the pioneers were far less extravagant than their descendants in such matters, the homespun and buckskin garments that they discarded would not be very elegant or serviceable. In his later years, however, he seems to have thought that even this kind of second-hand raiment was too luxurious, as his principal garment was made of a coffee sack, in which he cut holes for his head and arms to pass through, and pronounced it "a very serviceable cloak, and as good clothing as any man need wear." In the matter of head-gear his taste was equally unique; his first experiment was with a tin vessel that served to cook his mush, but this was open to the objection that it did not protect his eyes from the beams of the sun; so he constructed a hat of pasteboard with an immense peak in front, and having thus secured an article that combined usefulness with economy, it became his permanent fashion.

Thus strangely clad, he was perpetually wandering through forests and morasses, and suddenly appearing in white settlements and Indian villages; but there must have been some rare force of gentle goodness dwelling in his looks and breathing in his words, for it is the testimony of all who knew him that, notwithstanding his ridiculous attire, he was always treated with the greatest respect by the rudest frontiersman, and, what is a better test, the boys of the settlements forbore to jeer at him. With grown-up people and boys he was usually reticent, but manifested great affection for little girls, always having pieces of ribbon and gay calico to give to his little favorites. Many a grandmother in Ohio and Indiana can remember the presents she received when a child from poor homeless Johnny Appleseed. When he consented to eat with any family he would never sit down to the table until he was assured that there was an ample supply for the children; and his sympathy for their youthful troubles and his kindness toward them made him friends among all the juveniles of the borders.

The Indians also treated Johnny with the greatest kindness. By these wild and sanguinary savages he was regarded as a "great medicine man," on account of his strange appearance, eccentric actions, and, especially, the fortitude with which he could endure pain, in proof of which he would often thrust pins and needles into his flesh. His nervous sensibilities really seem to have been less acute than those of ordinary people, for his method of treating the cuts and sores that were the consequences of his barefooted wanderings through briers and thorns was to sear the wound with a red-hot iron, and then cure the burn. During the war of 1812, when the frontier settlers were tortured and slaughtered by the savage allies of Great Britain, Johnny Appleseed continued his wanderings, and was never harmed by the roving bands of hostile Indians. On many occasions the impunity with which he ranged the country enabled him to give the settlers warning of approaching danger in time to allow them to take refuge in their block-houses before the savages could attack them. Our informant refers to one of these instances, when the news of Hull's surrender came like a thunder-bolt upon the frontier. Large bands of Indians and British were destroying everything before them and murdering defenseless women and children, and even the block-houses were not always a sufficient protection. At this time Johnny travelled day and night, warning the people of the approaching danger. He visited every cabin and delivered this message: "The Spirit of the Lord is upon me, and he hath anointed me to blow the trumpet in the wilderness, and sound an alarm in the forest; for, behold, the tribes of the heathen are round about your doors, and a devouring flame followeth after them." The aged man who narrated this incident said that he could feel even now the thrill that was caused by this prophetic announcement of the wild-looking herald of danger, who aroused the family on a bright moonlight midnight with his piercing voice. Refusing all offers of food and denying himself a moment's rest, he traversed the border day and night until he had warned every settler of the approaching peril.

His diet was as meagre as his clothing. He believed it to be a sin to kill any creature for food, and thought that all that was necessary for human sustenance was produced by the soil. He was also a strenuous opponent of the waste of food, and on one occasion, on approaching a log-cabin, he observed some fragments of bread floating upon the surface of a bucket of slops that was intended for the pigs. He immediately fished them out, and when the housewife expressed her astonishment, he told her that it was an abuse of the gifts of a merciful God to allow the smallest quantity of any thing that was designed to supply the wants of mankind to be diverted from its purpose. . . .

It was his custom, when he had been welcomed to some hospitable log-house after a weary day of journeying, to lie down on the puncheon floor, and, after inquiring if his auditors would hear "some news right fresh from heaven," produce his few tattered books, among which would be a New Testament, and read and expound until his uncultivated hearers would catch the spirit and glow of his enthusiasm, while they scarcely comprehended his language. A lady who knew him in his later years writes in the following terms of one of these domiciliary readings of poor, self-sacrificing Johnny Appleseed: "We can hear him read now, just as he did that summer day, when we were busy quilting up stairs, and he lay near the door, his voice rising denunciatory and thrilling—strong and loud as the roar of wind and waves, then soft and soothing as the balmy airs that quivered the morning-glory leaves about his gray beard. His was a strange eloquence at times, and he was undoubtedly a man of genius." What a scene is presented to our imagination! The interior of a primitive cabin, the wide, open fire-place, where a few sticks are burning beneath the iron pot in which the evening meal is cooking; around the fire-place the attentive group, composed of the sturdy pioneer and his wife and children, listening with a reverential awe to the "news right fresh from heaven"; and reclining on the floor, clad in rags, but with his gray hairs glorified by the beams of the setting sun that flood through the open door and the unchinked logs of the humble building, this poor wanderer, with the gift of genius and eloquence, who believes with the faith of apostles and martyrs that God has appointed him a mission in the wilderness to preach the Gospel of love, and plant apple seeds that shall produce orchards for the benefit of men and women and little children whom he has never seen. If there is a sublimer faith or a more genuine eloquence in richly decorated cathedrals and under brocade vestments, it would be worth a long journey to find it. . . .

Thus died one of the memorable men of pioneer times, who never inflicted pain or knew an enemy—a man of strange habits, in whom there dwelt a comprehensive love that reached with one hand downward to the lowest forms of life, and with the other upward to the very throne of God. A laboring, self-denying benefactor of his race, homeless, solitary, and ragged, he trod the thorny earth with bare and bleeding feet, intent only upon making the wilderness fruitful. Now "no man knoweth of his sepulchre"; but his deeds will live in the fragrance of the apple blossoms he loved so well, and the story of his life, however crudely narrated, will be a perpetual proof that true heroism, pure benevolence, noble virtues, and deeds that deserve immortality may be found under meanest apparel, and far from gilded halls and towering spires.*

Davy Crockett

A much less gentle hero of the frontier than Johnny Appleseed was that mixture of history and legend and hero of his own tall tales, David Crockett (1786–1836), always known as Davy. Congressman, Indian fighter, and storyteller, Crockett was executed by General Santa Anna after the Battle of the Alamo in March 1836.

*Haley, 830–36.

*Crockett did a great deal to create his own legend during his lifetime,
with his coonskin hat and his exaggerated "tall talk." His legend grew
among the folk until he became a Paul Bunyan–like backwoods giant
figure performing the most amazing of feats. It was said, for instance,
that he planned to tear the tail off Halley's Comet in 1835 to save the
the world from destruction.*

*The kind of humor embodied by Crockett in his own stories about
himself and in stories told about him is peculiarly American and typical
of the frontier. It is rustic, unintellectual, boastful, uncouth, and full of
a kind of backwoods wisdom that looks down upon eastern elitism and
snobbery. Its primary vehicle is the tall tale, or "windy," an absurd and
impossibly exaggerated extended straight-faced anecdote marked by tall
talk—a combination of slang, dialect, exaggeration, and word coinage
that resulted in words like* rampageous *or* explatterate—*and in lies.
Writers such as Artemus Ward (Charles Farrar Browne) and Mark
Twain (Samuel Clemens) would make literary use of the tradition;
Twain's "Celebrated Jumping Frog of Calaveras County" is an example.
One of the favorite Crockett stories is the one about the coonskin trick.*

While on the subject of election matters, I will just relate a little anecdote
about myself, which will show the people to the East how we manage
these things on the frontiers. It was when I first run for Congress; I was
then in favor of the Hero [Andrew Jackson], for he had chalked out his
course so sleek in his letter to the Tennessee legislature that, like Sam
Patch, says I, "There can be no mistake in him," and so I went ahead.
No one dreamt about the monster and the deposits at that time, and so,
as I afterward found, many like myself were taken in by these fair promises, which were worth about as much as a flash in the pan when you
have a fair shot at a fat bear.

But I am losing sight of my story. Well, I started off to the Cross
Roads dressed in my hunting shirt, and my rifle on my shoulder. Many
of our constituents had assembled there to get a taste of the quality of
the candidates at orating. Job Snelling, a gander-shanked Yankee, who
had been caught somewhere about Plymouth Bay, and been shipped to
the West with a cargo of codfish and rum, erected a large shantee, and
set up shop for the occasion. A large posse of the voters had assembled
before I arrived, and my opponent had already made considerable headway with his speechifying and his treating, when they spied me about a
rifle shot from camp, sauntering along as if I was not a party in business.
"There comes Crockett," cried one. "Let us hear the colonel," cried
another; and so I mounted the stump that had been cut down for the
occasion, and began to bushwhack in the most approved style.

I had not been up long before there was such an uproar in the crowd that I could not hear my own voice, and some of my constituents let me know that they could not listen to me on such a dry subject as the welfare of the nation until they had something to drink, and that I must treat them. Accordingly I jumped down from the rostrum, and led the way to the shantee, followed by my constituents, shouting, "Huzza for Crockett!" and "Crockett forever!"

When we entered the shantee Job was busy dealing out his rum in a style that showed he was making a good day's work of it, and I called for a quart of the best; but the crooked crittur returned no other answer than by pointing to a board over the bar, on which he had chalked in large letters, *"Pay to-day and trust to-morrow."* Now that idea brought me up all standing; it was a sort of cornering in which there was no back-out, for ready money in the West, in those times, was the shyest thing in all natur, and it was most particularly shy with me on that occasion.

The voters, seeing my predicament, fell off to the other side, and I was left deserted and alone, as the Government will be, when he no longer has any offices to bestow. I saw as plain as day that the tide of popular opinion was against me, and that unless I got some rum speedily I should lose my election as sure as there are snakes in Virginny; and it must be done soon, or even burnt brandy wouldn't save me. So I walked away from the shantee, but in another guess sort from the way I entered it, for on this occasion I had no train after me, and not a voice shouted, "Huzza for Crockett!" Popularity sometimes depends on a very small matter indeed; in this particular it was worth a quart of New England rum, and no more.

Well, knowing that a crisis was at hand, I struck into the woods, with my rifle on my shoulder, my best friend in time of need; and, as good fortune would have it, I had not been out more than a quarter of an hour before I treed a fat coon, and in the pulling of a trigger he lay dead at the foot of the tree. I soon whipped his hairy jacket off his back, and again bent my steps towards the shantee, and walked up to the bar, but not alone, for this time I had half a dozen of my constituents at my heels. I threw down the coon-skin upon the counter, and called for a quart, and Job, though busy dealing out rum, forgot to point at his chalked rules and regulations; for he knew that a coon was as good a legal tender for a quart in the West as a New York shilling any day in the year.

My constituents now flocked about me, and cried, "Huzza for Crockett!" "Crockett forever!" and finding the tide had taken a turn, I told them several yarns to get them in a good humor; and having soon dispatched the value of the coon, I went out and mounted the stump without opposition, and a clear majority of the voters followed me to hear what I had to offer for the good of the nation. Before I was half through one of my constituents moved that they would hear the balance of my speech after they had washed down the first part with some more of Job Snelling's extract of cornstalk and molasses, and the question being put, it was carried unanimously. It wasn't considered necessary to tell the yeas and nays, so we adjourned to the shantee, and on the way I began to reckon that the fate of the nation pretty much depended upon my shooting another coon.

While standing at the bar, feeling sort of bashful while Job's rules and regulations stared me in the face, I cast down my eyes, and discovered one end of the coon-skin sticking between the logs that supported the bar. Job had slung it there in the hurry of business. I gave it a sort of quick jerk, and it followed my hand as natural as if I had been the rightful owner. I slapped it on the counter, and Job, little dreaming that he was barking up the wrong tree, shoved along another bottle, which my constituents quickly disposed of with great good humor, for some of them saw the trick; and then we withdrew to the rostrum to discuss the affairs of the nation.

I don't know how it was, but the voters soon became dry again, and nothing would do but we must adjourn to the shantee; and as luck would have it, the coon-skin was still sticking between the logs, as if Job had flung it there on purpose to tempt me. I was not slow in raising it to the counter, the rum followed, of course, and I wish I may be shot if I didn't, before the day was over, get ten quarts for the same identical skin, and from a fellow, too, who in those parts was considered as sharp as a steel trap and as bright as a pewter button.

This joke secured me my election, for it soon circulated like smoke among my constituents, and they allowed, with one accord, that the man who could get the whip hand of Job Snelling in fair trade, could outwit Old Nick himself, and was the real grit for them in Congress. Job was by no means popular; he boasted of always being wide awake, and that any one who could take him in was free to do so, for he came from a stock that, sleeping or waking, had always one eye open, and the other not more than half closed. The whole family were geniuses. His father was the inventor of wooden nutmegs, by which Job said he might have made a fortune, if he had only taken out a patent and kept the business in his own hands; his mother, Patience, manufactured the first white oak pumpkin seeds of the mammoth kind, and turned a pretty penny the first season; and his aunt Prudence was the first to discover that corn husks, steeped into tobacco water, would make as handsome Spanish wrappers as ever came from Havana, and that oak leaves would answer all the purpose of filling, for no one could discover the difference except the man who smoked them, and then it would be too late to make a stir about it. Job himself bragged of having made some useful discoveries, the most profitable of which was the art of converting mahogany sawdust into cayenne pepper, which he said was a profitable and safe business; for the people have been so long accustomed to having dust thrown in their eyes that there wasn't much danger of being found out.

The way I got to the blind side of the Yankee merchant was pretty generally known before election day, and the result was that my opponent might as well have whistled jigs to a milestone as attempt to beat up for votes in that district. I beat him out and out, quite back into the old year, and there was scarce enough left of him, after the canvass was over, to make a small grease spot. He disappeared without even leaving a mark behind; and such will be the fate of Adam Huntsman, if there is a fair fight and no gouging.

After the election was over, I sent Snelling the price of the rum, but took good care to keep the fact from the knowledge of my constituents. Job refused the money, and sent me word that it did him good to be taken in occasionally, as it served to brighten his ideas; but I afterwards learnt when he found out the trick that had been played upon him, he put all the rum I had ordered in his bill against my opponent, who, being elated with the speeches he had made on the affairs of the nation, could not descend to examine into the particulars of a bill of a vender of rum in the small way.*

Mike Fink

Another well-known subject of the tall tale was Mike Fink, "king of the keelboatmen" on the Mississippi. Fink was born in 1770 and became an Indian scout and then a boatman. His boasting made him a legend: "I can out-run, out-jump, out-shoot, out-brag, out-drink, an' out-fight, rough-an'-tumble, no holts barred, ary man on both sides the river from Pittsbugh to New Orleans an' back ag'in to St. Louiee†" Fink was essentially a bully and a particularly cruel one at that, as this tale indicates.

Mike, at one time, had a woman who passed for his wife; whether she was truly so, we do not know. But at any rate, the following anecdote is a rare instance of conjugal discipline.

*Crockett, 240–45.
†American Folklore, p. 144.

Some time in the latter part of autumn, a few years after the close of the late war with Great Britain, several keelboats landed for the night near the mouth of the Muskingum, among which was that of Mike. After making all fast, Mike was observed, just under the bank, scraping into a heap the dried beech leaves which had been blown there during the day, having just fallen from the effects of the early autumn frosts. To all questions as to what he was doing he returned no answer, but continued at his work until he had piled them up as high as his head. He then separated them, making a sort of an oblong ring, in which he laid down, as if to ascertain whether it was a good bed or not. Getting up, he sauntered on board, hunted up his rifle, made great preparations about his priming, and then called in a very impressive manner upon his wife to follow him. Both proceeded up to the pile of leaves, poor *"Peg"* in a terrible flutter as she had discovered that Mike was in no very amiable humor.

"Get in there and lie down," was the command to Peg, topped off with one of Mike's very choicest oaths. "Now, *Mr.* Fink,"—she always mistered him when his blood was up—"what have I done? I don't know, I'm sure—"

"Get in there and lie down, or I'll shoot you," with another oath, and drawing up his rifle to his shoulder. Poor Peg obeyed, and crawled into the leaf pile, and Mike covered her up with the combustibles. He then took a flour barrel and split the staves into fine pieces, and lighted them at the fire on board the boat, all the time watching the leaf pile, and swearing he would shoot Peg if she moved. So soon as his splinters began to blaze he took them into his hand and deliberately set fire, in four different places, to the leaves that surrounded his wife. In an instant the whole mass was on fire, aided by a fresh wind which was blowing at the time, while Mike was quietly standing by enjoying the fun. Peg, through fear of Mike, stood it as long as she could; but it soon became too hot, and she made a run for the river, her hair and clothing all on fire. In a few seconds she reached the water and plunged in, rejoiced to know she had escaped both fire and rifle so well. "There," said Mike, "that'll larn you not to be winkin' at them fellers on t'other boat."*

Paul Bunyan

The most famous of the backwoods American heroes probably never existed at all. Folklorists are fond of referring to the stories of the giant lumberjack Paul Bunyan as "faketales," because they seem to have been

*Howe, 277–78.

Paul Bunyan. U.S. postage stamp. By permission: U.S. Postal Service.

an invention of newspapermen, lumber companies, and chambers of commerce rather than the folk. But whatever the source of the stories, Paul Bunyan tales have become a part of American folklore. And there is some indication that Bunyan may have a genuine literary if not folkloric source in Gargantua and Pantagruel, giants in the works of the medieval French writer François Rabelais. This theory finds added support among those who argue that the legendary Bunyan was based on a French Canadian logger of the same name.

Among the Bunyan legends are that he formed the Grand Canyon by dragging his pick along the ground and a fairly recent one in which he builds the last seven stories of a high-rise hotel on hinges "so's they could be swung back for to let the moon go by."

Joe Magarac

A Bunyan-like character who emerges from the immigrant population is Joe Magarac (magarac mean "jackass" in Hungarian). Joe was a steelworker who claimed to have been born in an ore mountain. He was literally a "man of steel" and a giant besides. People said he made rails for the railroads by squeezing white-hot steel with his bare hands. As that other worker hero John Henry contested a machine, Magarac fought against iron ore itself and made better steel. Joe Magarac also resembles Paul Bunyan in that he seems not to be based on a real person but rather to be a creation of steelworkers, representing their sense of their own worth.

Mountain Men

Other heroes of the frontier were the so-called mountain men, about whom tall tales were told.

In search of beaver pelts to make felt, this strange collection of men—some down-and-outers, others of high skill and daring—opened up vast tracts of the mountain West, reaching even to California in their quest. During their relatively brief period of existence, these trappers numbered among them many legendary names: Jim Bridger, William Sublette, Jedediah Smith, Joseph Meeker. Their feats were amazing, all the more so when exaggerated in later years, and of course a number of great fortunes were made, as a result of their efforts, by men who financed their explorations, including John Jacob Astor.

In 1846, a merchant-trapper described this distinctive American type:

> *His skin, from constant exposure, assumes a hue almost as dark as that of the Aborigine, and his features and physical structure attain a rough and hardy cast. His hair, through inattention, becomes long, coarse, and bushy, and loosely dangles on his shoulders. His head is surmounted by a low crowned wool-hat, or a rude substitute of his own manufacture. His clothes are of buckskin gaily fringed at the seams with strings of the same material, cut and made in a fashion peculiar to him and his associates. The deer and buffalo furnish him the required covering for his feet which he fabricates at the impulse of want. His waist is encircled with a belt of leather, holding encased his butcher-knife and pistols—while from his neck is suspended a bullet-pouch securely fastened to the belt in front,*

and beneath the right arm hangs a powder-horn traversely from his shoulder, behind which, upon the strap attached to it, are affixed his bullet-mould, ball-screw, wiper, awl, &c. With a gun-stick made of some hard wood, and a good rifle placed in his hands, carrying from thirty-five balls to the pound, the reader will have him a correct likeness of a genuine mountaineer when fully equipped.

This costume prevails not only in the mountains proper, but also in the less settled portions of Oregon and California. The mountaineer is his own manufacturer, tailor, shoemaker, and butcher—and, fully accoutred and supplied with ammunition in good game country, he can always feed and clothe himself and enjoy all the comforts his situation affords.*

Presumably thus clad, Jedediah Smith sallied forth into the life of the trapper at age twenty-four, and he soon became a legend in his own time. He was the first American to enter California from the east, crossing the Mohave Desert from the Great Salt Lake in the 1820s. Thwarted by the Mexican governor of California, he gave up his plan to go north into Oregon and instead returned to the Great Salt Lake via the Sierra Nevadas, becoming the first American to return from California by land as well. In 1831, he was killed on the Santa Fe Trail by Comanches. One of his escapades was described by James Clyman in his diary:

Late in the afternoon while passing through a Brushy bottom a large Grssely came down the vally we being in single file men on foot leding pac horses he struck us about the center then turning ran paralel to our line. Capt. Smith being in the advanc he ran to the open ground and as he immerged from the thicket he and the bear met face to face Grissly did not hesitate a moment but sprung on the capt taking him by the head first pitc[h] sprawling on the earth he gave him a grab by the middle fortunately cat[c]hing him by the ball pouch and Butcher Kife which he broke but breaking several of his rubs and cutting his head badly none of us having any surgical Knowledge what was to be done one Said come take hold and he wuld say why not you so it went around I asked the Capt what was best he said one of 2 [go] for water and if you have a needle and thread git it out and sew up my wounds around my head which was bleeding freely I got a pair of scissors and cut of his hair and the began my first Job of d[r]essing wounds upon examination I [found] the bear had taken nearly all his head in his

S. E. Hollister Fighting a Bear. Courtesy of The Bancroft Library.

capcious mouth clos to his left eye on one side and clos to his right ear on the other and laid the skull bare to neat the crown of the head leaving a a white streak whare his teeth passed one of his ears was torn from his head out to the other rim arter stitching all the other wounds in the best way I was capabl and according to the captains directions the ear being the last I told him I could do nothing for his Eare O you must try to stitch up some way or other said he then I put in my needle stitching it through and through and over and over laying the lacerated parts together as nice as I could with my hands water was found in about one mile when we all moved down and encamped the captain being able to mount his horse and ride to campt whare we pitched a tent the onley one we had and made him as comfortable as circumstances would permit this gave us a lisson the chatacter of the grissly Baare which we did not forget.*

Grizzlies were the largest and most dangerous animals in North America and were found from New Mexico to Alaska and well to the east. It is natural that they commanded respect among the people on the

*Camp, 122–23, quoted as given here in Cleland, 58–59.

frontier, and also were the center of many a legend. In this anonymous tale that comes down from frontier days, the hero of the story is, in fact and rarity, a heroine.

> *One day when Oak Wing's sister war going to a baptizing, and had her feed n a bag under her arm, she seed a big bear that had come out from a holler tree, and he looked fust at her, then at the feed, as if he didn't know which to eat fust. He kinder poked out his nose, and smelt of the dinner which war sassengers maid of bear's meat and crocodile's liver. She stood a minute and looked at him, in hopes he would feel ashamed of himself and go off; but he then cum up and smelt her, and then she thort twr time to be stirring. So she threw the dinner down before him, and when he put his nose to it, to take a bite, she threw herself on him an caught the scuff of his neck in her teeth; and the bear shot ahead, for it felt beautiful, as her teeth war as long an as sharp as nales. He tried to run, an she held on with her teeth, an it stript the skin clear off of him, and left him as naked as he was born, she hung on with her teeth till it cum clear off the tale. The bear seen a week afterwards up in Muskrat Hollow, running without his skin. She made herself a good warm petticoat out of the pesky varmint's hide.* *

Miners

Throughout the West, legends tell of lost mines and hidden or missing caches of gold and silver. Of course, Coronado, the conquistador, first ventured up into the American Southwest and beyond in search of the fabled seven cities of gold. These never materialized, and Coronado eventually returned to Mexico City something of a disgrace. But gold was found throughout the mountain West and in California and Alaska, and to this day prospectors still roam the remote areas looking for it. Inevitably tales of fabulous lost riches have arisen, and these legends still have the power to drive men into the wilderness at risk of their fortune and lives.

In the Southwest, many of these legends are connected with reports by Apaches. The Apache knew every inch of this unforgiving land, the whereabouts of every spring, every canyon. They had no use for gold themselves but spoke often about it. Geronimo claimed to know several

*From Anonymous, *Twenty-five Cents Worth of Nonsense*, Philadelphia, New York, Boston: Fisher & Bros. C. 1840, reprinted in Haynes and Haynes, 335.

places where he could find the precious metal, one of them perhaps the legendary Lost Dutchman Mine in the Superstition Mountains, east of present-day Phoenix. Another legendary one is the Lost Sublett Mine of New Mexico.

Seems that a mountain man named William Caldwell Sublette drifted west with his frail wife and two children and fetched up finally in west Texas, where he did odd jobs for the railroad. Soon as he had a small stake he'd disappear for a while into the mountains, and when his money ran out he'd come home. He'd tell everyone he was looking for gold on those trips, hinted that he was looking in the nearby Guadalupe Mountains, and every so often he'd come home with an actual gold nugget to show for his effort.

Finally Sublette's wife gave up the ghost and Sublett handed his children over to some neighbors in Odessa. Sublett went right back into the mountains and came back empty-handed again. People called him the "crazy man"; all he talked about was the gold he was going to find.

One day he came back to Odessa after having been gone for several weeks, and he sauntered into a saloon where his credit had been canceled and ordered drinks for the house. Nobody paid him any mind, of course, but he threw a sack of nuggets on the bar and said, "I'm rich, I'm rich! Drinks for everybody."

So Sublett would keep going back to his secret mine and returning with more nuggets. Somebody offered him ten thousand dollars for a share in his mine, but he said he could get more gold than that in just a week. No amount of whiskey would loosen him up, and he never told anyone where the mine was. People came from all over to find it, but Sublett never let on and never let anyone follow him.

Apparently he took his son Rolth there when Rolth was nine years old. Rolth was too young then to remember the mine's location, but he did recall seeing his father climb down a rope ladder into a cave. Later Rolth tried many times to get his father to tell him where the mine was, but the old man would say, "Boy, if you want the mine, go out and find it like I did."

William Sublett died in 1892, when he was about fifty-seven. He never told anyone the location of his source of gold nuggets, and his son Rolth never did find it, either. Nor has anyone else to this day, even though people keep mounting expeditions to the Guadalupe Mountains looking for it.*

*Rewritten from Penfield, 46–49.

Betsey and the Mole

An offshoot of the tall tale on the frontier was the distinctly off-color tale, sometimes involving a trick appropriate to Native American tricksters such as Coyote and Iktome the spider. American folklore is full of tales where the girl is won by a trick. "Betsey and the Mole" was recorded in Eureka Springs, Arkansas, from a man named Robert Wyrick, who said he had heard it himself in 1910.

Once a fellow was going with a pretty schoolmarm named Betsey, and they was a real loving couple except that he did considerable grumbling. Trouble was, Betsey liked to play with his pecker but she wouldn't let him get it in her. She said that was sinful.

"Listen," he says, "you got to oil a man's tool every so often or it'll turn on him like a wild animal."

Betsey just laughed and said that was an old superstition that no one with any kind of education believed in anymore. No matter how many times he complained, Betsey wouldn't let him do any diddling.

So finally the fellow went to see old Gram French and she told him to go kill a mole and skin it. She told him to put it on his pecker with the sharp teeth sticking out front and see what happened. He did what she told him, and that night he and Betsey went out walking. Pretty soon, like she usually did, she slipped her hand into his britches, but this time she shrieked and pulled it out, and burst into tears. The fellow lit a match and showed her what was in there and said, "I'm gonna go to the doctor tomorrow and get me an operation."

Well, Betsey figured that was the end of him, he was gonna be ruined, and it was her fault. He went on into town the next day and stayed there a few days. When he got back he showed her that his pecker was as good as new, and she was so happy he was cured that she said she'd do whatever he said. So after that she gave him all he wanted and they never had no more trouble at all.*

The Yankee Pedlar

Other trickster tales of the frontier involved the ubiquitous figure of the salesman who was also a con artist. This story is a product of the 1850s.

*Rewritten from Randolph, 47.

Yes! I have laughed this morning, and that heartily, but I fear I shall scarce be able to amuse you at second-hand with what depends altogether on certain *un-writable* turns of countenance and manner. The hero of the occasion was an old pedlar, who came jogging along in his hearse-shaped cart, soon after breakfast, and before this dripping humour beset the weather. He stopped his cart on seeing several men at work, and it was not long before the laughter of the men, who usually pursue their business in solemn silence, drew my attention. The aspect of the pedlar secured it, for he was a personification of Momus. His face was very red, and of a most grotesque turn, and his nutcracker nose and chin were like nobody but Punch. His grey eyes twinkled through a pair of mock spectacles made of a strip of tin twisted into the requisite form and placed far down his nose, so that he was obliged to throw his head back in order to look through them. When I went to the window, he was enumerating the contents of his covered cart with a bewildering rapidity, but as soon as he observed me, he stopped short, pulled off the remains of an old straw hat, and made a very low bow in the style of Sir Pertinax, who thought the world was to be won by "booing."

"My dear beautiful lady," said he, "could I sell you anything this morning? I sell things for nothing, and I've got most everything you ever heard tell on. Here's fashionable calicoes,"—holding up a piece of bright scarlet,—"splendid French work collars and capes,"—and here he displayed some hideous things, the flowers on which were distinctly traceable from where I stood,—"elegant milk pans, and Harrison skimmers, and *ne plus ultry* dippers! patent pills, cure anything you like—ague bitters—Shaker yarbs—essences, winter green, peppermint, lobely—tapes, pins, needles, hooks and eyes—broaches and brasslets—smelling bottles—castor ile—corn-plaster—mustard—garding seeds—silver spoons—pocket combs—tea pots—green tea—saleratus—tracts, songbooks—thimbles—babies' whistles—copybooks, slates, playin' cards—puddin' sticks—butter-prints—baskets—wooden bowls—"

"Any wooden nutmegs, daddy?" said one of the men.

"No, but as I come past I see your father a turnin some out o' that piece o' lignum vitae you got him last week," said the pedlar quietly; then turning again to the window—"Can I suit you today, ma'am? I've all sorts o' notions—powder and shot, (but I s'pose you do all your shootin' at home), but may be your old man goes a gunnin'—I shan't offer you lucifers, for ladies with sich eyes never buys matches,—but you can't ask me for any thing I haven't got, I guess."

While I was considering my wants, one of the men must try a fall with this professed wit.

"Any goose-yokes, mister?" said he.

"I'm afraid I've sold the last, sir; there is so many wanted in this section of the country. But I'll take your measure, and fetch you a supply next time I come along." This of course produced a laugh.

"Well! I want a pair o' boots, any how," said the prostrate hero rallying, to show that he was not discomforted. "These here old ones o' mine lets in gravel, but won't let it out again. If you've got any to fit me. I'll look at 'em." And thus saying he stretched out a leg of curious wire drawn appearance. "Any to fit, old boss?"

"Fit you like a whistle, sir," said the pedlar, fumbling among his wares, and at length drawing forth a pair of *candle moulds*, much to the amusement of the bystanders.

The rain which had begun to fall now cut short our conference. I bought a few trifles, and the pedlar received his pay with a bow which was almost a salaam. Mounting his blue hearse, he drove off in triumph, not minding the rain, from which he was completely sheltered by a screen of boughs fitted in the sides of his wagon, and meeting over his head,—a protection against sun and rain which I much admired.*

Western Outlaws and Lawmen

Perhaps the richest source for legendary heroes in the American experience is the "Wild West." Noble lawmen, admirable and not-so-admirable outlaws, gun-slinging women who toss off hard talk, and lonely cowboys are the material out of which western heroes are made. It is important to note that legends of the American West, as extreme as they sometimes appear to be, are relatively close to historical fact, as they have not had the time to be transformed significantly. The West was a rough place to be, law enforcement was often nonexistent or executed by unauthorized individuals or groups, and the life of the cowboy was hard, as was the life of the settler.

Outlaws have always been favorite American heroes. As one of several categories of the much-admired "self-made man" (poor boy makes bad), they are defiant individualists, and Americans like to pay homage to rugged individualism, especially if it challenges authority. American outlaw heroes often have good reasons for being "bad"; they are in one way or another victims of society. Finally, they are frequently shown to have hearts of gold beneath their apparent bloodthirstiness; they are the

*Haliburton, 212–15.

Robin Hoods of the New World, robbing the rich, helping the poor, achieving their own kind of "justice" in the face of general corruption.

Billy the Kid

The premier outlaw figure in the vast panoply of outlaws who spattered the West with lead and derring-do was a youth born to the name of Henry McCarty in New York City in 1859. In fact, two Henry McCartys were born that year in New York, neither with any record of a father, and no one knows which one of them became Billy the Kid and was shot dead at Fort Sumner in New Mexico twenty-one years later.

Upon hearing of his death in 1881, the New York Daily Graphic *wrote that "he had built up a criminal organization worthy of the underworld of any of the European capitals. He defied the law to stop him and he stole, robbed, raped and pillaged . . . he became, in the short span of his twenty-one years, the master criminal of the American southwest."*

Even before his death, journalists referred to him as a "young demon" and "urged by a spirit hideous as hell." Indeed, thanks to the voracious hunger in the East for news of the rawboned West, and thanks to the florid prose and perfervid imaginations of western editors, Billy the Kid was a legend in his own time, purportedly the cold-blooded killer of as many as forty men. Others said twenty-one, one for each year of his life. In truth, Billy the Kid probably killed four men single-handedly and participated in shoot-outs that resulted in the death of five others, most of this violence occurring during what was called the Lincoln County Wars. These "wars," in effect, pitched two rival gangs against each other, each representing one side in what amounted to a disagreement over who would have the rights to run a large commercial cattle operation in the vast and underpopulated region called Lincoln County in southern New Mexico. Relatively short-lived (the wars lasted from 1877 to 1880) and tawdry, the conflict was also called "Lincoln County's War of the Roses."

Between 1881, when he died, and 1906, a dozen dime novels portrayed Billy the Kid as Satan's lieutenant on earth, an utterly ruthless, bloodthirsty killer whose death at the hands of Pat Garrett symbolized the welcome end of savagery and lawlessness in the West.

During the Lincoln County Wars, Billy the Kid was in the service of John Chisum, a Pecos Valley cattle baron, and Alex McSween, a storekeeper. According to one account, Chisum and McSwain in a happy moment hired the Kid, and his daredevil ways, his deadly marks-*

*Page, "Was Billy the Kid a Superhero—or a Superscoundrel?" 137–48.

*manship, and his perfect command of a horse, combined with what
seemed to be an absolute delight in murder, soon caused him to be made
the leader of his faction.*

Early in 1879 Chisum arranged for the appointment of The Kid as dep-
uty constable and clothed in this authority he was given a warrant for
the arrest, on a trivial charge, of Billy Morton and Frank Baker, two
herders employed by Tom Catron. This Catron, by the way, used to live
in Lafayette county, Missouri, and was the partner of Hon. Stephen B.
Elkins, himself a Missouri boy, later delegated to Congress from New
Mexico and now one of the moneyed men of New York. The Kid sad-
dled his horse, when told what was to be done, and, without a word to
any of his comrades, silently rode off to the range in search of his prey,
accompanied by one McCluskey. He found Morton and his companion
in a camp near the eastern boundary of the county and showing him
the warrant said:

"You are my prisoners. Come along."

"What do you want of me?" said Morton, in a threatening tone.

"Shut up, or I'll blow your brains out. You have been working
against Chisum. That's enough."

"We'll see about this pretty soon, young man," said Baker. "It's a
free country and no man arrests me without I know what it's for."

"Haven't I told your white-livered friend the reason. Hold your
tongue or I'll stop it forever with a bullet."

At this point McCluskey interfered and remonstrated with the young
desperado.

"You don't mean to kill a defenseless man do you?" he said.

"If I wish to, yes; and you, too."

With these words The Kid drew his revolver and before the astonished McCluskey could move his hand shot him in his tracks.

"You see how I treat men who fool with me, do you?" the murderer
said, as he scornfully kicked the lifeless form at his feet. "Be careful
what you do or I'll serve you as I have him."

Chaining the two men together by the wrists and carefully securing
them to the saddle he placed them both upon McCluskey's horse and
started back at a slow trot towards Chisum's ranch. The feelings of the
prisoners can easily be imagined. Should they be taken into camp the
vengeance of Chisum would be upon their heads. There was, at least, a
chance of escape. If the handcuffs could only be loosened and the chain
parted a successful break might be made. Those "ifs" must be gotten
out of the way in the next twenty miles. The men worked cautiously
and had almost freed themselves, when the watchful eye of The Kid

espied their movements. Without saying a word he coolly drew his rifle to his shoulder and fired twice at them. As the distance was only ten feet and his aim sure the reports were followed by the simultaneous fall of both Morton and Baker, and in a moment their souls had flown to what we may hope was a greener range, where even the cow-boy has a place. Shot dead without hardly an excuse. Thus The Kid added two more to the list of those who had felt his deadly power. Thus far he had killed four men and the career of this pseudo James boy had hardly begun. Fearful in its beginning the reader must judge the righteousness of the end.

Riding into camp The Kid informed Chisum of what he had done and asked that two men be sent out to bury them.

"Where is McCluskey?" asked Chisum.

"None of your —— business," replied The Kid.

"It is my business and I will know. I am not afraid of you and you may as well understand it now as any time."

"Come, come, old feller," he said, changing his tone and manner, "I was just bantering you a little. Now to be honest about it I killed Mc."

"Killed him!"

"That's the racket."

"Why, what had he done?"

"Too infernally inquisitive. Didn't know his place, either. Thought he'd try to boss the job, but I settled him quick."

"He was my best man, next to you," said Chisum, after a pause, in which he eyed The Kid closely and rubbed his chin reflectively.

"Don't care if he was, he had to go."

"Do you know, Kid, that this affair will leak out and the officers will be down here to inquire into it and arrest you?"

"Chisum, you must think I'm a fool. I care no more for Brady and Hindman than I do for a dog. If they get the drop on me—all right, but The Kid won't be caught napping and don't you forget it."

"I'm afraid they'll bring the troops down on us!"

"Let them do it. If we can't whip any company of 'blue coats,' why then I'll change my name and herd sheep in the States," and with this assertion The Kid carelessly sauntered down to his tent and threw himself down to catch a few hours' sleep before morning should dawn.*

Interest lapsed in the Kid until the publication in 1925 of The Saga of Billy the Kid, *by Walter Noble Burns (the initial selection of the newly*

*From one of the tales quoted in Botkin, 98–99.

formed Book-of-the-Month Club), which repopularized Billy as the romantic idealist symbolizing a lost pastoral world—a kind of Robin Hood figure whose first killing, it was said, was to avenge an insult to his mother, while the other killings were to avenge the death of his employer.

The Robin Hood theme resonated especially with the long-held Hispanic notion of the Kid. In the 1930s, a seventy-seven-year-old woman, Lorencita Herrera de Miranda, recounted her memories of the Lincoln County Wars:

> My husband and I were living on our farm just above Lincoln all during the Lincoln County War. We liked both factions so we never took any part in the war. I remember the day the McSween home was burned. We could see the flames and the smoke from our house but we stayed home for we were scared to death to stick our heads out of the house. We could also hear some of the shooting. Billy the Kid came to our house several times and drank coffee with us. We liked him for he was always nice to the Spanish people and they all liked him.

A former shepherd of the time recalled that the outlaw was a very generous man.

> All the Mexican people, they like him. He give money, horses, drinks—what he have . . . always very polite, very much of a gentleman. Once lots of mens, they go together after Billy the Keed to shoot him. They pay us—we go—sure. But we don't want to shoot Billy. We always be glad he too smart for us.*

Hollywood has weighed in with interpretations of Billy and the legends surrounding him. John Mack Brown's 1930 movie Billy the Kid showed the good outlaw, increasingly isolated and serving the cause of justice if not the law. (Aaron Copland's 1938 ballet of the same title returned Billy to the class of relentless, amoral killers.) In the 1940s, a string of B-movies starring the likes of Buster Crabbe presented Billy as a populist hero protecting the countryside in the manner of the Lone Ranger. In the 1950s, Paul Newman played the Kid twice, in a Gore Vidal television drama and in a movie—both times as a James Dean-like rebel without a cause. (The movie, The Left-handed Gun, perpetuated the notion that the Kid was a southpaw—which was derived from the one certain photograph of Billy, a tintype taken in 1879 at Fort

*See Weigle and White, 353–54.

Sumner by an itinerant photographer. Because tintype images are reversed, Billy's holster appears to be on his left side.)

Billy was a doomed avenger in John Wayne's *Chisum,* a symbol of the loss of individual freedom in Sam Peckinpah's *Pat Garrett and Billy the Kid,* and in the 1980s little more than an attractive-looking but troubled and short-tempered adolescent in *Young Guns,* the message of which was, essentially, "Say no to violence." In all, the Kid has been the subject of more than forty movies, including one in 1996 that had him heroically warding off Count Dracula.

On July 14, 1881, Billy the Kid was spending the night in Fort Sumner, New Mexico, where he had many friends. That night, perhaps after a nocturnal tryst with a young Hispanic woman, he wandered out of his room in his stocking feet and into that of the house's owner, a man named Pete Maxwell. Noting another presence in the gloom, he asked in Spanish, "Quien es?"

The answer was a bullet that conclusively dispatched him, a bullet from the gun of Pat Garrett, who had not long before been made sheriff of Lincoln County expressly to rid society of the young troublemaker. When told that Pat Garrett had killed Billy the Kid, the shepherd quoted before said:

> You think Billy the Keed let himself be shot in the dark like that? No, señora,—Billy the Keed?—never. I see Billy the Keed with these eyes. Many times, with these eyes. That Billy, tenia un agilesa in su mente—in su mente aquí. *[He pointed to his forehead and then made a quick motion to the sky.]* Un function electrica.*

Many others have refused to believe that Billy was so easily killed. A coroner's report of his death exists, but there never was a death certificate. What is supposed to be his grave has a marker at Fort Sumner, but it is not clear that he is under the marker. The site was flooded once, and another time soldiers used his grave marker for target practice, perhaps erecting another. Just as his origin is murky, so (some would have it) is his death, as befits a figure of myth.

In the 1950s a man named Brushy Bill Roberts from Hico, Texas, claimed to be Billy the Kid and was so convincing that arrangements were made to have the New Mexico governor give him the pardon the Kid always wanted. But Brushy Bill could neither speak Spanish nor read, two of Billy's known talents, so he was dismissed. Meanwhile, a man named John Miller, who lived on a Ramah, New Mexico, ranch until his death in 1937, told several people that he was the Kid. He was

*Weigle and White, 353–55.

a reclusive man with a hidden stash of money, and he gave to a Canadian lawman a gun that wound up in the hands of another Canadian who realized it was an 1880 army revolver that could have been the Kid's. But forensic anthropologists, comparing photos of Miller and Billy with the help of computers, have shown conclusively that Miller was not who he claimed.

No matter. Whether he was indeed shot by Pat Garrett or whether he escaped, as many would believe, he was ever the nonconformist, rebellious youth. And he continues to ride across the landscape of the American consciousness—elusive, irrepressible, lethal, an insouciant reminder that in matters of conformity and rebellion, violence and civility, justice and corruption, we Americans cannot make up our minds.

Jesse James

Another famous American Robin Hood was Jesse James.

Born in Clay County, Missouri, in 1847, Jesse James fought (and plundered) with Quantrill's Raiders in the Civil War and continued plundering once the war ended, forming a gang with his older brother Frank and a pair of brothers named Younger. The gang specialized in robbing banks, and then trains as well, until 1882. Virtually every bank robbery in Missouri in those years was attributed, however inaccurately, to the flamboyant James gang.

While their criminal activities resulted in the death of numerous innocent people, they became lionized as heroes in part because the railroads, one of their chief targets, were deeply hated for seizing private lands in Missouri under condemnation orders. Soon enough, the Pinkertons were on their trail. In 1875, thinking the James brothers were hiding in their mother's house, the Pinkertons set off a bomb (or perhaps a flare) that killed their little half-brother and blew off their mother's arm, bringing forth yet more sympathy for the James boys.

In 1882, while hanging a picture on a wall in his house in St. Joseph and planning yet more robberies (under the alias of Howard), Jesse James was assassinated by a new gang member, Bob Ford, to whom the state governor had promised a $10,000 reward. Mournfully, the Kansas City Star bid farewell with a banner headline: "Goodbye Jesse."

A controversy grew up over whether Ford had killed Jesse or a look-alike gang member and has never been resolved to all the doubters' satisfaction. His brother Frank, however, was arrested and aquitted in several trials for murder. In the meantime, the legend grew that the James brothers had been American Robin Hoods, robbing from the wealthy (generally true) and giving to the poor (which never happened).

"One day," says Sam Allender, "Frank James told me that on a certain occasion he and his pals were traveling on horseback somewhere in northern Missouri. It being about noon, they were hungry. They pulled off the main road and found a lone woman in charge of a small farmhouse. They asked her if she could supply them with something to eat.

"At first the woman hesitated. The men displayed money and assured her they would be glad to pay for what they ate. She then proceeded to prepare such scant food as she had on hand. As she was making coffee and cooking eggs, the James crowd sat around the room. They noticed that she was weeping; tears were rolling down her cheeks, sobs were heaving her bosom.

" 'Jesse,' said Frank in telling me the story, 'was always tenderhearted—couldn't stand a woman's tears. He asked her why she was crying. She tried to smile it off, and said that seeing us men around the house reminded her of the happy time when her husband was living and had other men now and then helping him do the farm work; she was just thinking how sadly things had changed since his death, and that was what made her cry, so she said.

" 'Jesse kept on asking questions. The woman said she had several children at school, some miles down the road; there was a mortgage on her farm, she went on to say, for $1,400; it was overdue, and this was the last day of grace.

" ' "Aha!" said Jesse, "and so that's really what's making you cry—you're afraid you're going to lose your home. I see."

" 'Yes, that was it, she admitted. That very afternoon, said the weeping widow, the man who held the mortgage was coming out from town to demand his money. He was a hardhearted old miser, she stated, and she didn't have a dollar to apply on the debt. The man would be sure to foreclose and turn her and her helpless little ones out.

" ' "Huh!" said Jesse, "that so?" his eyes blinking fast and furiously. "Well, now ma'am, I don't know about that; I—well, now, I think maybe you won't lose your farm after all."

" 'The widow looked rather puzzled. She put the food on the table and all of us sat down and turned to. After we finished eating, Jesse produced a sack and counted out on the table $1,400.

" ' "Here, lady," said Jesse, "you take this money and pay off your mortgage."

" 'The lady was amazed. "I can't ever pay you back," she said, "and so I won't borrow it."

" ' "But it's no loan," said Jesse; "it's a gift."

" 'The widow said she couldn't believe it was anything but a dream—things never happened that way—but Jesse assured her it was no dream; the money was good money and it was for her use. Jesse then sat down and wrote out a form of receipt, which he had the woman copy in her own handwriting. He put the original into his pocket, so that his handwriting wouldn't get into other hands. Jesse instructed the woman to pay the mortgage-holder the $1,400 and have him sign the receipt—in ink. He then handed her a handful of cash for her immediate needs.

" 'Jesse asked the grateful widow to describe the man who held the mortgage. She did so, telling the kind of rig he drove and about what hour she expected him, and the road by which he would come out from town. We then bade her good day and mounted our horses. The widow was still weeping, but weeping for joy.

" 'We rode some distance from the house and hid in the bushes beside the rocky road along which the mortgage man was to come in his buggy. Presently we saw him driving toward the widow's house, and pretty soon driving back, looking prosperous. He was humming "Old Dan Tucker was a fine old feller" as he came opposite. We stepped out into the road, held him up and recovered the $1,400.'

"I asked Frank James," said Sam Allender, "if they had any more difficulty in getting the money on that occasion than they had had on the occasion when they first acquired it; and he replied, with a laugh:

" 'Now, Sam, I'm not being sweated.' "*

Jesse James's life and death were immortalized in a ballad, of which the following version is the best-known.

Jesse James was a lad who killed many a man,
He robbed the Glendale train.
He stole from the rich and he gave to the poor,
He had a hand, a heart, and a brain.

Poor Jesse had a wife to mourn for his life,
Two children, they were brave,
But that dirty little coward that shot Mister Howard
Had laid poor Jesse in his grave.

With his brother Frank they robbed the Gallatin bank,
They caried the money from the town.
And in this very place they had a little race,
For they shot Captain Sheets to the ground.

*Love, 289–92.

It was on a Wednesday night, the moon was shining bright,
They robbed the Glendale train.
And the people they did say for many miles away,
It was robbed by Frank and Jesse James.

It was Robert Ford, the dirty little coward,
I wonder how he does feel.
For he ate of Jesse's bread and he slept in Jesse's bed,
Then he laid Jesse James in his grave.

It was on a Saturday night, poor Jesse was at home,
Talking to his family brave.
Robert Ford watched his eye, and shot him on the sly,
And he laid Jesse James in his grave.

The people held their breath when they heard of Jesse's death,
And wondered how he ever came to die.
Robert Ford's pistol ball brought him tumbling from the wall,
For he shot poor Jesse on the sly.

Jesse went to rest with his hand upon his breast,
The Devil will be down upon his knee.
He was born one day in the county of Clay,
And he came from a solitary race.

This song was made by Billy Gashade,
Just as soon as the news did arrive.
He said there was no man with the law in his hand
That could take Jesse James when alive.*

Wild Bill Hickok

In a society as lawless as the West, lawmen took on special importance. Central to the stereotypical picture of the Wild West is the beleaguered sheriff facing down—often alone—those who would threaten the security of his town.

James Butler Hickok (1837–1876), known as Wild Bill, was the premier sheriff of the old West. Known, like most great lawmen and outlaws, for his marksmanship, he drove stagecoaches over the Santa Fe and Oregon trails. It was on the Oregon trail that he was said to have bravely fought the famous McCanles Gang, killing David McCanles. Later, during the Civil War, Hickok became a Union spy and scout, and

*Erbsen, 26.

served under General Custer. In the late 1860s he began his career as a U.S. marshal in various Kansas towns and became famous as a card shark and as a "quick draw." There were many exaggerated stories about Hickok's gunfights. He showed off his marksmanship in the Wild West Show of Buffalo Bill Cody in the early 1870s. On August 2, 1876, in Deadwood, South Dakota, he was shot in the back during a poker game as he held what ever since has been called a "dead man's hand."

Wyatt Earp

Wyatt Earp (1849–1929) is best known for the famous shoot-out at the O.K. Corral in Tombstone, Arizona. The fight was between Earp and his brothers, helped by John H. "Doc" Holliday, and the popular Ike Clanton and his friends. It took only a few seconds for the Earp side to kill three of their opponents and for two of the Earp brothers to be wounded. In this case the town did not appear to value the "protection" of the noble lawman, and sympathies tended to run with the "outlaw" Clanton. In fact, there was a serious attempt to lynch the Earps and Holliday for their part in the fight, and they soon left town.

The Hanging Judge

Another archetypal character in the old West made so famous in the cinema genre of the western is the figure of the eccentric judge. Judges occupied a position of singular power in the Wild West.

What is surely the most devastating sentence ever handed down by a sitting American judge is attributed to one Judge Parker, the "hanging judge" of Fort Smith, Arkansas, in a case in which a Mexican cook shot and killed a cowboy in an argument over a card game across the border in the Indian Territory (now Oklahoma):

José Manuel Miguel Xavier Gonzales, in a few months it will be spring, the snow of winter will flee away, the ice will vanish, and the air will become soft and balmy. In short, José Manuel Miguel Xavier Gonzales, the annual miracle of the year's awakening will come to pass, but you won't be here. The rivulet will run its purling course to the sea, the timid desert flowers will put forth their tender shoots, the glorious valleys of this imperial domain will blossom as the rose, still you won't be here. From every treetop, some desert songster will carol his mating song, butterflies will sport in the sunshine, the busy bee will hum happily as it pursues its accustomed vocation, the gentle breezes will tease the tassels of the wild grasses, and all nature, José Manuel Miguel Xavier Gonzales, will be glad but you won't be here to enjoy it; for I command the sheriff or some other officer or officers of this county to lead you out to some remote spot, swing you up by the neck to a nodding bough of some sturdy oak, and there let you hang till you are dead, dead, dead. And then, José Manuel Miguel Xavier Gonzales, I command further that such officer or officers retire quietly from your swinging, dangling corpse, that the vultures may descend upon your filthy body and pick the putrid flesh therefrom till nothing remain but the bare, bleached bones of a cold-blooded, copper-colored, blood-thirsty, chili-eating, guilty, sheep-herding Mexican son-of-a-bitch.

Variants of this same sentence have been attributed to Judge Kirby Benedict of Santa Fe, New Mexico, as well as to Judge Roy Bean (though, in fact, Judge Bean never condemned anyone to death). *

The Cowboy

Much romanticized, the West and its most notable icon, the cowboy, have come in for a considerable amount of revisionist thinking by modern historians. Some of these quite rightly emphasize the role of women, labor movements, blacks, and other elements that played important roles in opening up the western lands. At the same time, revisionist historians have deplored the European American dispossession of the original inhabitants of the West, as well as the destructive ecological processes they brought along with them. As part of this new view, they have also debunked the notion of the individualist heroes, who, from the time of the mountain men on through the closing of the frontier, are now seen as mere puppets dancing to the tune of Eastern establishment capitalists, from John Jacob Astor to absentee ranch owners.

Nevertheless, the cowboy persists, working ranchlands throughout the western states, and continues to live out what others consider a "mythical" existence, a major feature of which is, and always has been, humor. A new/old genre called cowboy poetry has risen to some prominence in the West.

The Cowboy's Prayer

Charles Badger Clark was a South Dakota cowboy poet who spent the years from 1906 to 1910 in southern Arizona, where he wrote "The

---

*Lomax, "Stop-Over," 407–18.

Cowboy's Prayer," which subsequently often appeared on postcards and elsewhere without attribution, as if the author were unknown. It is a classic celebration of the romantic—and romanticized—attachment to the wide open western spaces. The first verse:

> Lord, I've never lived where churches grow.
> I love Creation better as it stood
> That day You finished it so long ago
> And looked upon Your work, and called it good.
> I know that others find You in the light
> That's sifted down through tinted window panes,
> And yet I seem to feel You near tonight
> In this dim, quiet starlight on the plains.*

Pecos Bill

Pecos Bill is the Paul Bunyan of cowboys. His story is a long tall tale, a comic version of the archetypal hero's life with its Herculean escapades.

There was a time when there wasn't no cowboys. That's right, no such thing. There was some people herded their few straggly cows around with sticks and such, but none of that ever did amount to much. The cowboy as we know him took some inventin' and that was done by one man, name of Pecos Bill.

Why don't you put another stick or two on that fire and I'll tell you about him. There.

Watch them sparks! Well, don't worry, there ain't nothin' around here that's gonna burn.

Now Bill wasn't much more than a crawlin' infant when his daddy decided to move west. He packed up the family—the missus and all their children, they say there was eleven of 'em, with Bill being the youngest—put 'em all in the wagon and off they went. They got to the bank of a river, the Pecos River, about thirty mile north of where it runs into the Rio Grande, down near Del Rio, you been there?—and that's when little Bill just fell out the back of the wagon into the grass.

It seems that nobody noticed. I guess they was all thinkin' about how to cross the river and all, which they did do, leavin' little Bill on the riverbank. Wasn't till three weeks later they realized he was missin' and by then it was too late to go back lookin' for him.

*Entire poem appears in Clark, 112.

Pecos Bill. U.S. Postage stamp. By permission: U.S. Postal Service.

They wouldn't of found him if they did go back because some coyotes came upon the boy and took him home. So Bill grew up among the varmints, sittin' on the hillsides yipping the way they do, howlin', huntin' with them, even learned their language. They say Bill thought he was a coyote and there's no reason to doubt it.

By the time Bill was thirteen, he'd grown bigger than most men, and every critter in the West knew about him. He'd won fights with rattlesnakes, grizzly bears, and even mountain lions, and the critters were beginnin' to think of him as the king.

But there was one big, mean mountain lion who thought *he* was the king, and he decided he'd show this coyote upstart a thing or two. He clumb up on some rocks above where Bill was howlin' one day, and when Bill threw his head back for a big long howl, the lion leaped down on him, knocked him onto the ground. But Bill just grabbed that big ole cat around the waist and said, "I can squeeze you to death right here and now, done it hundreds of times with bears and lions. But I got somethin' else in mind for you."

With that said, he threw the lion down and clumb up on its back, saying, "I'm gonna ride you wherever I want to go." Well, that old lion shook, and spat, and screamed and jumped and twisted hisself practically in knots, but he couldn't shake Bill off, and finally the lion gave up, said, "You win, you win. I guess I'll just have to carry you wherever you want."

And Bill said that would be fine till he got a better idea, which of course he did, but that comes later.

One day not long after, Bill was up on a hill and he saw another two-legged coyote runnin' hell bent for leather across the plain. He was bein' chased by as mean-looking a bull as anyone had ever seen, and he was shoutin', "Help, help!"

Bill gave out a whistle, and all the rattlesnakes nearby came slitherin' over to him. One after the other, he tied them sidewinders together and made a loop at one end. Swingin' the snake rope over his head, he went plungin' down the hill on his mountain lion and galloped over to where the two-legged coyote was gaspin' on the dusty ground and that bull was about to get him. Bill swung the snake loop over the bull's horns and pulled him to a stop so sudden it raised dust a mile in the air. Now you can imagine that bull was eye-rate to beat hell, and he yanked, and pulled, and kicked and snorted and all, till Bill gave the rope another tug and swung that bull around in the air and let him loose to fly head over back end over the plain for five miles. He landed with a thump so loud it shook the mountains nearby.

All of Bill's friends, the coyotes, had gathered around by this time and everyone was havin' a good laugh. The two-legged coyote, who was a man of course, got up off the ground and thanked Bill and then asked him why he wasn't wearin' no clothes and why he was hangin' around with varmints.

"Well, I *am* a varmint," Bill said. "I got fleas and I howl at night."

"That don't prove nothin'. So does every man in Texas," the man said. "But coyotes have tails. You ain't got no tail, so you must be a man."

Bill craned his neck around and said, "Dang if you're not right. I guess I better throw myself in with you."

So that's how Bill came to live among humans, and they called him Pecos Bill 'cause that's where he came from. It wasn't long before Bill had invented the lasso made of rope, not sidewinders, and had tamed the horse for ridin'. A horse has got more endurance than a lion any day.

Bill proceeded to start ranchin' and pretty soon he and his cattle had ate all the grass in Texas, so he went west across the Pecos and staked out New Mexico to be his new place. Fenced off Arizona to be his calf pasture. Now New Mexico was as dry as a bone and Bill took to fetchin' water for his cows from the Gulf of California, but he grew tired of that, so he dug the Rio Grande to get water from the Rocky Mountains flowing through. It was there in New Mexico he found a special horse when it was just a colt. He raised that colt on a diet of nitroglycerin and called it Widow-maker 'cause he was the only man who could get a leg over it without killin' hisself.

One time a feller did try to ride Widow-maker and that horse just throwed that boy so high he came down on top of Pike's Peak. He was in a real fix up there 'cause he couldn't get down and faced a lingerin' death from starvation and cold. But Bill got his lasso, which some say was as long as the equator but others say was shorter than that at one end, and he threwed the loop up there. Got the man around the neck and tugged it gently so the man fell to safety in the valley twenty thousand feet below. The man was grateful and went to work on Bill's ranch as a horse wrangler.

There are some stories you might hear about how Pecos Bill invented outlawin' in the West, holdin' up stagecoaches and rustlin' cattle, and none of those stories are true, I guarantee that. They invented rustlin' in the Bible, they did. Bill did invent the centipede and the scorpion, just as a joke on his friends, and it's true that he put the thorns on cactus and the horns on toads, but he also invented the fencepost and the hitchin' rail and other things like ten-gallon hats that make a cowboy's life possible. He invented the buckin' bronco too, and how that man could ride. Only got throwed once and that was when he decided to ride a tornado.

It seems that a tornado appeared one day on the horizon and turned the sky all black and green, and it was kickin' up a roar so loud they tell me it woke up the king of France. Bill just grabbed that tornado by the ear and pushed it down to the ground—that was up near Kansas where this occurred—and clumb on its back. Well, sir, that tornado jumped like it was stuck with a cactus spine, and it took to flippin', sidewindin',' sunfishin' the entire length of Texas. It tied the rivers into knots and it just swiped all the timber down on the Staked Plains where there used to be forests, and it whirled and leaped and then headed west while Bill sat up there, kickin' the tornado in the withers with the spurs he'd invented.

Finally the tornado realized it wasn't gonna get this hombre off its back so it just rained itself out to nothin'. There was so much rain that the flash flood that resulted dug out Grand Canyon. And Pecos Bill fell off over in California, where he hit the dirt so hard it sank the ground down below sea level. They call the place Death Valley. That was the origins of rodeo, but nobody's ever seen rodeoin' like that again, let me tell you.

Now Pecos Bill was like any other man in one way. He did love women. In his long and excitin' life he found time to have many wives, and there're plenty of women alive today who *claim* that Bill married them, you know how that is. But Bill never fell so hard in love as he did with the woman who became his first wife, and he never did forget her either.

She was Slue-foot Sue.

You say you know a song about Slue-foot Sue? Sing it for us, will you?

> *There once was a girl I knew*
> *Her name was Slue-foot Sue.*
> *She was chief engineer at the shirt-tail factory*
> *Down by the riverside view.*
> *Her form was all she had*
> *Her face was like a softshell crab*
> *Every night she'd hustle*
> *With her grandmother's bustle . . .*
> *Boy, she was bad.*

Well, now that's right pretty but I reckon it's some other Slue-foot Sue you're singin' about. Sounds like one of them New England songs, maybe.

Anyway this Slue-foot Sue I was tellin' you about was a famous rider herself, and Bill just plumb lost his heart to her the time he saw her first. She was ridin' one of them huge Rio Grande catfish downriver, holdin' the rope with one hand and firin' a sixgun in the other, shootin' holes in the clouds overhead. They was married the next day, and Bill was never so happy.

But Slue-foot Sue insisted that she get to ride Widow-maker, and Bill let her against his better judgment. As you can imagine, that old horse bucked like a maniac, threw Slue-foot Sue so high she cracked her head on the moon. Fortunately, she was still wearin' her weddin' dress and it had one of them big springy bustles. So when Sue hit the ground, she bounced, and ever' time she came down she bounced again, and Bill was callin' to her, tellin' her to quit bouncin'.

But she kept on bouncin' farther and farther away, crying tears like two creeks in spring and throwin' kisses to her lover man. For three days and four night more, Sue kept bouncin' and it was clear she was gonna starve to death, so Bill had to shoot her. Damn if that wasn't tragic.

Bill did marry again, as I said before, lots of times, but no one ever did fill the place in his heart that had been occupied by Slue-foot Sue, no sir.

Bill didn't take to drinkin' then, like some will tell you. No, Bill had drunk all his life. His mother weaned him on whiskey, and gave him a Bowie knife to cut his teeth on. That was before he fell off the wagon back when. Came a time when whiskey just didn't get the hairs up on him anymore so he took to drinkin' wolf poison, but that didn't do him no harm. Surely, it didn't kill him.

I'll tell you how Pecos Bill died.

One day he was walkin' along the sidewalk in Laredo and he met a feller from Boston who'd just arrived in town. This feller had got hisself a mail-order cowboy outfit or somethin'. Had him a new hat, and a new pair of jeans, just like them you're wearin'. Boots made of lizard skin and not a speck of dust, and a big old belt buckle made of brass. Yep, just like that one of yours.

And poor Bill, he took a look at the feller and laid down on the sidewalk and laughed hisself to death.*

Women of the Frontier

Because of the dominance of men in a society governed by the gun and sheer physical power, and because of the preponderance of male-generated legends and tall tales, heroines are somewhat rare in western lore. A few do exist, however. To the extent that they are heroic, they act like men, although their hardness often veils a soft heart for love.

---

*Rewritten based on Botkin, 80ff, and Marcatante and Potter, 199ff.

Annie Oakley

Phoebe Anne Oakley Mozee, known as Annie Oakley (1860–1926), learned marksmanship as a child, hunting rabbits for the family supper. After she defeated the famous marksman Frank E. Butler in a contest in Cincinnati she married him, and together they became a part of the Buffalo Bill Wild West Show. It was said that Annie Oakley could shoot a dime thrown into the air, and once she shot a cigarette out of her husband's mouth. She could shoot a playing card full of holes as it floated through the air, hence the name "Annie Oakley" for a complimentary ticket already punched.

Calamity Jane

A more raucous woman of the West was Martha Jane Cannary Burke (1852–1903), otherwise known as Calamity Jane, probably because of her hard luck in life. She became an orphan at fifteen and began a hard life hanging out in saloons. Calamity dressed and swore and shot like a man. According to legend, she had a love affair with Wild Bill Hickok in Deadwood, South Dakota. Her last years were spent peddling a book of exaggerated tales of her life.

Bad Men and Bad Women

Legends about bad men and bad women sometimes had more urban settings. Americans have always loved tales of gangsters and their molls (more poor boys and girls "making bad").

Ma Barker

Born Arizona Donnie Clark in 1872 near Springfield, Missouri, and the wife of an itinerant farm worker, "Kate" or "Ma" Barker was labeled "a veritable beast of prey" by J. Edgar Hoover. So fixed is she in the American mind as the evil matriarch that film actor Warren Beatty described the often-hostile film critic Pauline Kael and her retinue as "Ma Barker and her boys." The Encyclopaedia Britannica *has this to say about her:*

> Matriarch of an outlaw gang of brothers and allies, engaged in kidnapping and in payroll, post-office, and bank robberies in the 1920s and '30s. The activities of the gang, which included her sons,

the "Bloody Barkers"—Herman (1894–1927), Fred (1902–35), and Arthur, known as "Doc" (1899–1939)—ranged throughout the the midwestern United States from Minnesota to Texas. All met violent deaths. Ma Barker and Fred were killed at a Florida resort in a gun battle with the FBI; Arthur was killed in an attempted escape from Alcatraz; Herman, cornered by Kansas police, shot himself. A fourth brother, Lloyd (1896–1949), a loner, spent 25 years in Leavenworth prison (1922–47) and, after release, was killed by his wife. (The father of the Barker boys, George Barker, was never a gang member and was abandoned by Ma Barker in 1927.)*

According to the FBI, Ma planned all the gang's jobs, running their affairs with iron discipline, never even allowing the presence of any girlfriends in her son's lives. She was adept at getting her sons released from arrest by weeping histrionically and sometimes screaming. Ma Barker met her death on January 16, 1935, when the FBI tracked her and her favorite son, Freddie, to a cottage at Fort Weir, Florida. In a four-hour gun battle, Freddie was riddled with bullets and Ma Barker, evidently wielding a tommy gun, died with a single bullet in her—or perhaps three.

Another view, according to other criminals of the period as well as members of the Barker gang, is that Ma Barker was a dumpy and insignificant woman who did weep to get her boys out of jail but otherwise was harmless, even feckless. For one thing, the gang's hideouts were always filled with whores, about which Ma did nothing. As one gang member wrote in his memoirs:

> *Ma was always somebody in our lives. Love didn't enter into it really. She was somebody we looked after and took with us when we moved from city to city, hideout to hideout.*
>
> *It's no insult to Ma's memory that she just didn't have the brains or know-how to direct us on a robbery. It wouldn't have occurred to her to get involved in our business, and we always made a point of only discussing our scores when Ma wasn't around. We'd leave her at home when we were arranging a job, or we'd send her to a movie. Ma saw a lot of movies.*

From such accounts, it seems that in the case of their "Bloody Mama," the very quintessence of the evil matriarch, the FBI engaged in its own bit of legend making.†

**New Encyclopaedia Britannica*, volume 1, 899.
†Sifakis, 51.

Bonnie and Clyde

Gangster lovers who captured the American imagination, Bonnie Parker and Clyde Barrow rampaged through the Midwest in the 1930s, robbing and murdering and, to a great degree, creating their own legendary celebrity by sending out snapshots of themselves pointing guns at each and by undertaking various other publicity stunts.

They met up at a time when ninety-pound, nineteen-year-old Bonnie, married to a man serving a ninety-nine-year sentence for murder, was, as she said, "bored crapless." Soon they turned to crime (most of the robberies they perpetrated were minor) and Clyde was caught, tried, and jailed. With his brother, Bonnie arranged to smuggle a gun into the prison and Clyde escaped. The jail experience had turned Clyde into a confirmed homosexual, while Bonnie was something of a nymphomaniac, so thereafter they often worked with a male partner both could share.

Nevertheless, the two were devoted to each other. On many occasions when they were trapped in shoot-outs with the law, Clyde heroically fought his way back to save her rather than abandon his woman.

In May 1934, they were betrayed by Henry Methvin, a convict they had helped escape from prison but who informed the Texas Rangers of a rendezvous near Gibland, Louisiana. The pair arrived—Clyde driving in his socks and Bonnie eating a sandwich in a car that held a small arsenal. The waiting lawmen opened fire and the pair died instantly, with a total of forty-eight bullets in their bodies.

Bonnie had predicted this in an oddly modern way a bit earlier, when she sent copies of the popular song "The Ballad of Bonnie and Clyde" to several newspapers. The ballad ended:

> The road gets dimmer and dimmer,
> Sometimes you can hardly see,
> Still it's fight man to man,
> And do all you can,
> For they know they can never be free.
>
> If they try to act like citizens
> And rent them a nice little flat,
> About the third night they are invited to fight
> By a submachine-gun rat-tat-tat.
>
> They don't think they are too tough or desperate,
> They know the law always wins,
> They have been shot at before

But they do not ignore
That death is the wages of sin.

From heartbreaks some people have suffered,
From weariness some people have died,
But take it all in all,
Our troubles are small,
Till we get like Bonnie and Clyde.

Some day they will go down together,
And they will bury them side by side.
To a few it means grief,
To the law it's relief
But it's death to Bonnie and Clyde. *

The Comic Book Hero

Along with Ma Barker, Bonnie and Clyde, Al Capone, John Dillinger, Pretty Boy Floyd, and a host of other criminal "heroes," America has produced a group of purely fictional "comic book" law-enforcing heroes endowed with great intelligence and/or the superhuman powers associated with the heroes of ancient mythology. Dick Tracy and Sam Spade are detectives who exemplify the first type. Characters such as Wonder Woman, Batman, and Superman represent the second.

Superman

The Superman "myth" comes complete with a miraculous birth in another world (the planet Krypton), abandonment of the child (in a space basket sent to Earth), care by people of a "lower order," and miraculous powers, such as immense strength and the ability to see through solid matter. Superman, who takes ordinary human form as Clark Kent, loves fellow reporter Lois Lane. But until recently in the movies, Superman, in the tradition of the true American hero from Natty Bumppo to the Lone Ranger, has resisted sexual entanglements. His concern is to protect his city, Metropolis, and indeed the world from the gangsters and maniacs who attempt to undermine it. Superman's background, his endless crusade against evil, and his his apparent invincibility render him truly heroic, if not godlike.

*Source of information and ballad is Sifakis, 87.

Jesus and Elvis, by Coral Lynn Deibler. Media Xerox, ink, and watercolor on paper. © 1989 Cora Lynn Deibler. Published by Nobleworks, Inc. 1996.

The Rock Hero

Mythic characteristics have been attributed in popular lore to more real and less supernatural figures than Superman. The great rock star Elvis Presley ("the King") has been endowed with Arthurian characteristics, specifically his role as the "once and future king," as in this song by Greg Brown.

Elvis—"Jesus and Elvis"

Jesus had some water, said "Wine'd be better yet."
Elvis picked up a guitar and made all the women wet.

Elvis he died young—Jesus he died younger.
Elvis died of too much—Jesus died of hunger.

Jesus sang down through the ages: "Do like you'd have 'em do to
you."
Elvis rocked the universe with be-bop-a-lu-la—

Now here they are on black velvet, in a parking lot in Missouri—
rocking my soul with rock 'n' roll, soulful harmony.

Jesus went to heaven to be the King of Kings,
but I hear the King of Rock 'n' Roll is still restlessly roaming.

Go on home to Jesus, El—he's waiting there you'll find.
You two can jam on old gospel songs—them are the best kind.*

Among the ways contemporary Americans have indicated a longing for
a mythic hero is by creating and embracing film sagas such as *Star Wars,*
which mythologist Joseph Campbell placed in the context of the traditional hero myth. The movie is "not a simple morality play, it has to do
with the powers of life as they are either fulfilled or broken and sup-
pressed through the action of man."† He compares the film hero's being
trapped in a garbage compressor on the space station to Jonah's being
in the belly of the whale, the heroic "descent into the dark." The evil
Darth Vader is like Mephistopheles, attempting to halt the hero quest
before the achievement of wholeness.

---

*Lyrics by Greg Brown.
†Campbell, *Power*, 145.

African American

The expression of the hero concept among African Americans has necessarily reflected the restricted place of people of African descent in American society. Black heroes around whom legends have developed have included leaders of rebellion or reform, animal tricksters, blues lovers, and workers.

The Slave Rebels

Primary heroes for the slaves were leaders such as Toussaint L'Ouverture of Haiti, who defeated the troops of Napoleon and freed the slaves of his country, or slaves like Gabriel Prosser, Denmark Vesey, Peter Poyas, and Nat Turner, who led rebellions against slave owners in the American South of the early 1800s.

Gabriel Prosser and Denmark Vesey

Gabriel Prosser was a tall man who, it was said, wore his hair long in imitation of his biblical hero, Samson. Prosser's planned rebellion in Richmond in 1800 failed when he was betrayed by a fellow slave and by what the white Virginians called "an act of God," a severe storm that washed out bridges and roads between Richmond and the rendezvous spot of Prosser's army.

Denmark Vesey, like Prosser, was fond of quoting scripture, especially the lines from Joshua that read, "And they utterly destroyed all that was in the city, both man and woman, young and old, and ox, and sheep, and ass, with the edge of the sword." Vesey, who was ably as-

sisted by Peter Poyas, planned an attack on military establishments in Charleston, South Carolina, in July 1822, but they were betrayed and hanged. On the day of his execution Poyas was said to have refused to reveal information about fellow plotters, and he ordered those who were to be hanged with him to "die silent as you shall see me do." Black educator and diplomat Archibald Grimké would say of Poyas's words that "considering the circumstances under which they were spoken, [they] were worthy of a son of Sparta or Rome, when Sparta and Rome were at their highest levels as breeders of men."

Nat Turner

The question of Nat Turner is more complex. The legend begins with the story of Nat's mother's having been tied up to prevent her murdering her son rather than allow him to be born into slavery. Nat grew up in slavery and, like Gabriel Prosser and Denmark Vesey, felt he was called by God "to lead his people out of bondage." Turner, who was always called "the Prophet," was a mystic who had visions—of black and white spirits wrestling in the sky, of blood spouting in streams from ears of corn. According to the story, a spirit came to him and told him that upon receiving a clear sign he must "slay my enemies." It was always said that Turner quoted Jesus's words before the final entry into Jerusalem: "From that time began Jesus to show into his disciples, that he must go unto Jerusalem . . . and be killed." The county seat of South-ampton County, Virginia, was in fact called Jerusalem, and after receiving a sign in the form of a solar oddity that took place on August 13, 1831, he planned his rebellion for August 21.

After a night of ruthless killing of white slave owners and their families, the rebellion was put down and an equally ruthless massacre of slaves followed. Turner himself managed to go into hiding. His presence somewhere in the southern landscape spawned rumors of the imminent arrival of the Prophet and a new army of death. The story is told of how when a small boy in Murfreesboro, North Carolina, called out, "Nat's coming!" the town panicked and several old men died of heart attacks. We are also told that when Turner was finally caught and people in Southampton County cried out, "Nat's caught!" and fired their guns in joy, many women fled the town, thinking that the guns were Turner's and that the cry was, "Nat's coming." The prophet was hanged in Je-rusalem, Virginia, on November 11, 1831. The story goes that Turner had said it would rain when he died, and it did.

Nat Turner's modern hero descendants are figures such as Malcolm X and Martin Luther King, Jr., one expressing the prophet as warrior, one the prophet as preacher, both standing for the liberation of a people in bondage.

Tricksters and the Black Tall Tale

Reactions against slavery were also veiled by the comic stories of animal heroes like the tricksters Brer Rabbit or Aunt Nancy (the Gullah pronunciation of Anansi, the African spider trickster), who, in spite of their small size, often take on and defeat larger and more powerful adversaries by way of their cunning and wit. Aunt Nancy has definite African roots, and Brer Rabbit is clearly based on the Hare stories of East Africa and Native America. Heroes do not always come out on top, especially trickster heroes.

Brer Rabbit and the Tar Baby

This is the famous story of Brer Rabbit and the Tar Baby, which is very similar to a story about Anansi and the Gum Doll, also of African origin. Like so many of the Brer Rabbit tales, it became a part of American folklore in general when it was published by Joel Chandler Harris in the Atlanta Constitution *in the late nineteenth century. The tales were collected in 1880 in* Uncle Remus, His Songs and His Sayings: The Folklore of the Old Plantation *and in* Nights With Uncle Remus and Brer Rabbit.

"Didn't the fox *never* catch the rabbit, Uncle Remus?" asked the little boy the next evening. "He come mighty nigh it, honey, sho's you born— Brer Fox did. One day Brer Fox went ter wuk en got 'im some tar, en mix it wid some turkentime, en fix up a contrapshun w'at he call a Tar-Baby, en he tuck dish yer Tar-Baby en he sot 'er in de big road, en den he lay off in de bushes fer to see what de news wuz gwine ter be. En he didn't hatter wait long, needer, Kaze bimeby here come Brer Rabbit pacin' down de road—lippity-clippity, clippity-lippity—dez ez sassy ez a jaybird. Brer Fox, he lay low. Brer Rabbit come prancin' long twel he spey de Tar-Baby, en den he fotch up on his behime legs like he wuz 'stonished. De Tar-Baby, she sot dar, she did, en Brer Fox, he lay low.
    " 'Mawnin'!' sez Brer Rabbit, sezee—'nice wedder dis mawnin',' sezee. Tar-Baby ain't sayin' nothin', en Brer Fox, he lay low. 'How duz yo' sym'tums seem ter segashuate?,' 'sez Brer Rabbit, sezee. Brer Fox, he wink his eye slow en lay low, en de Tar-Baby, she ain't sayin' nothin'. 'How you come on, den? Is you deaf?' sez Brer Rabbit, sezee. 'If you is, I kin holler louder.' Tar-Baby stay still, en Brer Fox, he lay low.

Brer Fox Laughing at Brer Rabbit Tangled in the Tar Baby. From Joel Chandler Harris, *Uncle Remus, His Songs and His Sayings,* New York: Grossett and Dunlap, 1921. Illustration by A. B. Frost. Courtesy Picture Collection, The Branch Libraries, The New York Public Library.

" 'You er stuck up, dat's w'et you is,' says Brer Rabbit, sezee, 'en I'm gwine ter kyore you, dat's w'at I'm a-gwine ter do,' sezee. Brer Fox, he sorter chuckle in his stummick, he did. 'I'm gwine ter larn you how ter talk ter 'spectubble folks ef hit's de las' ack. Ef you don't take off dat hat en tell me howdy I'm gwine ter bus' you wide open,' sezee. Tar-Baby stay still, en Brer Fox, he lay low. Brer Rabbit keep on axin' im, en de Tar-Baby, she keep on sayin' nothin', twel present'y Brer Rabbit draw back wid his fis', he did, en blip he tuck 'er side er de head. Right dar's whar he broke his merlasses jug. His fis' stuck, en he can't pull loose. De tar hilt 'im. But Tar-Baby, she stay still, en Brer Fox, he lay low. 'Ef you don't lemme loose, I'll knock you agin,' sez Brer Rabbit, sezee, en wid dat he fotch 'er a swipe wid de udder han', en dat stuck. Tar-Baby, she ain't sayin' nothin', en Brer Fox, he lay low. 'Tu'n me loose 'fo' I kick de natchul stuffin' outen you,' sez Brer Rabbit, sezee, but de Tar-Baby, she ain't sayin' nothin'. She des hilt on, en den Brer Rabbit lose de use er his feet in de same way. Brer Fox, he lay low. Den Brer Rabbit squall out dat ef de Tar-Baby don't tu'n 'im loose he butt 'er cranksided. En den he butted, en his head got stuck. Den Brer Fox, he sa'ntered fort', lookin' des ez innercent ez a mockin'bird.

" 'Howdy, Brer Rabbit,' sez Brer Fox, sezee. 'You look sorter stuck up dis mawnin',' sezee, en den he rolled on de groun' en laughed en laughed twel he couldn't laugh no mo'.' "

Here Uncle Remus paused and drew a two-pound yam out of the ashes. "Did the fox eat the rabbit?" asked the little boy to whom the story had been told. "Dat's all de fur de tale goes," replied the old man. "He mought, en den again he moughtent. Some say Jedge B'ar come along en loosed 'im—some say no. I hear Miss Sally callin'. You better run 'long."

Stagolee

Stagolee (Staggerlee, Stackalee) is the epitome of the "bad" (in every sense of that word) "nigger." He is the tall-tale postslavery urban representation—usually comic—of the black man who refuses to accept a second-place position in society—a version of the beloved outlaw so popular in other segments of American society as well. He is afraid of neither white nor black and he gets away with it. In an old ballad, based on a real incident, Stagolee (in real life, probably Stacker Lee of Memphis or St. Louis) kills a man, Billy Lyons, for stealing the magic Stetson that gives him trickster or shape-shifting capabilities. This version of the Stagolee–Billy Lyons legend is told by scholar Julius Lester.

Stagolee was, undoubtedly and without question, the baddest nigger that ever lived. Stagolee was so bad that the flies wouldn't even fly around his head in the summertime, and snow wouldn't fall on his house in the winter. He was bad, jim.

Stagolee grew up on a plantation in Georgia, and by the time he was two, he'd decided that he wasn't going to spend his life picking cotton and working for white folks. Uh-uh. And when he was five, he left. Took off down the road, his guitar on his back, a deck of cards in one pocket and a .44 in the other. He figured that he didn't need nothing else. When the women heard him whup the blues on the guitar he could have whichever one he laid his mind on. Whenever he needed money, he could play cards. And whenever somebody tried to mess with him, he had his .44. So he was ready. A man didn't need more than that to get along with in the world.

By the time Stack was grown, his reputation had spread around the country. It got started one night in one of them honky-tonks down there in Alabama, and Stagolee caught some dude trying to deal from the bottom of the deck. Ol' Stack pulled out his .44 and killed him dead, right there on the spot. Then he moved the dead guy over to the center of the room and used the body as a card table. Another time, something similar happened, and Stack pulled the body over next to him, so a buddy of his, who was kinda short, would have something to sit on. Didn't take long for the word to get around that this was one bad dude! Even white folks didn't mess with Stagolee.

Well, this one time, Stagolee was playing cards with a dude they called Billy Lyons. Billy Lyons was one of them folk who acted like they were a little better than anybody else. He'd had a little education, and that stuff can really mess your mind up. Billy Lyons had what he called a "scientific method" of cardplaying. Stagolee had the "nigger method." So they got to playing, and, naturally, Stagolee was just taking all of Billy Lyons's money, and Billy got mad. He got so mad that he reached over and knocked Stagolee's Stetson hat off his head and spit in it.

What'd he do that for? He could've done almost anything else in the world, but not that. Stack pulled his .44, and Billy started copping his plea. "Now, listen here, Mr. Stagolee. I didn't mean no harm. I just lost my head for a minute. I was wrong, and I apologize." He reached down on the ground, picked up Stack's Stetson, brushed it off, and put it back on his head. "I didn't mean no harm. See, the hat's all right. I put it back on your head." Billy was tomming like a champ, but Stack wasn't smiling. "Don't shoot me. Please, Mr. Stagolee! I got two children and a wife to support. You understand?"

Stack said, "Well, that's all right. The Lawd'll take care of your children. I'll take care of your wife." And, with that, Stagolee blowed Billy Lyons away. Stagolee looked at the body for a minute and then went off to Billy Lyons's house and told Mrs. Billy that her husband was dead and he was moving in. And that's just what he did, too. Moved in.

Now there was this new sheriff in town, and he had gotten the word about Stagolee, but this sheriff was a sho' nuf' cracker. He just couldn't stand the idea of Stagolee walking around like he was free—not working, not buying war bonds, cussing out white folks. He just couldn't put up with it, so, when he heard that Stagolee had shot Billy Lyons, he figured that this was his chance.

Sheriff told his deputies, said, "All right, men. Stagolee killed a man tonight. We got to get him."

The deputies looked at him. "Well, sheriff. Ain't nothing wrong with killing a man every now and then," said one.

"It's good for a man's health," added another.

"Well," said the sheriff, "that's all right for a white man, but this is a nigger."

"Now, sheriff, you got to watch how you talk about Stagolee. He's one of the leaders of the community here. You just can't come in here and start talking about one of our better citizens like that."

The sheriff looked at them. "I believe you men are afraid. Afraid of a nigger!"

Deputies thought it over for half a second. "Sheriff. Let's put it this way. We have a healthy respect for Stagolee. A long time ago, we struck a bargain with him. We promised him that if he let us alone, we'd let him alone. And everything has worked out just fine."

"Well, we're going to arrest Stagolee," the sheriff said. "Get your guns, and let's go."

The deputies stood up, took their guns, and laid 'em on the shelf. "Sheriff, if you want Stagolee, well, you can arrest him by yourself." And they went on out the door and over to the undertaker's parlor and told him to start making a coffin for the sheriff.

When all the other white folks heard what the sheriff was going to do, they ran over to talk to him. "Sheriff, you can't go around disturbing the peace." But couldn't nobody talk no sense into him.

Now Stagolee heard that the sheriff was looking for him, and, being a gentleman, Stagolee got out of bed, told Mrs. Billy he'd be back in a little while, and went on down to the bar. He'd barely gotten the first drink down when the sheriff came stepping through the door.

He walked over to the bartender. "Barkeep? Who's that man down at the other end of the bar? You know there's a law in this town against drinking after midnight. Who is that?"

Bartender leaned over the counter and whispered in his ear, "Don't talk so loud. That's Stagolee. He drinks when he gets thirsty and he's generally thirsty after midnight."

Sheriff walked over to Stagolee. Stagolee didn't even look around. Sheriff fired a couple of shots in the air. Stagolee poured himself another drink and threw it down. Finally, the sheriff said, "Stagolee, I'm the sheriff, and I'm white. Ain't you afraid?"

Stagolee turned around slowly. "You may be the sheriff, and you may be white, but you ain't Stagolee. Now deal with that."

The sheriff couldn't even begin to figure it out, no less deal with it, so he fell back in his familiar bag. "I'm placing you under arrest for the murder of Billy Lyons."

"You and what army? And it bet' not be the United States Army, 'cause I whupped them already."

"Me and this army," the sheriff growled, jabbing the pistol in Stack's ribs.

Before the sheriff could take another breath, Stagolee hit him upside the head and sent him flying across the room. Stagolee pulled out his gun, put three bullets in him, put his gun away, had another drink, and was on his way out the door before the body hit the floor.

The next day, Stagolee went to both of the funerals to pay his last respects to the sheriff and Billy Lyons, and then he settled down to living with Mrs. Billy. She really didn't mind too much. All the women knew how good-looking Stack was. And he was always respectful to women, always had plenty of money, and, generally, he made a good husband, as husbands go. Stagolee had one fault, though. Sometimes he drank too much. About once a month, Stagolee would buy up all the available liquor and moonshine in the county and proceed to get wasted, and when Stagolee got wasted, he got totally wasted.

The new sheriff waited until one of those nights when Stagolee was so drunk he was staggering in his sleep, and he was lying flat in the bed. If Judgment Day had come, the Lord would have had to postpone it until Stagolee had sobered up. Otherwise, the Lord might've ended up getting Gabriel shot and his trumpet wrapped around his head. When the sheriff saw Stagolee that drunk, he went and got together the Ku Klux Klan Alumni Association, which was every white man in four counties. After the sheriff had assured them that Stagolee was so drunk he couldn't wake up, they broke in the house just as bad as you please. They had the lynching rope all ready, and they dropped it around his neck. The minute that rope touched Stack's neck, he was wide awake and stone cold sober. When white folks saw that, they were falling over each other getting out of there. But Stack was cool. He should've been. He invented it.

"Y'all come to hang me?"

The sheriff said that that was so. Stagolee stood up, stretched, yawned, and scratched himself a couple of times. "Well, since I can't seem to get no sleep, let's go and get this thing over with so I can get on back to bed."

They took him on out behind the jail where the gallows was built. Stagolee got up on the scaffold, and the sheriff dropped the rope around his neck and tightened it. Then the hangman opened up on the trap door, and there was Stack, swinging ten feet in the air, laughing as loud as you ever heard anybody laugh. They let him hang there for a half-hour, and Stagolee was still laughing.

"Hey, man! This rope is ticklish."

The white folks looked at each other and realized that Stack's neck just wouldn't crack. So they cut him down, and Stagolee went back home and went back to bed.

After that, the new sheriff left Stagolee in peace, like he should've done to begin with.

Stagolee lived on and on, and that was his big mistake. 'Cause Stagolee lived so long, he started attracting attention up in Heaven. One day, St. Peter was looking down on the earth, and he happened to notice Stack sitting on the porch picking on the guitar. "Ain't that Stagolee?" St. Peter said to himself. He took a closer look. "That's him. That's him. Why, that nigger should've been dead a long time ago." So St. Peter went and looked it up in the record book, and sure enough, Stagolee was supposed to have died thirty years before.

St. Peter went to see the Lord.

"What's going on, St. Peter?"

"Oh, ain't nothing shaking Lord. Well, that's not totally true. I was just checking out earth, and there's a nigger down there named Stagolee who is way overdue for a visit from Death."

"Is that so?"

"It's the truth, Lord."

"Well, we have to do something about that."

The Lord cleared his throat a couple of times and hollered out, "HEY, DEATH! HEEEEY, DEATH!"

Now Death was laying up down in the barn catching up on some sleep, 'cause he was tired. Having to make so many trips to Vietnam was wearing him out, not to mention everywhere else in the world. He just couldn't understand why dying couldn't be systematized. He'd tried his best to convince God either to get a system to dying or get him some assistants. He'd proposed that, say, on Mondays, the only dying that would be done would be, say, in France, Germany, and a few other counties. Tuesday it'd be some other countries, and on like that. That way, he wouldn't have to be running all over the world twenty-four hours a day. But the Lord had vetoed the idea. Said it sounded to him like Death just wanted an excuse to eventually computerize the whole operation. Death had to admit that the thought had occurred to him. He didn't know when he was going to catch up on all the paperwork he had to do. A computer would solve everything. And now, just when he was getting to sleep, here come the Lord waking him up.

So Death got on his pale white horse. He was so tired of riding a horse he didn't know what to do. He'd talked to God a few months ago about letting him get a helicopter or something. But the Lord just didn't seem to understand. Death rode on off down through the streets of Heaven, and when folks heard him coming, they closed their doors, 'cause even in Heaven, folks were afraid of Death. And that was the other thing. Death was mighty lonely. Didn't nobody talk to him, and he was getting a little tired of it. He wished the Lord would at least let him wear a suit and tie and look respectable. Maybe then he could meet some nice young angel and raise a family. The Lord had vetoed that idea, too.

"What took you so long, Death?"

"Aw, Lord. I was trying to get some sleep. You just don't realize how fast folks are dying these days."

"Don't tell me you gon' start complaining again."

"I'm sorry, Lord, but I'd like to see you handle the job as well as I do with no help, no sleep, no wife, no nothing."

"Well, I got a special job for you today."

"Can't wait until tomorrow?"

"No, it can't wait, Death! Now hush up. There's a man in Fatback, Georgia, named Stagolee. You should've picked him up thirty years ago, and I want you to send me a memo on why you didn't."

"Well, I got such a backlog of work piled up."

"I don't want to have to be doing your job for you. You get the lists every day from the Record Bureau. How come you missed this one? If he's escaped for thirty years, who knows who else has been living way past their time. Speaking of folks living past their time. St. Peter, have the librarian bring me all the files on white folks. Seems to me that white folks sho' done outlived their time. Anyway, Death, go on down there and get Stagolee."

Death headed on down to earth. A long time ago, he used to enjoy the ride, but not anymore. There were so many satellites and other pieces of junk flying around through the air that it was like going through a junkyard barefooted. So he didn't waste any time getting on down to Fatback, Georgia.

Now on this particular day, Stagolee was sitting on the porch, picking the blues on the guitar, and drinking. All of a sudden, he looked up and saw this pale-looking white cat in this white sheet come riding up to his house on a white horse. "We ain't never had no Klan in the daytime before," Stagolee said.

Death got off his horse, pulled out his address book, and said, "I'm looking for Stagolee Booker T. Washington Nicodemus Shadrack Nat Turner Jones."

"Hey, baby! You got it down pat! I'd forgotten a couple of them names myself."

"Are you Stagolee Booker T. Wash—"

"You ain't got to go through the thing again. I'm the dude. What's going on?"

"I'm Death. Come with me."

Stagolee started laughing. "You who?"

"I'm Death. Come on, man. I ain't got all day."

"Be serious."

Death looked at Stagolee. No one had ever accused him of joking before. "I *am* serious. It's your time to die. Now come on here!"

"Man, you ain't bad enough to mess with me."

Death blinked his eyes. He'd never run up on a situation like this before. Sometimes folks struggled a little bit, but they didn't refuse. "Stagolee, let's go!" Death said in his baddest voice.

"Man, you must want to get shot."

Death thought that one over for a minute. Now he didn't know how to handle this situation, so he reached in his saddlebags and pulled out his *Death Manual.* He looked up *resistance* and read what it said, but wasn't a thing in there about what to do when somebody threatens you. Then he looked up *guns* but that wasn't listed. He looked under everything he could think of, but nothing was of any help. So he went back to the porch. "You coming or not, Stagolee?"

Stagolee let one of them .44 bullets whistle past ol' Death's ear, and Death got hot. Death didn't waste no time getting away from there. Before he was sitting in the saddle good, he had made it back to Heaven.

"Lord! You must be trying to get me killed."

"Do what? Get you killed? Since when could you die?"

"Don't matter, but that man Stagolee you just sent me after took a shot at me. Now listen here, Lord, if you want that man dead, you got to get him yourself. I am not going back after him. I knew there was some reason I let him live thirty years too long. I'd heard about him on the grapevine and, for all I care, he can live three hundred more years. I am not going back—"

"O.K. O.K. You made your point. Go on back to sleep." After Death had gone, God turned to St. Peter and asked, "We haven't had any new applications for that job recently?"

"You must be joking."

"Well, I was just checking." The Lord lit a cigar. "Pete, looks like I'm going to have to use one of my giant death thunderbolts to get that Stagolee."

"Looks that way. You want me to tell the work crew?"

The Lord nodded, and St. Peter left. It took 3,412 angels 14 days, 11 hours, and 32 minutes to carry the giant death thunderbolt to the Lord, but he just reached down and picked it up like it was a toothpick.

"Uh, St. Peter? How you spell Stagolee?"

"Lord, you know everything. You're omnipotent, omniscient, omni—"

"You better shut up and tell me how to spell Stagolee."

St. Peter spelled it out for him, and the Lord wrote it on the thunderbolt. Then he blew away a few clouds and put his keen eye down on the earth. "Hey, St. Peter. Will you look at all that killing down there? I ain't never seen nothing like it."

"Lord, that ain't Georgia. That's Vietnam."

The Lord put his great eye across the world. "Tsk, tsk, tsk. Look at all that sin down there. Women wearing hardly no clothes at all. Check that one out with the black hair, St. Peter. Look at her! Disgraceful! Them legs!"

"LORD!"

And the Lord put his eye on the earth and went on across the United States—Nevada, Utah, Colorado, Kansas, Missouri—

"Turn right at the Mississippi, Lord!"

The Lord turned right and went on down into Tennessee.

"Make a left at Memphis, Lord!"

The Lord turned left at Memphis and went on up through Nashville and on down to Chattanooga into Georgia. Atlanta, Georgia. Valdosta. Rolling Stone, Georgia, until he got way back out in the woods to Fatback. He let his eye go up and down the country roads until he saw Stagolee sitting on the porch.

"That's him, Lord! That's him!"

And the Great God Almighty, the God of Nat Turner and Rap Brown, the God of Muddy Waters and B. B. King, the God of Aretha Franklin and The Impressions, this great God Almighty Everlasting, *et in terra pax hominibus,* and all them other good things, drew back his mighty arm—

"Watch your aim now, Lord."

And unloosed the giant thunderbolt. BOOM!

That was the end of Stagolee. You can't mess with the Lord.

Well, when the people found out Stagolee was dead, you ain't never heard such hollering and crying in all your life. The women were beside themselves with grief, 'cause Stagolee was nothing but a sweet man.

Come the day of the funeral, and Stagolee was laid out in a $10,000 casket. Had on a silk mohair suit and his Stetson hat was in his hand. In his right coat pocket was a brand new deck of cards. In his left coat pocket was a brand new .44 with some extra rounds of ammunition and a can of Mace. And by his side was his guitar. Folks came from all over the country to Stack's funeral, and all of 'em put little notes in Stagolee's other pockets, which were messages they wanted Stagolee to give to their kinfolk when he got to Hell.

The funeral lasted for three days and three nights. All the guitar pickers and blues singers had to come sing one last song for Stagolee.

All the backsliders had to come backslide one more time for Stagolee. All the gamblers had to come touch Stack's casket for a little taste of good luck. And all the women had to come shed a tear as they looked at him for the last time. Those that had known him were crying about what they weren't going to have any more. And those that hadn't known him were crying over what they had missed. Even the little bitty ones was shedding tears.

After all the singing and crying and shouting was over, they took Stagolee on out and buried him. They didn't bury him in the cemetery. Uh-uh. Stagolee had to have a cemetery all his own. They dug his grave with a silver spade and lowered him down with a golden chain. And they went on back to their homes, not quite ready to believe that Stack was dead and gone.

But you know, it's mighty hard to keep a good man down, and long about the third day, Stagolee decided to get on up out of the grave and go check out Heaven. Stack just couldn't see himself waiting for Judgment Day. The thought of the white man blowing the trumpet on Judgment Day made him sick to his stomach, and Stagolee figured he was supposed to have his own Judgment Day, anyhow.

He started on off for Heaven. Of course it took him a long time to get there, 'cause he had to stop on all the clouds and teach the little angels to play Pittat and Coon-Can and all like that, but, eventually, he got near to Heaven. Now as he got close, he started hearing all this harp music and hymn singing. Stagolee couldn't believe his ears. He listened some more, and then he shrugged his shoulders. "I'm approaching Heaven from the wrong side. This can't be the black part of Heaven, not with all that hymn singing and harp music I hear."

So Stack headed on around to the other side of heaven, and when he got there, it was stone deserted. I mean, wasn't nobody there. Streets was as empty as the President's mind. So Stack cut on back around to the other side of Heaven. When he got there, St. Peter was playing bridge with Abraham, Jonah, and Mrs. God. When they looked up and saw who it was, though, they split, leaving St. Peter there by himself.

"You ain't getting in here!" St. Peter yelled.

"Don't want to either. Hey, man. Where all the colored folks at?"

"We had to send 'em all to Hell. We used to have quite a few, but they got to rocking the church service, you know. Just couldn't even sing a hymn without it coming out and sounding like the blues. So we had to get rid of 'em. We got a few nice colored folks left. And they nice, respectable people."

Stagolee laughed. "Hey, man. You messed up."

"Huh?"

"Yeah, man. This ain't Heaven. This is Hell. Bye."

And Stagolee took off straight for Hell. He was about 2,000 miles away, and he could smell the barbecue cooking and hear the jukeboxes playing, and he started running. He got there, and there was a big BLACK POWER sign on the gate. He rung on the bell, and the dude who come to answer it recognized him immediately. "Hey, everybody! Stagolee's here!"

And the folks came running from everywhere to greet him.

"Hey, baby!"

"What's going down!"

"What took you so long to get here?"

Stagolee walked in, and the brothers and sisters had put down wall-to-wall carpeting, indirect lighting, and best of all, they'd installed air-conditioning. Stagolee walked around, checking it all out. "Yeah. Y'all got it together. Got it uptight!"

After he'd finished checking it out, he asked "Any white folks down here?"

"Just the hip ones, and ain't too many of them. But they all right. They know where it's at."

"Solid." Stagolee noticed an old man sitting over in a corner with his hands over his ears. "What's his problem?"

"Aw, that's the Devil. He just can't get himself together. He ain't learned how to deal with niggers yet."

Stagolee walked over to him. "Hey, man. Get your pitchfork, and let's have some fun. I got my .44. C'mon. Let's go one round."

The Devil just looked at Stagolee real sadlike, but didn't say a word.

Stagolee took the pitchfork and laid it on the shelf. "Well, that's hip. I didn't want no stuff out of you nohow I'm gon' rule Hell by myself!"

And that's just what he did, too.*

John Henry

John Henry was a black tall-tale rival to Paul Bunyan and Stagolee. He is the legendary expression of the black man's strength in the new Industrial Age. Henry's story is in all likelihood based on real events associated with the building of the Big Bend Tunnel of the Chesapeake and Ohio Railroad in West Virginia in the 1870s. It is a celebration of African American potency and strength in the face of continued mockery and oppression. John Henry is the black Herakles. His tragic victory

---

*From Lester, *Black Folktales*. Quoted in Worley and Perry, 57–65.

John Henry. U.S. postage stamp. By permission: U.S. Postal Service.

has, through the ballad bearing his name, become a standard element of American folklore.

> John Henry was a li'l baby, uh-huh,
> Sittin' on his mama's knee, oh, yeah,
> Said: "De Big Bend Tunnel on de C. & O. road
> Gonna cause de death of me,
> Lawd, Lawd, gonna cause de death of me."
>
> John Henry, he had a woman,
> Her name was Mary Magdalene,
> She would go to de tunnel and sing for John,
> Jes' to hear John Henry's hammer ring,
> Lawd, Lawd, jes' to hear John Henry's hammer ring.
>
> John Henry had a li'l woman,
> Her name was Lucy Ann,

John Henry took sick an' had to go to bed,
Lucy Ann drove steel like a man,
Lawd, Lawd, Lucy Ann drove steel like a man.

Cap'n says to John Henry,
"Gonna bring me a steam drill 'round,
Gonna take dat steam drill out on de job,
Gonna whop dat steel on down,
Lawd, Lawd, gonna whop dat steel on down."

John Henry tol' his cap'n,
Lightnin' was in his eye:
"Cap'n, bet yo' las' red cent on me,
Fo' I'll beat it to de bottom or I'll die,
Lawd, Lawd, I'll beat it to de bottom or I'll die."

Sun shine hot an' burnin',
Wer'n't no breeze a-tall,
Sweat ran down like water down a hill,
Dat day John Henry let his hammer fall,
Lawd, Lawd, dat day John Henry let his hammer fall.

John Henry went to de tunnel,
An' dey put him in de lead to drive;
De rock so tall an' John Henry so small,
Dat he lied down his hammer an' he cried,
Lawd, Lawd, dat he lied down his hammer an' he cried.

John Henry started on de right hand,
De steam drill started on de lef'—
"Before I'd let dis steam drill beat me down,
I'd hammer my fool self to death,
Lawd, Lawd, I'd hammer my fool self to death."

White man tol' John Henry,
"Nigger, damn yo' soul,
You might beat dis steam an' drill of mine,
When de rocks in dis mountain turn to gol',
Lawd, Lawd, when de rocks in dis mountain turn to gol'."

John Henry said to his shaker,
"Nigger, why don' you sing?
I'm throwin' twelve poun's from my hips on down,

Jes' listen to de col' steel ring,
Lawd, Lawd, jes' listen to de col' steel ring."

Oh, de captain said to John Henry,
"I b'lieve this mountain's sinkin' in."
John Henry said to his captain, oh my!
"Ain' nothin' but my hammer suckin' win',
Lawd, Lawd, ain' nothin' but my hammer suckin' win'."

John Henry tol' his shaker,
"Shaker, you better pray,
For, if I miss dis six-foot steel,
Tomorrow'll be yo' buryin' day,
Lawd, Lawd, tomorrow'll be yo' buryin' day."

John Henry tol' his captain,
"Looka yonder what I see—
Yo' drill's done broke an' yo' hole's done choke,
An' you cain' drive steel like me,
Lawd, Lawd, an' you cain' drive steel like me."

De man dat invented de steam drill,
Thought he was mighty fine.
John Henry drove his fifteen feet,
An' de steam drill only made nine,
Lawd, Lawd, an' de steam drill only made nine.

De hammer dat John Henry swung
It weighed over nine pound;
He broke a rib in his lef'-han' side,
An' his intrels fell on de groun',
Lawd, Lawd, an' his intrels fell on de groun'.

John Henry was hammerin' on de mountain,
An' his hammer was strikin' fire,
He drove so hard till he broke his pore heart,
An' he lied down his hammer an' he died,
Lawd, Lawd, he lied down his hammer an' he died.

All de womens in de Wes',
When de heared of John Henry's death,
Stood in de rain, flagged de eas'-boun' train,
Goin' where John Henry fell dead,
Lawd, Lawd, goin' where John Henry fell dead.

John Henry's li'l mother,
She was all dressed in red,
She jumped in bed, covered up her head,
Said she didn' know her son was dead,
Lawd, Lawd, didn' know her son was dead.

John Henry had a pretty li'l woman,
An' de dress she wo' was blue,
An' de las' words she said to him:
"John Henry, I've been true to you,
Lawd, Lawd, John Henry, I've been true to you."*

Blues Lovers and Legends in Cool

"Frankie and Johnny"

Frankie and her unfortunate boyfriend Johnny (sometimes called Albert) are the protagonists of a blues ballad that, like the Stagolee legend, emerged from the post–Civil War urban life of African Americans. It was probably based on a true incident in St. Louis. The "hero" of this version of the archetypal tale of the tragic love affair is Frankie, who shoots her man dead for his infidelities.

Frankie and Johnny were lovers, O Lordy, how they could love.
Swore to be true to each other, true as the stars above;
He was her man, but he done her wrong.

Frankie she was a good woman, just like everyone knows.
She spent a hundred dollars for a suit of Johnny's clothes.
He was her man, but he done her wrong.

Frankie and Johnny went walking, Johnny in a brand-new suit.
"Oh, good Lord," says Frankie, "but don't my Johnny look cute?"
He was her man, but he done her wrong.

Frankie went down to Memphis, she went on the evening train.
She paid one hundred dollars for Johnny's watch and chain.
He was her man, but he done her wrong.

*Lomax and Lomax, 5–9.

Frankie lived in the crib house, crib house had only two doors;
Gave all her money to Johnny, he spent it on those call-house
   whores.
He was her man, but he done her wrong.

Johnny's mother told him, and she was mighty wise,
"Don't spend Frankie's money on that parlor Alice Pry.
You're Frankie's man, and you're doing her wrong."

Frankie and Johnny were lovers, they had a quarrel one day,
Johnny he up and told Frankie, "Bye-bye, babe, I'm going away.
I was your man, but I'm just gone."

Frankie went down to the corner to buy a glass of beer.
Says to the fat bartender, "Has my lovingest man been here?
He was my man, but he's doing me wrong."

"Ain't going to tell you no story, ain't going to tell you no lie,
I seen your man 'bout an hour ago with a girl named Alice Pry.
If he's your man, he's doing you wrong."

Frankie went down to the pawnshop, she didn't go there for fun;
She hocked all of her jewelry, bought a pearl-handled forty-four
   gun
For to get her man who was doing her wrong.

Frankie she went down Broadway, with her gun in her hand,
Sayin', "Stand back, all you livin' women, I'm a-looking for my
   gambolin' man.
For he's my man, won't treat me right."

Frankie went down to the hotel, looked in the window so high,
There she saw her loving Johnny a-loving up Alice Pry.
Damn his soul, he was mining in coal.

Frankie went down to the hotel, she rang that hotel bell.
"Stand back, all of you chippies, or I'll blow you all to hell.
I want my man, who's doing me wrong."

Frankie threw back her kimono, she took out her forty-four,
Root-a-toot-toot three times she shot right through that hotel
   door.
She was after her man who was doing her wrong.

Johnny grabbed off his Stetson, "Oh, good Lord, Frankie, don't
   shoot!"

But Frankie pulled the trigger and the gun went root-a-toot-toot.
He was her man, but she shot him down.

Johnny he mounted the staircase, crying, "Oh, Frankie, don't you
    shoot!"
Three times she pulled that forty-four a-root-a-toot-toot-toot-toot.
She shot her man who threw her down.

First time she shot him he staggered, second time she shot him he
    fell.
Third time she shot him, O Lordy, there was a new man's face in
    hell.
She killed her man who had done her wrong.

"Roll me over easy, roll me over slow,
Roll me over on my left side for the bullet hurt me so.
I was her man, but I done her wrong."

"Oh my baby, kiss me, once before I go.
Turn me over on my right side, the bullet hurt me so.
I was your man, but I done you wrong."

Johnny he was a gambler, he gambled for the gain,
The very last words that Johnny said were, "High-low Jack and
    the game."
He was her man, but he done her wrong.

Frankie heard a rumbling away down in the ground.
Maybe it was Johnny where she had shot him down.
He was her man and she done him wrong.

Oh, bring on your rubber-tired hearses, bring on your rubber-tired
    hacks,
They're taking Johnny to the cemetery and they ain't a-bringing
    him back.
He was her man, but he done her wrong.

Eleven macks a-riding to the graveyard, all in a rubber-tired hack,
Eleven macks a-riding to the graveyard, only ten a-coming back.
He was her man, but he done her wrong.

Frankie went to the coffin, she looked down on Johnny's face,
She said, "Oh, Lord, have mercy on me. I wish I could take his
    place.
He was my man and I done him wrong."

Frankie went to Mrs. Halcomb, she fell down on her knees,
She said to Mrs. Halcomb, "Forgive me if you please.
I've killed my man for doing me wrong."

"Forgive you, Frankie darling, forgive you I never can.
Forgive you, Frankie darling, for killing your only man.
He was your man, though he done you wrong."

The judge said to the jury, "It's as plain as plain can be.
This woman shot her man, it's murder in the second degree.
He was her man, though he done her wrong."

Now it was not murder in the second degree, it was not murder in
   the third.
The woman simply dropped her man, like a hunter drops his bird.
He was her man and he done her wrong.

"Oh, bring a thousand policemen, bring them around today,
Oh, lock me in that dungeon and throw the key away.
I killed my man 'cause he done me wrong."

"Oh, put me in that dungeon. Oh, put me in that cell,
Put me where the northeast wind blows from the southwest corner
   of hell.
I shot my man 'cause he done me wrong."

Frankie walked up the scaffold, as calm as a girl can be,
And turning her eyes to heaven she said, "Good Lord, I'm coming
   to thee.
He was my man, and I done him wrong."*

✳

In addition to the songs that have become classics, African American
music—particularly blues and jazz, born of urban life—has produced
several real-life heroes who have become legends.

Bessie Smith

*Bessie Smith (1894–1937) was the "Empress of the Blues." She learned
much from the "Mother of the Blues," Gertrude "Ma" Rainey. The
stories about Bessie Smith are part legend, part fact. It is said that she
started singing and dancing at the age of ten outside the White Elephant*

---

*Battle, 218–21.

saloon in the slums of Chattanooga, Tennessee. As men threw her coins she would respond with witticisms like, "That's right Charlie, give to the Church." Some say that the eleven-year-old Bessie was kidnapped in a burlap bag and delivered to Ma Rainey, who gave her singing lessons. By the 1920s Bessie Smith was generally hailed as "Queen of the Blues." Later she was called "Empress." Alcohol had become a problem for her by that time, too, and there are countless stories of drunken scenes. Smith died after an automobile accident in Clarksdale, Mississippi; according to one story, because she was black she was refused admittance to a hospital and so bled to death. Both the real and legendary aspects of the Bessie Smith story convey a true-to-life facet of the lives of black people in America.

Billie Holiday—"Lady Sings the Blues"

The story of Billie Holiday (1915–1959) can stand as another blues representation of life for black Americans. She sang often with another jazz myth, "Count" William Basie (1904–1984), who learned from Thomas "Fats" Waller (1904–43). Known as "Lady Day," Holiday lived the life of a tragic heroine. A performer from the age of fifteen, overworked, abused by unscrupulous promoters and lovers, she died in misery. Her signature song, "Lady Sings the Blues," speaks not only for blues heroines such as Billie Holiday, Bessie Smith, Ma Rainey, and Nina Simone, but for black women, women in general, and a whole race, for whose condition the song is an elaborate metaphor.

> Lady sings the blues
> She's got them bad
> She feels so sad
> Wants the world to know
> Just what her blues is all about.
>
> Lady sings the blues
> She tells her side
> Nothing to hide
> Now the world will know
> Just what her blues is all about.
>
> The blues ain't nothing
> But a pain in your heart
> When you get a bad start
> You and your man have to part
> I ain't gonna just sit around and cry

And I know I won't die
Because I love him

Lady sings the blues
She's got them bad
She feels so sad
But now the world will know
She's never gonna sing 'em no more
No more.

The jazz world has also been a venue for the "cool" male hero. Trumpeter John Birks "Dizzy" Gillespie (1917–1993) was the "King of Bop," and he mythologized himself, not only by developing bop with Charlie "Bird" or "Yardbird" Parker (1920–1955) in the 1940s, but by wearing a goatee, a beret, and heavy glasses, a style that was copied by his admirers.

The image of the "cool" African American man whose clothes, walking style, gestures, and speech patterns are copied by others is ubiquitous in American life. Whether athletes such as Wilt Chamberlain and Michael Jordan or singers such as Sam Cook, Otis Redding, and Marvin Gay, whole mythologies are built around these heroes—mythologies that include such themes as mysterious origins, great amorous powers, amazing physical feats, and tragic deaths.

Leader Heroes

African Americans have never been short of great leader heroes. Booker T. Washington, although accepting political submission, was a leader for economic improvement in the late nineteenth and early twentieth centuries. W. E. B. DuBois was a more radical champion of black rights in the same period and beyond, and so was the much less well known Monroe Trotter. Mary McLeod Bethune was an important leader for civil rights in the 1930s and 1940s, and Thurgood Marshall provided leadership at the NAACP and later from his seat on the Supreme Court. Of the early-twentieth-century leaders, Marcus Garvey was the most charismatic and visionary. Garvey organized the first mass black nationalist movement and coordinated significant economic and political activity in black communities. He celebrated his movement with elaborate parades, a black nationalist flag, corps of "Black Star" nurses, and African Legion marchers in uniform.

But it is two great leaders in the later twentieth century, Martin Luther King, Jr. (1929–1968) and Malcolm X (1925–1965), who have most successfully found their way into what can be called American myth and legend as a whole. King and Malcolm X represent different approaches to the problem of black deprivation, but they have both achieved the level of the heroic. In part this is because, like white leaders John F. Kennedy and Robert Kennedy, they were victims of assassins' bullets in a volatile age. But mostly it was because both men possessed the vision and charisma of a Marcus Garvey and the intelligence and the persuasive genius of a W. E. B. DuBois. People did not just listen to Martin and Malcolm; they believed in them, and still do.

Martin Luther King, Jr.—"I Have a Dream"

King, with other mainline black leaders, led the fight for the desegregation and integration of American society in the 1960s. His movement was marked by nonviolent protest influenced by India's Mahatma Gandhi. As such, it was a movement in which progressive whites felt welcome. In terms of American legend, as opposed to the political and social reality, which was much more complex, King's movement and his heroism reached its zenith during his keynote address to the 250,000 people who attended his great March on Washington on August 28, 1963. In that speech King articulated his vision of a new America of community, sharing, and gentleness—a new American dream to replace the old one of manifest destiny and the almighty dollar. It was a speech that echoed but went beyond the famous Gettysburg Address of the "Great Emancipator," Abraham Lincoln, whose speech had begun "Fourscore and seven years ago. . . ."

I am happy to join with you today in what will go down in history as the greatest demonstration for freedom in the history of our nation.

Five score years ago a great American in whose symbolic shadow we stand today signed the Emancipation Proclamation. This momentous decree is a great beacon light of hope to millions of Negro slaves who had been seared in the flames of withering injustice. It came as a joyous daybreak to end the long night of their captivity. But 100 years later the Negro still is not free. One hundred years later the life of the Negro is still badly crippled by the manacles of segregation and the chains of discrimination. One hundred years later the Negro lives on a lonely island of poverty in the midst of a vast ocean of material prosperity. One hundred years later the Negro is still languished in the corners of American society and finds himself in exile in his own land. So we've come here today to dramatize a shameful condition.

In a sense we've come to our nation's capital to cash a check. When the architects of our Republic wrote the magnificent words of the Constitution and the Declaration of Independence, they were signing a promissory note to which every American was to fall heir. This note was a promise that all men—yes, black men as well as white men—would be guaranteed the unalienable rights of life, liberty, and the pursuit of happiness. It is obvious today that America has defaulted on this promissory note insofar as her citizens of color are concerned. Instead of honoring this sacred obligation, America has given the Negro people a bad check which has come back marked "insufficient funds."

But we refuse to believe that the bank of justice is bankrupt. We refuse to believe that there are insufficient funds in the great vaults of opportunity of this nation. So we've come to cash this check, a check that will give us upon demand the riches of freedom and the security of justice.

We have also come to this hallowed spot to remind America of the fierce urgency of now. This is no time to engage in the luxury of cooling off or to take the tranquilizing drug of gradualism. Now is the time to make real the promises of democracy. Now is the time to rise from the dark and desolate valley of segregation to the sunlit path of racial justice. Now is the time to lift our nation from the quicksands of racial injustice to the solid rock of brotherhood.

Now is the time to make justice a reality for all of God's children. It would be fatal for the nation to overlook the urgency of the moment. This sweltering summer of the Negro's legitimate discontent will not pass until there is an invigorating autumn of freedom and equality— 1963 is not an end but a beginning. Those who hope that the Negro needed to blow off steam and will now be content will have a rude awakening if the nation returns to business as usual.

There will be neither rest nor tranquility in America until the Negro is granted his citizenship rights. The whirlwinds of revolt will continue to shake the foundations of our nation until the bright day of justice emerges. And that is something that I must say to my people who stand on the worn threshold which leads into the palace of justice. In the process of gaining our rightful place we must not be guilty of wrongful deeds. Let us not seek to satisfy our thirst for freedom by drinking from the cup of bitterness and hatred.

We must forever conduct our struggle on the high plane of dignity and discipline. We must not allow our creative protests to degenerate into physical violence. Again and again we must rise to the majestic heights of meeting physical force with soul force. The marvelous new militancy which has engulfed the Negro community must not lead us to distrust all white people, for many of our white brothers, as evidenced by their presence here today, have come to realize that their destiny is tied up with our destiny.

They have come to realize that their freedom is inextricably bound to our freedom. We cannot walk alone. And as we walk we must make the pledge that we shall always march ahead. We cannot turn back. There are those who are asking the devotees of civil rights, "When will you be satisfied?" We can never be satisfied as long as the Negro is the victim of the unspeakable horrors of police brutality.

We can never be satisfied as long as our bodies, heavy with the fatigue of travel, cannot gain lodging in the motels of the highways and the hotels of the cities.

We cannot be satisfied as long as the Negro's basic mobility is from a smaller ghetto to a larger one. We can never be satisfied as long as our children are stripped of their adulthood and robbed of their dignity by signs stating "For Whites Only."

We cannot be satisfied as long as the Negro in Mississippi cannot vote and the Negro in New York believes he has nothing for which to vote.

No, no, we are not satisfied and we will not be satisfied until justice rolls down like waters and righteousness like a mighty stream.

I am not unmindful that some of you have come here out of great trials and tribulation. Some of you have come fresh from narrow jail cells. Some of you have come from areas where your quest for freedom left you battered by the storms of persecution and staggered by the winds of police brutality. You have been the veterans of creative suffering.

Continue to work with the faith that unearned suffering is redemptive. Go back to Mississippi, go back to Alabama, go back to South Carolina, go back to Georgia, go back to Louisiana, go back to the slums and ghettos of our Northern cities, knowing that somehow this situation can and will be changed. Let us not wallow in the valley of despair.

I say to you today, my friends, though, even though we face the difficulties of today and tomorrow, I still have a dream. It is a dream deeply rooted in the American dream. I have a dream that one day this nation will rise up, live out the true meaning of its creed: "We hold these truths to be self-evident, that all men are created equal."

I have a dream that one day on the red hills of Georgia sons of former slaves and the sons of former slave-owners will be able to sit down together at the table of brotherhood. I have a dream that one day even the state of Mississippi, a state sweltering with the heat of injustice, sweltering with the heat of oppression, will be transformed into an oasis of freedom and justice.

I have a dream that my four little children will one day live in a nation where they will not be judged by the color of their skin but by the content of their character. I have a dream . . . I have a dream that one day in Alabama, with its vicious racists, with its governor having his lips dripping with the words of interposition and nullification, one day right there in Alabama little black boys and black girls will be able to join hands with little white boys and white girls as sisters and brothers.

I have a dream today . . . I have a dream that one day every valley shall be exalted, every hill and mountain shall be made low. The rough places will be made plain, and the crooked places will be made straight. And the glory of the Lord shall be revealed, and all flesh shall see it together. This is our hope. This is the faith that I go back to the South with. With this faith we will be able to hew out of the mountain of despair a stone of hope. With this faith we will be able to transform the jangling discords of our nation into a beautiful symphony of brother-hood. With this faith we will be able to work together, to pray together, to struggle together, to go to jail together, to stand up for freedom to-gether, knowing that we will be free one day.

This will be the day when all of God's children will be able to sing with new meaning, "My country, 'tis of thee, sweet land of lib-erty, of thee I sing. Land where my fathers died, land of the pilgrim's pride, from every mountain side, let freedom ring." And if America is to be a great nation, this must become true. So let freedom ring from the prodigious hilltops of New Hampshire. Let freedom ring from the mighty mountains of New York. Let freedom ring from the heighten-ing Alleghenies of Pennsylvania. Let freedom ring from the snow-capped Rockies of Colorado. Let freedom ring from the curvacious slopes of California.

But not only that. Let freedom ring from Stone Mountain of Geor-gia. Let freedom ring from Lookout Mountain of Tennessee. Let freedom ring from every hill and molehill of Mississippi, from every mountain side. Let freedom ring. . . .

When we allow freedom to ring—when we let it ring from every city and every hamlet, from every state and every city, we will be able to speed up that day when all of God's children, black men and white men, Jews and Gentiles, Protestants and Catholics, will be able to join hands and sing in the words of the old Negro spiritual, "Free at last, Free at last, Great God a-mighty, We are free at last."*

Malcolm X—"To Mississippi Youth"

Malcolm X (born Malcolm Little) became an important leader in the Nation of Islam and later led his own movement for justice. Malcolm spoke for that aspect of the collective African American psyche that said, "Enough is enough." Nonviolence was the proper response to nonviolence, he said, but violence was justified in order to meet violence. Desegregation and integration were not nearly as important as justice. If King was a "good" black hero leader in the eyes of America as a whole, Malcolm was at least a dangerous one. It was only with the publicity achieved by Spike Lee's film about him and the gradual mythologizing of his personality, his life, and his words that the American public has begun to assimilate him as one of its folk heroes.

Malcolm delivered this speech to a group of black Mississippi teenagers visiting Harlem in December 1964—two months before his assassination. The speech is supportive of the civil rights struggle in the South, and, among other things, it speaks of the falseness of the American myth of the melting pot.

One of the first things I think young people, especially nowadays, should learn is how to see for yourself and listen for yourself and think for yourself. Then you can come to an intelligent decision for yourself. If you form the habit of going by what you hear others say about someone, or going by what others think about someone, instead of searching that thing out for yourself and seeing for yourself, you will be walking west when you think you're going east, and you will be walking east when you think you're going west. This generation, especially of our people, has a burden, more so than any other time in history. The most important thing that we can learn to do today is think for ourselves.

It's good to keep wide-open ears and listen to what everybody else has to say, but when you come to make a decision, you have to weigh all of what you've heard on its own, and place it where it belongs, and come to a decision for yourself; you'll never regret it. But if you form the habit of taking what someone else says about a thing without checking it out for yourself, you'll find that other people will have you hating your friends and loving your enemies. This is one of the things that our people are beginning to learn today—that it is very important to think

*Worley, 313–16.

out a situation for yourself. If you don't do it, you'll always be maneuvered into a situation where you are never fighting your actual enemies, where you will find yourself fighting your own self.

I think our people in this country are the best examples of that. Many of us want to be nonviolent and we talk very loudly, you know, about being nonviolent. Here in Harlem, where there are probably more black people concentrated than any place in the world, some talk about nonviolent talk too. But we find that they aren't nonviolent with each other. You can go out to Harlem Hospital, where there are more black patients than any hospital in the world, and see them going in there all cut up and shot up and busted up where they got violent with each other.

My experience has been that in many instances where you find Negroes talking about nonviolence, they are not nonviolent with each other, and they're not loving with each other, or forgiving with each other. Usually when they say they're nonviolent, they mean they're nonviolent with somebody else. I think you understand what I mean. They are nonviolent with the enemy. A person can come to your home, and if he's white and wants to heap some kind of brutality on you, you're nonviolent; or he can come to take your father and put a rope around his neck, and you're nonviolent. But if another Negro just stomps his foot, you'll rumble with him in a minute. Which shows you that there's an inconsistency there.

I myself would go for nonviolence if it was consistent, if everybody was going to be nonviolent all the time. I'd say, okay, let's get with it, we'll all be nonviolent. But I don't go along with any kind of nonviolence unless everybody's going to be nonviolent. If they make the Ku Klux Klan nonviolent, I'll be nonviolent. If they make the White Citizens Council nonviolent, I'll be nonviolent. But as long as you've got somebody else not being nonviolent, I don't want anybody coming to me talking any nonviolent talk. I don't think it is fair to tell our people to be nonviolent unless someone is out there making the Klan and the Citizens Council and these other groups also be nonviolent.

Now, I'm not criticizing those here who are nonviolent. I think everybody should do it the way they feel is best, and I congratulate anybody who can be nonviolent in the face of all that kind of action in that part of the world. I don't think that in 1965 you will find the upcoming generation of our people, especially those who have been doing some thinking, who will go along with any form of nonviolence unless nonviolence is going to be practiced all the way around.

If the leaders of the nonviolent movement can go into the white community and teach nonviolence, good. I'd go along with that. But as long as I see them teaching nonviolence only in the black community, we can't go along with that. We believe in equality, and equality means that you have to put the same thing over here that you put over there. And if black people alone are going to be the ones who are nonviolent, then it's not fair. We throw ourselves off guard. In fact, we disarm ourselves and make ourselves defenseless. . . .

The Organization of Afro-American Unity is a nonreligious group of black people who believe that the problems confronting our people in this country need to be re-analyzed and a new approach devised toward trying to get a solution. Studying the problem, we recall that prior to 1939 all of our people, in the North, South, East, and West, no matter how much education we had, were segregated. We were segregated in the North just as much as we were segregated in the South. Even now there's as much segregation in the North as there is in the South. There's some worse segregation right here in New York City than there is in McComb, Mississippi; but up here they're subtle and tricky and deceitful, and they make you think you've got it made when you haven't even begun to make it yet.

Prior to 1939, our people were in a very menial position or condition. Most of us were waiters and porters and bellhops and janitors and waitresses and things of that sort. It was not until war was declared with Germany, and America became involved in a manpower shortage in regards to her factories plus her army, that the black man in this country was permitted to make a few strides forward. It was never out of some kind of moral enlightenment or moral awareness on the part of Uncle Sam. Uncle Sam only let the black man take a step forward when he himself had his back to the wall.

In Michigan, where I was brought up at that time, I recall that the best jobs in the city for blacks were waiters out at the country club. In those days if you had a job waiting tables in the country club, you had it made. Or if you had a job at the State House. Having a job at the State House didn't mean that you were a clerk or something of that sort; you had a shoeshine stand at the State House. Just by being there you could be around all those big-shot politicians—that made you a big-shot Negro. You were shining shoes, but you were a big-shot Negro because you were around big-shot white people and you could bend their ear and get up next to them. And ofttimes you were chosen by them to be the voice of the Negro community.

Around that time, 1939 or '40 or '41, they weren't drafting Negroes in the army or navy. A Negro couldn't join the navy in 1940 or '41. They wouldn't take a black man in the navy except to make him a cook. He couldn't just go and join the navy, and I don't think he could just go and join the army. They weren't drafting him when the war first started. This is what they thought of you and me in those days. For one thing, they didn't trust us; they feared that if they put us in the army and trained us in how to use rifles and other things, we might shoot at some targets that they hadn't picked out. And we would have. Any thinking man knows what target to shoot at. If a man has to have someone else to choose his target, then he isn't thinking for himself—they're doing the thinking for him.

The Negro leaders in those days were the same type we have today. When the Negro leaders saw all the white fellows being drafted and taken into the army and dying on the battlefield, and no Negroes were dying because they weren't being drafted, the Negro leaders came up and said, "We've got to die too. We want to be drafted too, and we demanded that you take us in there and let us die for our country too." That was what the Negro leaders said back in 1940. I remember. A. Philip Randolph was one of the leading Negroes in those days who said it, and he's one of the Big Six right now; and this is why he's one of the Big Six.

So they started drafting Negro soldiers then, and started letting Negroes get into the navy. But not until Hitler and Tojo and the foreign powers were strong enough to put pressure on this country, so that it had its back to the wall and needed us, [did] they let us work in factories. Up until that time we couldn't work in the factories; I'm talking about the North as well as the South. And when they let us work in the factories, at first they let us in only as janitors. After a year or so passed by, they let us work on machines. We became machinists, got a little more skill. If we got a little more skill, we made a little more money, which enabled us to live in a little better neighborhood. When we lived in a little better neighborhood, we went to a little better school, got a little better education and could come out and get a little better job. So the cycle was broken somewhat.

But the cycle was not broken out of some kind of sense of moral responsibility on the part of the government. No, the only time that cycle was broken even to a degree was when world pressure was brought to bear on the United States government. They didn't look at us as human beings—they just put us into their system and let us advance a little bit father because it served their interests. They never let us advance a little bit farther because they were interested in us as human beings. Any of you who have a knowledge of history, sociology, or political science, or the economic development of this country and its race relations—go back and do some research on it and you'll have to admit that this is true.

It was during the time that Hitler and Tojo made war with this country and put pressure on it [that] Negroes in this country advanced a little bit. At the end of the war with Germany and Japan, then Joe Stalin and Communist Russia were a threat. During that period we made a little more headway. Now the point that I'm making is this: Never at any time in the history of our people in this country have we made advances or progress in any way based upon the internal good will of this country. We have made advancement in this country only when this country was under pressure from forces above and beyond its control. The internal moral consciousness of this country is bankrupt. It hasn't existed since they first brought us over here and made slaves out of us. They make it appear they have our good interests at heart, but when you study it, every time, no matter how many steps they take us forward, it's like we're standing on a—what do you call that thing?—a treadmill. The treadmill is moving backwards faster than we're able to go forward in this direction. We're not even standing still—we're going backwards.

In studying the process of this so-called progress during the past twenty years, we of the Organization of Afro-American Unity realized that the only time the black man in this country is given any kind of recognition, or even listened to, is when America is afraid of outside pressure, or when she's afraid of her image abroad. So we saw that it was necessary to expand the problem and the struggle of the black man in this country until it went above and beyond the jurisdiction of the United States. . . .

I was fortunate enough to be able to take a tour of the African continent during the summer. I went to Egypt, then to Arabia, Kuwait, Lebanon, Sudan, Ethiopia, Kenya, Tanganyika, Zanzibar, Nigeria, Ghana, Guinea, Liberia, and Algeria. I found, while I was traveling on the African continent, I had already detected it in May, that someone had very shrewdly planted the seed of division on this continent to make the Africans not show genuine concern with our problem, just as they plant seeds in your and my minds so that we won't show concern with the African problem. . . .

I also found that in many of these African countries the head of state is genuinely concerned with the problem of the black man in this country; but many of them thought if they opened their mouths and voiced their concern that they would be insulted by the American Negro leaders. Because one head of state in Asia voiced his support of the civil-rights struggle [in 1963] and a couple of the Big Six had the audacity to slap his face and say they weren't interested in that kind of help—which in my opinion is asinine. So the African leaders only had to be convinced that if they took an open stand at the governmental level and showed interest in the problem of black people in this country, they wouldn't be rebuffed.

And today you'll find in the United Nations, and it's not an accident, that every time the Congo question or anything on the African continent is being debated, they couple it with what is going on, or what is happening to you and me, in Mississippi and Alabama and these other places. In my opinion, the greatest accomplishment that was made in the struggle of the black man in America in 1964 toward some kind of real progress was the successful linking together of our problem with the African problem, or making our problem a world problem. Because now, whenever anything happens to you in Mississippi, it's not just a case of somebody in Alabama getting indignant, or somebody in New York getting indignant. The same repercussions that you see all over the world when an imperialist or foreign power interferes in some section of Africa—you see repercussions, you see the embassies being bombed and burned and overturned—nowadays, when something happens to black people in Mississippi, you'll see the same repercussions all over the world.

I wanted to point this out to you because it is important for you to know that when you're in Mississippi, you're not alone. As long as you think you're alone, then you take a stand as if you're a minority or as if you're outnumbered, and that kind of stand will never enable you to win a battle. You've got to know that you've got as much power on your side as that Ku Klux Klan has on its side. And when you know that you've got as much power on your side as the Klan has on its side, you'll talk the same kind of language with that Klan as the Klan is talking with you. . . .

I think in 1965, whether you like it, or I like it, or they like it, or not, you will see that there is a generation of black people becoming mature to the point where they feel that they have no more business being asked to take a peaceful approach than anybody else takes, unless everybody's going to take a peaceful approach.

So we here in the Organization of Afro-American Unity are with the struggle in Mississippi one thousand percent. We're with the efforts to register our people in Mississippi to vote one thousand percent. But we do not go along with anybody telling us to help nonviolently. We think that if the government says that Negroes have a right to vote, and then some Negroes come out to vote, and some kind of Ku Klux Klan is going to put them in the river, and the government doesn't do anything about it, it's time for us to organize and band together and equip ourselves and qualify ourselves to protect ourselves. And once you can protect yourself, you don't have to worry about being hurt. . . .

I hope you don't think I'm trying to incite you. Just look here: Look at yourselves. Some of you are teenagers, students. How do you think I feel—and I belong to a generation ahead of you—how do you think I feel to have to tell you, "We, my generation, sat around like a knot on a wall while the whole world was fighting for its human rights—and you've got to be born into a society where you still have the same fight." What did we do, who preceded you? I'll tell you what we did: Nothing. And don't you make the same mistake we made.*

*Worley, 141–46.

Asian American

The few American-based folktales and hero legends of Asian Americans were reactions to conditions faced by Chinese laborers on the western railroads in the nineteenth century. Both these tales and those imported, as most were, directly from the Old World served to remind the immigrants of old values in the face of new temptations and distractions. New tales focused on issues such as the difficulty in keeping the young from losing their Asian identity in the depraved and unruly atmosphere of the early West. The tales brought from Asia, although stressing what on the surface seem to be Asian values, are strangely familiar to all of us.

Yeh-Shen

Versions of fairy tales that predate the versions known in the Western world were and are particularly popular among Asian Americans. Through the heroes and heroines of these tales, young Asian Americans can be reminded of the importance of family togetherness and respect for parents. The Chinese Cinderella tale is a good example.

All this I will tell you happened long ago, long before the time when we wrote down the passing of each year—a time when most people of China dwelled in caves. Such was Wu, a cave chief who lived in southern China with his two wives, each of whom had presented Wu with a baby daughter.

But then one of the wives took sick and quickly died, leaving her daughter, Yeh-Shen. And Yeh-Shen was soon orphaned when her father Wu also took sick and died. So Yeh-Shen lived in her stepmother's home and grew into a beautiful girl with dark almond eyes and skin as smooth as cream. Her stepmother, whose own child was plain to look at and a tiresome chatterbox to boot, grew jealous of Yeh-Shen and gave her the most onerous chores around the house.

Yen-Shen had but one friend as she grew to girlhood, a lovely golden orange fish who lived in a pond nearby and would wait patiently for Yeh-Shen's daily visit. Yeh-Shen would slip away from her stepmother's house and share her small ration of food with the fish, and it grew large.

No one knows how the stepmother found out about the secret fish— it was probably Yeh-Shen's stepsister who told—but the woman flew into a rage, marched down to the pond, and tricked the fish into coming to the surface by holding out a morsel of food. As the fish rose to take the morsel she stabbed it with a dagger she held in her other hand and took it home, where she put it in a pot of boiling water.

Later that day, Yeh-Shen found that her friend, the fish, was missing, and she fell on the ground beside the pond in sorrow. Presently, she heard a voice.

"Excuse me," the voice said. Yeh-Shen looked up to see an old man standing nearby. He wore a cloak of matted fur, and his mustache ends hung down to his knees.

"This is a very sad time for you," the old man said. "Your step-mother killed your friend and is making soup out of him right at this very moment. But your fish had wondrous powers and these powers still reside in his bones. Whenever you are in great need, you can kneel before them and tell them what is in your heart." The old man smiled and added: "Even this cannot go on forever, though. Don't waste these gifts from the fish." And with that, the old man vanished.

By now, in the boiling water, the fish's flesh had fallen from its bones and the stepmother flung the bones out the kitchen door onto the waste pile. Yeh-Shen gathered them up and hid them in a secret place where, from time to time, she would talk to them, tell them of her fears and her hopes. But she never asked the bones for any favor, any gift.

The winter passed and spring arrived, and with it the time of festival when the people cooked delicacies and dressed in their finest clothes and promenaded about, listening to music and feasting. It was when young people often chose whom they would marry. Of course, the stepmother had no desire for any eligible young men to see the pretty Yeh-Shen and make the inevitable comparison with her own daughter, so she ordered Yeh-Shen to stay home and guard the household.

Once alone, Yeh-Shen marched off to her secret place and spoke to the bones of her long-dead friend.

"Dearest friend, my only friend, how I long to go to the festival.

But even if I were to disobey, I couldn't go dressed like this, in these rags."

She looked down in despair, but instead of rags she was wearing a flowing gown of blue silk embroidered with gold, and on her feet was a pair of sandals, delicate golden sandals that shimmered like the scales of a fish.

"Oh," she gasped, and thought she heard a voice, as if the bones were speaking.

"Don't lose your sandals," the voice cautioned. "Now go to the festival."

Overcome with gratitude, Yeh-Shen ran off to join the assembling crowds. Heads turned as she approached. No one had ever seen so beautiful a girl, much less one so beautifully clad. The other young women looked on jealously as the various swains took note and began to rustle and preen. People whispered: "Who could that be?"

Yeh-Shen was standing radiant in their midst when she heard the voice of her stepsister.

"Mother, isn't that Yeh-Shen?" she hissed. "How did she . . . ?"

Panicked, Yeh-Shen bolted, racing down the side of the hill where the banquet tables had been laid out. She stumbled and one sandal fell off, leaving the other on her left foot . . . and her clothes in rags! The beautiful blue gown was gone, vanished. She raced home, tears of humiliation flowing down her cheeks, and went to the secret place to tell the bones what had happened and promise she would find the other sandal.

The bones were silent. Just bones, lying there. The last vestiges of her friend's spirit were gone, and with them Yeh-Shen's hopes and dreams. She collapsed on the ground and wailed, weeping herself to sleep.

The stepmother stole back to her house and spotted Yeh-Shen lying in her rags. She returned to the festival and found her daughter.

"Whoever that was," she said, "it wasn't your stepsister. Now try and look pretty, will you? Stop that shaking, and for heaven's sake don't natter the next time a young man says hello. Just smile and bow your head."

The stepsister did her best, but the young men avoided her for the most part, knowing that a nattering girl often grows into a nagging woman. Meanwhile, one of the villagers found Yeh-Shen's golden sandal under a bush and quickly sold it to a merchant. In due course, the merchant presented it to the king to curry his favor.

The king was entranced. It was so delicate a slipper, so beautiful, and so light, even though made of gold. He decided he would find out who owned such an exquisite sandal. He ordered that all the women in his retinue try the shoe, but it was too small for all of them. He ordered that the search be continued farther afield, even among the cave women in the outlying countryside.

His lieutenants protested that there were thousands of such women in the hills and valleys of the kingdom and the search could take years.

"Then place the sandal in a pavilion near where it was found by that toady of a merchant," the king ordered. "Announce that the sandal is to be returned to its owner."

The king's men went off to do his bidding and the king, quietly and in secret, followed along to watch. Over the next day, hundreds of cave women and girls came forth to try the sandal. Yeh-Shen's stepsister was among them.

"Yes," she said in her nattering voice, "this will surely fit me, and then it will be mine, Mother, and . . ."

But of course the sandal hardly fit over her toes, much less onto her ungainly foot.

The stepmother snorted in disgust.

"Let me try it," she barked.

But the sandal was far too small for her as well. In his hiding place, the king breathed a sigh of relief and continued his vigil into the night.

Yeh-Shen heard of the sandal in the pavilion and guessed it was hers. If it was, and if she got it back, she would have the pair complete again, and perhaps her friend the fish would come to life through the bones again. In the darkest part of the night—an hour before dawn—she tiptoed up to the pavilion and peered carefully at the sandal. It looked like the one she had lost! She stood before it, her heart pounding.

Watching this girl in rags touch the sandal, thinking she was merely a thief, the king decided to have his lieutenants shoo her away, but in the first weak glow of dawn he noticed the beauty of her face, the delicate grace of her gestures. He watched the girl put the slipper on her tiny foot, the tiniest foot he had ever seen. It fit.

"Follow her," he ordered. "Find out who she is and where she lives."

Yeh-Shen, knowing nothing of this, went home and was about to hide the two sandals in her bed when she heard an imperious knocking at the door. It was, she found to her amazement, the king himself. She bowed, and he asked her gently if she would put both slippers on her feet. She did as she was told and—whisk!—she was again clad in her blue gown with filigrees of gold embroidery adorning it.

The king gasped at her beauty and took her hand in his. And before too many days passed, he took her hand in marriage. There were celebrations throughout the kingdom, great feasts, and music and dancing. But the king, knowing that Yeh-Shen's stepmother and stepsister had always been unkind to her, wouldn't let them attend the festivities. Instead, they were banished to a distant outlying cave in a poor village with a sickly well, and they both perished soon thereafter. Some said it was a dragon that ate them, others said it was an avalanche. But no one really cared.

The Guru

There has also been a tendency in America to endow certain Asian-American characters with great amounts of the mysterious "wisdom of the Orient," raising them to folk hero status. The detective Charlie Chan is an example, as is Mr. Miagi, the Japanese American karate teacher in the Karate Kid *film series. The tendency is particularly noticeable in connection with the Indian guru-heroes who have attracted huge followings and sometimes seemingly the status of gods, or at least saints, in the ashrams of America. The first of the gurus to proselytize successfully in America was Swami Vivekananda (1863–1902), a follower of the great Hindu guru and mystic Ramakrishna. Vivekananda founded the Vedanta Society in New York in 1895 and preached his own brand of "pure" Hinduism. Many gurus have come to America since.*

Conclusion

A journey through American myth and legend leaves us with the sense that we are, as a whole, a very young culture made up of many old cultures attempting to make sense of this New World and our place as a nation in it. The United States has come into its own as a world power in what might be called a nonmythological age. Furthermore, it is commonly understood that the great juggernaut of modern science leaves little room for myth, and certainly none for the creation of new myth. But this understanding is not altogether accurate. Historian James Gilbert of the University of Maryland has recently pointed out that Americans have long had a penchant for mixing religion and mythology with science.

In 1925, a young biology teacher named John Scopes challenged a Tennessee law that forbade the teaching of evolution in the public schools. The Scopes trial (one of the numerous ones before and since billed as the "trial of the century") pitted the brilliant defense lawyer Clarence Darrow against the equally brilliant fundamentalist Christian politician William Jennings Bryan. In literary versions later, such as the play *Inherit the Wind*, it was a titanic courtroom battle, with science finally triumphant. But the actual outcome was less than conclusive. Bryan, often depicted as the archenemy of science, believed himself to be an upholder of commonsense science, and believed as well that science and religion were not and need not be at odds. Human origins, he thought, were simply too important to be left in the hands of elite scientists.

Since then, and still today, the matter of evolution as a subject in schools is fought over in school district after school district, and fundamentalist Christian groups have sponsored a few institutes devoted to what is called "creation science," which purports to show that the exact story of creation as given in the Bible accords with proper scientific fact. This is, in a sense, the idea that in a democracy, anyone can do science however they see fit.

Another instance of this peculiar American penchant was the very popular works of Immanuel Velikovsky in the 1950s, which set out to prove that a collision between the earth and a comet had produced the opening of the Red Sea as described in Exodus, while another comet coming hard and fast after the first one caused rocks to fall on Joshua and stopped the earth's rotation, "stopping" the sun as in the biblical story.

Perhaps the greatest example of the freebooting mythologization of science or technology—and a nearly exclusively American phenomenon—is the plethora of UFO sightings that began in the late 1940s and has led recently to tales of alien abduction and, tragically, the death of thirty-nine members of the Heaven's Gate cult in 1997. Here, the cult members were inspired by a charismatic leader who was certain that salvation was on its way in the form of a spaceship hidden behind the rapidly approaching Hale-Bopp comet. The members committed suicide in a peaceful and orderly manner to free their "true selves" and ascend to the Level Above Human, to reach heaven via the spaceship.

From the very beginning of the UFO phenomenon, largely inaugurated by the alleged crash of a flying saucer near Roswell, New Mexico, a half century ago, the alien visitors have been imbued by many believers with religious significance. They are seen as messengers from a higher plane, be they evil or good. The assumption that such creatures have been actually found and then covered up by agencies of the government only adds to the tingling excitement of the story, particularly at a time in American political life when the government is seen, through some eyes, as something of a monster itself, conspiring against the people it is supposed to serve.

Professional scientists scoff and fume about UFOs the way they do about such beliefs as astrology, but polls repeatedly show that somewhere in excess of 50 percent of all Americans confidently believe in these phenomena.

In this new version of myth making, the oral tradition from which most myths have developed since time immemorial has been replaced by the even more rapid and certainly more far-reaching capacity of electronic messaging. Communities of interest may now be in instant touch with themselves, regardless of geography. And from these virtual communities, one can assume that new mythologies and new legends will arise and add to the already diverse realm of American myth. That it will become yet more diverse is predictable, given the fact that the United States is a society already made up of sometimes very separate groups, with very separate conceptions of what it is to be American.

BIBLIOGRAPHY

Abrahams, Roger D., ed. *Afro-American Folktales*. New York: Pantheon Books, 1985.

Adams, Henry. *The Education of Henry Adams*. Boston: Houghton Mifflin, 1946 [1907].

African American Literature. Austin, TX: Holt, Rinehart and Winston, 1992.

Alger, Horatio. *Abraham Lincoln: The Backwoods Boy*. New York: John R. Anderson and Henry S. Allen, 1883.

Allen, Donald M., ed. *The New American Poetry, 1945–1960*. New York: Grove Press, 1960.

American Folklore and Legend. Pleasantville, NY: Reader's Digest Association, 1978.

Battle, Kemp P. *Great American Folklore*. Garden City, NY: Doubleday, 1986.

Bierhorst, John. *The Red Swan: Myths and Tales of the American Indians*. New York: Farrar, Straus, and Giroux, 1976.

———. *The Mythology of North America*. New York: Morrow, 1985.

Boas, Franz. "Tsimshian Mythology." *Annual Reports of Bureau of American Ethnology* 31. Washington, 1916, 29–1037.

Boller, Paul F., Jr. *Not So!: Popular Myths About America from Columbus to Clinton*. New York: Oxford University Press, 1995.

Book of Mormon. Salt Lake City, UT: The Church of Latter-day Saints, 1968.

Botkin, B. A. *A Treasury of American Folklore*. New York: Crown, 1944.

Bright, William. *A Coyote Reader*. Berkeley: University of California Press, 1993.

Brown, Greg. "The Poet's Game," (compact disc) Brown-Feldman Publishing Co. ASCAP, 1994.

Camp, Charles L., ed. "James Clyman, His Diaries and Reminiscences." *California Historical Society Quarterly*, vol. IV (1925), pp. 122–23.

Campbell, Joseph. *The Hero with a Thousand Faces* (1959). Princeton, NJ: Princeton University Press, 1968 [1959].

———. *The Power of Myth*. New York: Doubleday, 1988.

Cannon, Hal, ed. *Cowboy Poetry: A Gathering*. Salt Lake City, UT: Peregine Smith Books, 1985.

Clark, Charles Badger. *Sun and Saddle Leather*. Tucson: University of Arizona Press, 1983.

Cleland, Robert Glass. *This Reckless Breed of Men*. Albuquerque: University of New Mexico Press, 1976.

Crockett, David. *The Life of Colonel David Crockett*. Philadelphia: G. G. Evans, 1860.

Deren, Maya. *Divine Horsemen: The Living Gods of Haiti*. New Paltz, NY: McPherson, 1983 [1953].

Dorson, Richard M., *Buying the Wind: Regional Folklore in the United States*. Chicago: University of Chicago Press, 1964.

———. *America in Legend: Folklore from the Colonial Period to the Present*. New York: Random House, 1973.

Elijah Muhammad. *Message to the Blackman in America*. Chicago: Nation of Islam, 1965.

———. *The Supreme Wisdom: Solution to the So-Called Negro Problem*. Chicago: Nation of Islam, 1957.

Emerson, Ralph Waldo. *The Complete Works of Ralph Waldo Emerson*, ed. E. W. Emerson, 12 vols., 1903–1904.

Emrich, Duncan. *Folklore on the American Land*. Boston: Little, Brown, 1972.

Erbsen, Wayne. *Outlaw: Ballad, Legends, and Lore*. Asheville, NC: Native Ground Music, 1996.

Erdoes, Richard, and Alfonso Ortiz. *American Myths and Legends*. New York: Pantheon, 1984.

Griffith, James S. *Southern Arizona Folk Arts*. Tucson: University of Arizona Press, 1988.

Haley, W. D. "Johnny Appleseed: A Pioneer Hero" *Harper's New Monthly Magazine*, November 1871, pp. 830–36.

Haliburton, T. C. *The Americans at Home*, vol. II. London: Hurst and Blackett, 1854.

Harris, Joel Chandler. *Nights with Uncle Remus, Myths and Legends of the Old Plantation*. Boston: James R. Osgood, 1883.

———. *The Tar Baby and Other Rhymes of Uncle Remus*. New York: Appleton, 1904.

Haynes, Bessie Doak, and Edgar Haynes. *The Grizzly Bear: Portraits from Life*. Norman: University of Oklahoma Press, 1966.

Howe, Henry. *The Great West*. New York: George F. Tuttle, 1857.

Jung, Carl. G. "On the Psychology of the Trickster Figure" (1954), trans. R. F. C. Hull. In *Four Archetypes*. Princeton, NJ: Princeton University Press, 1970.

Kay, Elizabeth. *Chimayo Valley Traditions*. Santa Fe, NM: Ancient City Press, 1987.

Leach, Maria, ed. *Funk and Wagnalls Standard Dictionary of Folklore Mythology and Legend*. San Francisco: Harper and Row, 1984.

Leeming, David A. *The World of Myth*. New York: Oxford University Press, 1990

Leeming, David A., and Margaret Leeming. *A Dictionary of Creation Myths*. New York: Oxford University Press, 1995.

Leeming, David A., and Jake Page. *Goddess: Myths of the Female Divine.* New York: Oxford University Press, 1994.

———. *God: Myths of the Male Divine.* New York: Oxford University Press, 1996.

———. *The Mythology of Native North America.* Norman: University of Oklahoma Press, 1998.

Lester, Julius, *Black Folktales.* New York: Grove, 1969

Lincoln, C. Eric. *The Black Muslims in America,* third edition. Grand Rapids, MI: William B. Eerdmans, 1994.

Lomax, John A. "Stop-Over at Abilene." *Southwest Review* 25 (1940), pp. 407–18.

Lomax, John A., and Alan Lomax. *American Ballads and Folk Songs.* New York: Macmillan, 1934.

Love, Robertus. *The Rise and Fall of Jesse James.* New York: G. P. Putnam's Sons, 1926.

Marcatante, John J., and Robert R. Potter. *American Folklore and Legends.* New York: Globe, 1971.

Marriott, Alice, and Carol K. Rachlin. *American Indian Mythology.* New York: Mentor Books, 1968.

Martinez, Reyes N. *New Mexico Federal Writers' Project,* WPA, 555 #29. Stanford, CA: Stanford University Publications, 1951.

Melville, Herman. *Moby Dick.* Boston: Houghton Mifflin, 1956 [1851].

Mr. Muhammad Speaks. 13 December 1958, 4 July 1959.

Muhammad, Elijah. See Elijah Muhammad

Napier, John. *Bigfoot: The Yeti and Sasquatch in Myth and Reality.* New York: E. P. Dutton, 1973.

The New Encyclopaedia Britannica. 1990.

One of the Kids. *The Cowboy's Career, or the Dare Devil Deeds of "Billy the Kid," The Noted New Mexico Desperado.* Chicago: Belford and Clarke, 1881.

Page, Jake. "In Pursuit of Bigfoot and Yeti," in *Mysterious Creatures.* New York: Time-Life Books, 1988.

———. "Was Billy the Kid a Superhero—or a Superscoundrel?" *Smithsonian Magazine* 21 (Feb. 1991), pp. 137–48.

Page, Jake, and Susanne Page. *Hopi.* New York: Abrams, 1982.

———. *Navajo.* New York: Abrams, 1995.

Penfield, Thomas. *A Guide to Treasure in New Mexico.* Deming, NM: True Treasure Library, 1981.

Puckett, Newbell Niles. *Folk Beliefs of the Southern Negro.* New York: Negro Universities Press, 1926.

Radin, Paul. *The Trickster: A Study in American Indian Mythology.* New York: Greenwood Press, 1969 [1956].

Randolph, Vance. *Pissing in the Snow.* New York: Avon, 1976.

Robertson, James Oliver. *American Myth, American Reality.* New York: Hill and Wang, 1980.

Sage, Rufus. *Scenes in the Rocky Mountains.* Chicago: Donohue, Henneberry, 1857.

San Souci, Robert D. *Cut From the Same Cloth: American Women of Myth, Legend, and the Tall Tale.* New York: Philomel Books, 1993.

Secakuku, Alph. *Following the Sun and Moon*. Flagstaff, AZ: Northland Publishing, 1995.

Shenkman, Richard, and Kurt Reiger. *One-Night Stands With American History*. New York: Quill, 1982.

Sifakis, Carl. *The Encyclopedia of American Crime,* New York: Smithmark, 1992.

Steele, Thomas J. *Santos and Saints*. Santa Fe, NM: Ancient City Press, 1982.

Stegner, Wallace. *Beyond the Hundredth Meridian*. Lincoln: University of Nebraska Press, 1953.

Still, Bayrd. *The West*. New York: Capricorn, 1961.

Thoreau, Henry David. *Walden*. New York: Collier, 1961 [1854].

Van Doren, Charles, and Roberet McHenry, ed. *Webster's Guide to American History*. Springfield, MA: Merriam, 1967.

Weems, Mason Locke. *The Life of George Washington*. Philadelphia: J. Allen 1828 [1806].

Weigle, Marta. *The Penitentes of the Southwest*. Santa Fe, NM: Ancient City Press, 1970.

Weigle, Marta, and Peter White. *The Lore of New Mexico*. Albuquerque: University of New Mexico Press, 1988.

Whicher, George F., ed. *Poetry of the New England Renaissance*. New York: Holt, Rinehart and Winston, 1962.

Worley, Demetrice A., and Jesse Perry, Jr., eds. *African American Literature*. Lincolnwood, IL: National Textbook Co., 1993.

TEXT CREDITS

INDEX